Trauma and Attachment Workbook

158 Attachment-Based Interventions to Heal Trauma

By Christina Reese, PhD

Copyright © 2021 Christina Reese
Published by
PESI Publishing
3839 White Ave
Eau Claire, WI 54703

Cover: Amy Rubenzer
Editing: Jenessa Jackson, PhD
Layout: Amy Rubenzer & Bookmasters
ISBN: 9781683733911

Printed in the United States of America

PESI Publishing
pesipublishing.com

About the Author

 **Dr. Christina Reese** has been working with children and families impacted by trauma for the last 20 years. She has worked with children in court-ordered drug treatment, in residential treatment centers, and in the community. She has provided both in-home and in-school therapy to address a variety of traumas. Dr. Reese has also worked with adoptive families and with children in foster care, focusing on attachment. She has been the director of a mental health clinic and has worked with homeless individuals and families. She is a licensed clinical professional counselor in Maine, Maryland, and Pennsylvania and is a licensed clinical supervisor.

Dr. Reese received her master's degree in community counseling from McDaniel College and her PhD in counselor education from George Washington University. Dr. Reese's research includes a study titled "A Qualitative Study of Gang Desistance in Former Gang Members." She travels nationally with PESI, is a continuing education provider, and trains mental health professionals in creating trauma-informed classrooms. She is a Trust-Based Relational Intervention (TBRI) practitioner and owns Felicity Counseling Services in Pennsylvania. Dr. Reese has authored several books, including *Attachment: 60 Trauma-Informed Assessment and Treatment Interventions Across the Lifespan*, *Puzzle Pieces: Parenting a Child Impacted by Attachment and Other Traumas*, and *The Attachment Connection: Technology, Mental Health and Our Current Attachment Crisis*.

Dedication

I dedicate this book to Jesus, who has given me the gifts I have and the ability to use them.

To my loving husband, Michael, and my sweet girl, Lina, who share me with my computer while I am writing.

To my parents, Brian and Cindy Rice, who raised me in a loving home and gave me the benefit of a healthy start in this life.

Love to you all!

Table of Contents

Acknowledgments

I would like to thank Marnie Sullivan and Meg Graf at PESI for believing in me four years ago and for introducing me to a job I love: sharing about children and trauma with professionals who are making a difference. Thank you to Patti Johnson, Shannon Todd, and Ryan Bartholomew for the continued opportunities. A special thanks to Karsyn Morse at PESI Publishing for working with me on two books and for seeing my vision with me. An extra special thanks to Jenessa Jackson, the editor who molds and shapes my thoughts. I have loved being a part of the PESI family. Who would have thought that in the last four years, I would have presented over 1,000 continuing education credit hours (spanning across 125 days and 21 states and 2 countries) and published 2 books with you! Thank you for making all of this possible.

I would also like to acknowledge researchers in this field who have filled my head with the healing information I now share with others. First, Drs. Karyn Purvis and David Cross, who have spent the last 20 years working with traumatized children and helping them to find healing with Trust-Based Relational Intervention (TBRI). You provide the foundation for everything I know about healing trauma. Dr. Dan Seigel for providing his insight into the brain and its development, as well as his guidance in explaining large scientific concepts to children—I use your "hand brain" every day! Dr. Bruce Perry and the work he has done in helping children to heal from trauma. His use of brain scans has allowed us to actually see the developmental delays caused by trauma, which has been eye-opening and inspiring as he finds ways to heal parts of the brain that are "offline." And, finally, Dr. Bessel van der Kolk, who reminds us that trauma is stored in the body. It is a mind-body connection, and we must be holistic in our treatment of trauma if we are to bring true healing. These professionals have shaped my thinking and beliefs about how to bring healing. Thank you all for your contributions.

Introduction

Robert was a 14-year-old white male whose foster parents brought him in for therapy. Robert was born into a home where his parents regularly abused substances. He would cry for hours as a newborn, often going hungry while his parents were passed out or had even left the home to seek out drugs. He lived in dirty diapers that were not changed for days, and he was seldom picked up and held. In fact, his parents often screamed at him to "shut up" when he cried. **Robert experienced extreme neglect as a baby, which was his first trauma.** When Robert was unable to build a trust-based relationship with his parents—because he was unable to trust that they would feed him and take care of his needs—he began to become more independent. By the time he was two years old, Robert knew how to find food in the kitchen and feed himself. His parents had not engaged in a healthy relationship with Robert and had not spent time teaching him about his environment or connecting to him in loving ways. **This resulted in Robert's second trauma: attachment trauma.**

As a toddler, Robert walked around the house and frequently got into things that most two-year-olds get into. He needed supervision, which was an age-appropriate need, but his parents were unable to provide that supervision due to their continued substance abuse. Robert's parents often became angry when he made a mess and would physically hit and slap him. **This resulted in Robert's third trauma: physical abuse.** He did not understand this abuse, as he did not know what he had done to make his parents so angry.

When Robert entered kindergarten at age five, his school recognized signs of abuse and neglect and made a report to child services. Robert was removed from his parents' custody and placed in foster care. This was an **additional attachment trauma**, as Robert was separated from the only parents he had ever known, his primary caregivers, the people he'd spent the most time with. Even though they did not adequately care for him, he loved them and wanted to be loved by them.

Since his placement in foster care nine years ago, Robert has lived in seven foster homes. Each time he has built a relationship with his foster parents, he has had to leave that relationship, resulting in **another attachment trauma**. As a result, he no longer seeks to build relationships with foster parents or other adults because he knows he will not have a long-term relationship with them. Robert's complex trauma occurred during his developmental years, which impacted his foundational belief system about the world and the people within that world. It also impacted the course of his development because while other children were learning to walk, talk, listen, and follow directions, Robert was busy learning survival skills and defense mechanisms. This resulted in developmental delays that became more apparent as he entered school and fell behind his peers both academically and emotionally.

As Robert's story illustrates, when a child does not trust adults to take care of them, to meet their needs, or to keep them safe, that child becomes independent and does not reach out for or accept help from adults. Children who have been abused or neglected have not experienced relationships as a safe place, which impacts their beliefs about who adults are, whether adults are safe people, and whether adults can meet their needs. Children then develop an internal working model of relationships that is maladaptive, dysfunctional, and based in trauma. This internal working model tints the lens through which they view all relationships moving forward, which can lead to relationship difficulties and poor social skills. For example, children may struggle to follow directions or to be respectful of adults. As these children move into adulthood, this inability to trust others is transferred to all authority figures, including law enforcement officers, employers, and landlords. This can lead to challenges holding a job, keeping a home, and providing for themselves and their families. It can also result in incarceration and other societal consequences.

However, trauma is not specific to abuse or neglect, as medical traumas can also impact a child's ability to feel safe with adults. For example, a child who undergoes a serious medical procedure may perceive that adults are inflicting pain on them, and based on their developmental age and stage, they may be unable to understand the reason for this pain. In addition, serious medical diagnoses—which adults cannot alleviate, control, or "fix"—can cause a child to feel fear and anxiety, especially if these diagnoses are life-threatening. Children look to adults to keep them safe, and if the adults in their lives have no power or control over the medical condition, this can undermine a child's ability to feel like adults can take care of them. The child may then begin to attempt to take care of themselves before they are developmentally ready to do so. This can result in behaviors that appear oppositional and challenging as the child attempts to make their own decisions while parents try to do the same. These children grow into highly anxious adults who need to have control over their relationships and their environment.

Trauma can also come in the form of natural disasters, such as tornadoes, floods, hurricanes, and fires. These traumas impact the entire family, and parents may face challenges in regulating their own emotions when attempting to assist their child in regulating theirs. Adults may parent out of anxiety, and children may begin to question their parents' ability to protect them. Realistically, there will be situations that parents cannot protect their children from. The solution is not for parents to be superhuman or to hold themselves to unrealistic expectations. Doing so only sets parents up for unattainable goals that result in feelings of failure and ineptitude. Rather, the solution is to help parents heal from the trauma so they can help their children heal too. It involves teaching parents emotion regulation skills so they can allow their child to find feelings of safety again. Even though parents cannot always keep their child safe, they themselves can be a safe haven for their child.

Finally, trauma can result from witnessing violence or from experiencing (or being exposed to) mass violence. For children and adults who are living in inner-city environments, where violence is a daily event, survival becomes a daily goal. When a child walks home from school and chooses to walk down one street instead of another to avoid crime and violence, that child is making a life-or-death decision every day. Likewise, when we fear walking into a department store, music festival, school, or restaurant because of the extensive history of mass violence in America, we as a society are being impacted by trauma.

Vicarious exposure to trauma also impacts us when we watch the news and have unlimited access to social media reports of mass violence and natural disasters. Watching live footage of these traumatic incidents can terrorize us over and over again, overwhelming our brains. Our own self-preservation systems initiate as our brain feels a threat, resulting in a release of adrenaline and feelings of anxiety about keeping ourselves safe. This can be especially overwhelming for children, who are unable to fully rationalize the reason behind these events.

Understanding the impact of all these types of trauma on adults and children is the first step to beginning the healing process. That is where this book comes in. This book seeks to teach children and adults the emotion regulation skills and coping strategies needed to heal from trauma. It is intended for mental health professionals working with individuals who have been exposed to various forms of trauma, including abuse, neglect, attachment trauma, domestic violence, medical traumas, natural disasters, and mass violence.

Although trauma is prevalent throughout society, we often don't recognize its impact because we don't see trauma for what it is. In therapy, trauma may unknowingly present itself in a variety of manners. It can manifest as aggressive, oppositional, or problematic behaviors, or it can manifest as a state of complete immobility or dissociation. For individuals who have experienced attachment trauma, it can manifest as relationship difficulties, poor social skills, and relationship dissatisfaction.

Trauma is based on someone's personal experience of the event, and regardless of the type of trauma or the manner in which it manifests, it impacts a person's ability to feel safe. It takes away their sense of security and causes them to fear things they never feared before. It brings anxiety and panic, leading people to doubt what they knew before. Therefore, the goal of this book is to help families and individuals restore a sense of safety—or in situations where this is not realistic (such as someone living in a neighborhood with daily exposure to violence), to create a sense of felt safety. **Felt safety is the concept of feeling safe (even in unsafe situations) by creating an atmosphere of emotional safety.**

However, before providing the tools to effectively help individuals heal from trauma, it is necessary to examine how trauma impacts the brain and how it influences a person's thought process and worldview. Trauma has the potential to change a person's belief system and to create an operating system based in anxiety and fear. How do we assess for trauma? How do we identify trauma symptoms in a person who has not disclosed a trauma history that we typically recognize? How do we know what questions to ask to identify various types of trauma? Let's begin our exploration of trauma and its impact on families and communities.

Part 1

Recognizing and Assessing the Impact of Trauma

1

Trauma

THE IMPACT OF TRAUMA ON THE BRAIN

We collect information about our environment through our five senses, which is then presented to the brain for categorization. The brain creates a groove to store new information, or it adds additional information to already established grooves. This is how memories are made. Our verbal memories begin around three or four years of age as we begin to develop the capacity for language and our brain begins to categorize information based on language. Prior to that, our memories are largely based on our senses. In particular, we have memories of what we saw, felt, smelled, heard, and tasted in relation to a particular event (Rettner, 2010). These sense memories explain why certain smells or sounds may evoke specific memories, such as the scent of freshly baked cookies that triggers memories of spending time with our grandmother.

Sense memories are associated with emotionally charged personal experiences, both those that are positive and negative, which explains why sense memories also play a role in trauma. The senses remember the trauma (van der Kolk, 2014). Therefore, certain sights, sounds, smells, feelings, or tastes may evoke memories of a trauma. This is known as preverbal trauma: when the senses remember the trauma but someone does not have a verbal memory of it.

Preverbal trauma is encoded in the brain, and depending on the frequency and duration of the trauma, it can impact the brain in various ways. For example, when a one-time trauma occurs, like a natural disaster or car accident, our senses collect information about the event, which is then recorded into a groove in the brain. It is a singly invested groove. Once the trauma is over, then healing can begin.

However, if trauma happens repeatedly, over a period of time, then that same groove is invested in over and over again. Neural pathways are created in the brain based on the trauma, and these pathways deepen and become a part of our belief system. For example, if someone experiences repeated abuse as a child, then that experience informs their belief system about relationships given that the trauma happened within a relationship. That person may come to believe that all relationships are characterized by mistreatment because that has been their only experience. In turn, they may seek out relationships that are abusive in nature since that has been normalized as part of their experience. Or they may avoid relationships altogether because they believe that pain and abuse are to be expected in connections with others. In these instances, healing cannot begin because the trauma continues to impact their belief system. It impacts their personality, their perspective, and their worldview. **Healing begins when a person is, and feels, safe.**

The impact of trauma on the brain is also dependent on age, and trauma that occurs during childhood can be particularly impactful for several reasons. First, children do not have an existing framework through which to interpret trauma. Everything they know about the world they learn through experience. These experiences create grooves, or neural pathways, in the brain from which context is built (Bremner, 2006). If trauma is a part of a child's early experiences, then that trauma becomes encoded as part of their context and beliefs about the world around them.

Second, children have not yet developed the capacity for abstract thinking, and they have difficulty differentiating fantasy from reality and struggle with problem solving. Because the prefrontal cortex does not fully develop until age 25, children do not yet have the capacity to rationalize and reason, which interferes with their ability to make sense of traumatic events that their brain is not developmentally ready for. For example, a child who moves into a new home following a house fire may worry that this new home will burn down as well.

Third, children have not fully developed the capacity for self-regulation, so they may have large feelings about the traumatic event and may not know how to manage those feelings. Children still need modeling and prompts from adults in order to use coping skills to regulate their emotions. In fact, when a child has experienced trauma, the largest factor in that child's recovery is their family. If their home life is stable and their needs are met consistently, then the child will have an improved likelihood of recovery. However, if the parents are so overwhelmed with their own feelings, then that child will not feel supported. This may occur when the family experiences a collective trauma. In this case, it can be difficult for parents to attend to the emotional needs of the child because they themselves are trying to manage their own feelings.

Finally, trauma is especially impactful for children because their brains are still developing. During childhood, the brain is growing exponentially, allowing children to learn, practice, and refine their executive functioning skills. However, when children are exposed to trauma, the brain is overwhelmed with keeping the child safe and with making sure their needs are met. This is especially the case when the parent is unwilling or unable (depending on the type of trauma) to complete those tasks for the child. In turn, the child begins to develop survival skills that are not age appropriate, which results in developmental delays and impairments.

THE IMPACT OF TRAUMA ON THE BODY

When we feel unsafe, the alarm system in our brain is activated, which prompts the release of adrenaline and cortisol into the body. These survival hormones serve to speed up heart rate, increase blood pressure, and constrict blood vessels. This biological response reflects the body's built-in fight, flight, or freeze response, which prepares us to respond to stressful or threatening situations by facing it head on (fight), running away from it (flight), or attempting to become "invisible" (freeze) if it is not possible to fight back or escape the situation. For example, in a state of freeze, someone may curl up into a small ball and go completely silent, hoping not to be seen.

However, when trauma becomes stuck in the body, this biological response gets repeated over and over again, causing individuals to stay in a state of heightened reactivity long after the event has passed. The body goes on overdrive as the fight, flight, or freeze response is constantly activated. The long-term effects of this continued state of arousal have been well-documented. In particular, the findings of the groundbreaking Adverse Childhood Experiences (ACE) Study demonstrated that individuals who experienced childhood trauma were at a higher risk for a variety of adverse physical outcomes later in life, including heart disease, cancer, pulmonary disease, and reduced life expectancy (Felitti et al., 1998). Simply put, trauma negatively impacts the body.

How we respond to someone in this survival mode greatly predicts our ability to work with them. Many times, when there is a child or adult who is becoming oppositional (fight), who is moving away from us (flight), or who is non-responsive (freeze), we respond with authority. Our voice becomes firm, we may speak a little louder, and we begin to give directions. When we respond in this manner, this only serves to amplify the fight, flight, or freeze response. It escalates feelings of non-safety, and that individual is not likely to respond to our directions. That is because **people do not follow directions given by someone with whom they do not feel safe**. Instead, they are now fully engaged in survival mode. When the fear response has been initiated in this manner, people often respond out of emotion versus logical thought because their executive functioning skills are "offline."

Therefore, we must remember that individuals in a state of fight, flight, or freeze are simply scared. With this recognition, we can engage that person in a completely different manner, as we react very differently to someone who is oppositional as opposed to someone who is afraid. In particular, we lower our volume, speak in a gentle tone of voice, and offer support and validation. This allows the person to disengage their defense mechanisms and to engage with us in a relational interaction that feels safe.

THE IMPACT OF TRAUMA ON EMOTION REGULATION

Finally, trauma can negatively affect an individual's ability to manage their emotions. Trauma is emotionally dysregulating. It creates large feelings of fear, sadness, and anger. When someone doesn't feel safe—when their sense of safety has been taken from them—the resulting emotions can feel overwhelming. These emotions can make it difficult to find emotional stability. Individuals feel out of control and struggle to find their balance again. This can create distress and impact their relationships, as they may become increasingly irritated with or easily triggered by others.

In addition, when people struggle to regulate their emotions, they may turn to unhealthy coping behaviors as a way to self-soothe. For example, they may abuse alcohol or other substances, develop disordered eating habits, engage in self-harm, or lash out with destructive anger. These dysfunctional coping behaviors may be particularly problematic for those who have experienced childhood trauma, given that children do not consistently make good decisions, especially when under large amounts of stress. If left to themselves to figure out how to manage these large emotions, they are likely to resort to unhealthy coping options that result in negative life outcomes.

RESILIENCY FACTORS IN TRAUMA

Despite the wide-ranging impacts of trauma on the body and the brain, it is possible to heal from the effects of trauma. However, being able to heal is dependent on several factors that influence resiliency (Nugent, Sumner, & Amstadter, 2014). **Personality** is one such factor that can impact whether a person can more easily overcome the trauma or whether they will experience more difficulties. For example, someone who is more extroverted may reach out for support and connection during the healing process, which can increase resilience by helping them feel like they are not alone. However, someone who is more introverted may find that recovery proves more challenging as they attempt to manage and heal from their symptoms on their own.

Similarly, being open can increase resilience, as healing often means trying new interventions and approaches. In contrast, individuals who are more closed off or rigid in their thinking may become "stuck" in their trauma because what happened to them does not fit into their perception of what life "should" be. Those with an anxious temperament may also struggle in the face of trauma compared to those with a more emotionally stable temperament, as the stress of the traumatic incident can exacerbate their underlying predisposition toward anxiety.

Context is another factor that can facilitate healing or serve as a barrier. If someone has a context of safety, and trauma is an isolated experience, then the context surrounding the trauma may lead to resilience. For instance, if someone experiences a car accident as an adult—after 30 or 40 years of safe driving experiences—then that trauma is filed within the context that driving is a safe activity. However, if someone gets into a car accident during one of their first experiences driving (or riding) in a car, then they may form the context that driving is not a safe activity. In turn, they may fear getting into another car. As another example, a child who experiences abuse or neglect forms the context that authority figures are not safe people. If that child encounters teachers who angrily rebuke students to maintain control of their classroom, this reinforces the context that authority figures are not safe. This belief can instigate and actually contribute to continued negative experiences with authority figures in adulthood, which further reinforces that belief. It is in this manner that context can impact recovery.

The ability to use healthy **coping skills** can also impact resilience and recovery from trauma. As discussed earlier, trauma creates a fear response that results in a host of physiological changes to the body, including increased adrenaline and cortisol (Harvard Health Publishing, 2011). When individuals use effective coping skills to manage these emotional and physical changes, they can more easily come back down to baseline. For example, regularly engaging in physical activity can burn off excess adrenaline and cortisol, as can maintaining good sleep and eating habits. Deep breathing exercises can also re-regulate our breathing and heart rate, which calms the nervous system and reduces adrenaline and cortisol. The use of coping skills can mitigate overwhelming emotional and physical responses, and it instills a sense of competence and confidence in being able to handle life's challenges. It helps individuals decrease the intensity of their emotions and gives them back control over a situation that feels out of control. It gives them the ability to feel mastery over their emotions.

Finally, **supportive connections** are a contributing factor to recovery from trauma. If someone feels like they have been left alone to cope with the effects of the trauma, it can result in feelings of depression, hopelessness, and despondency, which compound the experience of trauma. On the other hand, if someone has supportive relationships they can depend on, this can bring hope and comfort to a traumatic situation. Being able to talk about what happened and to have others offer emotional and physical support can greatly facilitate recovery. It can lessen the impact of the trauma and make challenges easier to cope with because others are helping carry the load.

Supportive connections are particularly important for children, as they cannot take care of themselves and depend on their parents to meet their needs. Parents need to provide for, protect, and prepare children. They can *provide for* their children by making sure they have food, clothing, shelter, and love. They can *protect* them by making sure they feel safe. They can *prepare* them by teaching them emotion regulation and social skills. These are things that all children need, but they're especially important if a child has experienced a trauma. If parents do not take care of children or meet their needs related to trauma, this can negatively impact the child's ability to heal from that trauma.

Trauma can bring changes to a person's brain, body, and emotions. In order to facilitate healing, we must address every area in which a person has experienced harm. Moving forward, interventions will be presented for each of these categories. Taking into account resiliency factors, we can also facilitate healing by exploring a person's internal and external supports and by assisting them in strengthening any supports that may be ineffective or even detrimental to the healing process. Given that relationships represent a large resiliency factor that can bring healing after trauma, a large portion of the healing interventions presented will focus on relationship development and restoration of impaired relationships (López-Zerón & Blow, 2017). Before discussing these interventions, though, we need to better understand how to identify someone who has experienced trauma.

②

Assessment and Diagnosis

Although trauma has wide-ranging effects on our brain, body, and emotions, not everyone who has experienced a traumatic event will be diagnosed with post-traumatic stress disorder (PTSD), seeing as there are many factors that impact symptomology. As discussed earlier, the presence of resiliency factors, such as having a strong support system, can mitigate the trauma response and protect against severe trauma reactions. Similarly, if trauma is a one-time event and healing can begin soon thereafter, then this can also facilitate a shorter recovery time.

When a trauma occurs, people may experience a few bothersome symptoms that impact their daily functioning but that do not otherwise impair them. Overwhelmingly, they may be able to manage their regular routine and accomplish tasks. They may exhibit several symptoms but not meet full criteria for a diagnosis. When such individuals seek help, they are often diagnosed with depression or anxiety even though the root issue is trauma. In these instances, the underlying trauma needs to be addressed before the depression and anxiety can subside. Otherwise, people can be in treatment for years for a co-occurring disorder that does not reflect the principal cause of their distress.

In children, the presence of unidentified trauma can be especially significant because they are not accurate reporters. They do not have conscious memories of the events that occurred in their life before they acquired the capacity for language. They also may not understand current events in their life or how these events impact them. For example, a child living in a neighborhood with a high incidence of violence may not be able to recognize or verbalize the fear they experience when walking home from school because that is their baseline. It is their sense of "normal." Similarly, parents may not realize that certain events, such as divorce, represent a type of trauma to children, and parents may even be unsupportive of labeling it as such despite its traumatic impact.

Given that children who have experienced trauma may experience developmental delays and impairments, it is imperative that we also assess the child's developmental age because this will often not match their chronological age. A child experiencing these impairments may be expected to behave in ways that they are developmentally unable to, which can create additional distress and unsafe feelings in a child who is already hypervigilant. Recognizing these delays, meeting the child where they are at, and moving them forward from that point is essential to bring healing.

DIAGNOSTIC CRITERIA

According to the latest edition of the *Diagnostic and Statistical Manual of Mental Disorders* (DSM-5˚), a diagnosis of PTSD is based on the following criteria (American Psychiatric Association, 2013), which must last for one month or more and not be related to another disorder:

- **A person must experience a stressful event that results in actual or perceived harm to themselves or someone with whom they are in a relationship.** The event can include death, a serious injury, or a sexual violation. The person may experience the event themselves, witness the event, or hear about it happening to a loved one. Although traumatic events can happen to anyone at any time, many individuals work in positions where trauma is a daily occurrence, such as law enforcement officers, firefighters, members of the armed forces, and emergency room staff.

- **A person experiences intrusive thoughts or feelings related to the event.** They will recall the trauma at times when they do not want to. This can be in the form of nightmares and flashbacks or an emotional reaction to sensory triggers. The person will experience physical reactivity as their brain responds to the threat and releases adrenaline and cortisol into the body, in turn activating the fight, flight, or freeze response. They may become agitated or non-responsive, or they may want to leave the area where they are experiencing the trigger. For example, an adult man who was physically abused by his mother as a child may unintentionally project feelings of anger onto every adult woman he meets because his brain is flashing back to the trauma and causing him to react as if he was being traumatized again.

  Children often manifest this symptom through play in which they relive or reenact the trauma. For example, children who are the victim of sexual abuse may become overly sexual in play because their boundaries have been distorted regarding appropriate sexuality. They may reenact sexual acts with dolls or recreate these acts in drawings, not realizing that other children would not play in the same way.

- **A person attempts to avoid people, places, or situations that remind them of the trauma.** They may even avoid certain emotions, such as fear, as this triggers feelings of danger. Children may not want to participate in school events that require them to be on stage with their classmates, or they may go to an amusement park and emotionally dysregulate when faced with a roller coaster that elicits similar feelings of panic. If the trauma was associated with a specific person, as in the case of abuse or neglect, then individuals may also avoid developing relationships with people who remind them of their abuser.

- **A person experiences negative changes to their thoughts and emotions.** For example, they may develop a negative worldview wherein they see everything through a lens of pain and grief. They may feel like only bad things happen to them, that they are being targeted, or that they cannot overcome their difficulties. They may isolate or have a decreased interest in things that used to bring them joy in the past. These persistent feelings of hopelessness can even lead to suicidal ideation when people believe their life will never improve.

  Individuals may also have difficulty recalling details of the trauma or deny their importance because their mind has compartmentalized that information and blocked it in an effort to protect them. They may have feelings of anger toward themselves for allowing the trauma to happen, though it was no fault of their own, or they may blame others who could have prevented the trauma but did not.

  In children, this symptom can manifest in terms of self-blame. Children may take responsibility for things that are not their fault. They may frequently say "I'm sorry" when they did nothing wrong. Children may also become anxious or escalate emotionally when they are separated from their parent.

- **A person experiences changes in emotional reactivity as evidenced by difficulty managing emotions like anger and sadness.** They may become more irritable or "moody," and their emotions may seem exaggerated and disproportionate. They may lash out aggressively, use substances, or engage in risky behaviors in an attempt to cope with overwhelming emotions. Their alarm system is overactive and on high alert, so they are likely to overreact to small incidents where there is a perceived threat. Because their internal alarm is on overdrive, they are likely to have difficulty concentrating or sleeping. They are also likely to experience relationship problems as a result of difficulties managing overwhelming emotions.

In children, angry outbursts are a common response to trauma. Because children are not yet able to regulate their emotions, these behaviors may appear aggressive or oppositional when they actually reflect underlying fear or sadness. They may become a danger to themselves or others, requiring repeated crisis response or hospitalization. Because increased reactivity interferes with concentration, children may be mistakenly diagnosed with attention-deficit/hyperactivity disorder (ADHD). However, ADHD medications will have no impact on trauma symptoms and can even exacerbate anxiety symptoms related to the trauma.

Even if someone does not meet criteria for PTSD, it is important to recognize that even one symptom can be dysregulating and impactful for that individual. For example, mood dysregulation or flashbacks can be significant enough to cause distress on their own, without the presence of other symptoms. Therefore, know that each separate symptom can substantially interfere with daily functioning, though all criteria need to be present for a diagnosis.

The section that follows includes several checklists that can assist you in identifying PTSD and assessing the impact of trauma. Even if a client does not meet full criteria for diagnosis, you can use these checklists to identify what areas of that person's life are being impacted so treatment can address that specific concern. Given that resiliency factors (such as personality, context, coping skills, and supportive connections) can also facilitate trauma recovery, a resiliency assessment is included in this section as well.

TRAUMA SYMPTOM QUESTIONNAIRES

There are a variety of reliable measures that have been developed and validated to assess trauma in children and adults. Two common instruments include the Clinician-Administered PTSD Scale for DSM-5 (CAPS-5) and the child/adolescent version of this same measure (CAPS-CA-5). These tools, which can be found at https://www.ptsd.va.gov/professional/assessment/documents/ptsd_trauma_assessments.asp, can inform diagnosis and help to distinguish PSTD from other co-occurring diagnoses. You can use these measures at intake via an interview format. Each tool contains 30 questions that correspond to the diagnostic criteria for PTSD. These tools must be administered by trained clinicians and should not be used by clients or by helping professionals who are not clinically trained. Instructions for conducting the interview and scoring the assessment are included.

In addition, the following section contains two **Traumatic Experience Inventories**—one for adults and one for children—that are intended to help categorize the types of trauma a client has experienced. If a client answers yes to any category, or endorses multiple categories of potentially traumatic events, then those responses warrant further exploration by asking additional clarifying questions. Often, clients may not identify an event in their life as being "traumatic." Therefore, when we ask them about their history, we can miss an important trauma if the client is not labeling it that way. For example, parents may not recognize that their child having been in the NICU for several weeks after birth was traumatic for both their child and themselves. In these instances, the Trauma Experience Inventories can assist in identifying the trauma that has been previously unrecognized.

Traumatic Experiences Inventory for Children

Identifying and treating trauma is important to maintain good mental and physical health. Please take a few minutes and think about whether you (if the child is completing) or your child (if the parent is completing) has ever experienced any of the items listed here, regardless of the age when the event happened. Place a check mark next to each item that was experienced. Note: Most children will need to consult with a parent/guardian to be able to complete this worksheet.

Type of Trauma	Check if "yes"
1. Spending time in the NICU or PICU as a baby	
2. Having a long-term medical diagnosis (e.g., asthma, epilepsy, diabetes)	
3. Having a parent or caregiver with a long-term medical diagnosis	
4. Undergoing a surgery or medical procedure (e.g., endoscopy, heart surgery)	
5. Being exposed to drugs or alcohol in utero	
6. Being exposed to high stress in utero (e.g., mother being treated violently or living in poverty)	
7. Difficult birth and delivery	
8. Lack of access to food (e.g., going to bed hungry, not being fed regularly as a baby)	
9. Lack of access to housing (e.g., homelessness, heat being turned off)	

10. Lack of parental nurturing (e.g., lack of love or affection, not being picked up as a baby)	
11. Verbal abuse (e.g., being yelled at, belittled, or called names by a parent or caregiver)	
12. Physical abuse (e.g., being hit or disciplined in a way that left a mark)	
13. Sexual abuse (e.g., being touched when touch was unwanted)	
14. Having a parent or caregiver who used drugs or alcohol	
15. Having a parent or caregiver who was incarcerated or arrested (e.g., jail, prison)	
16. Being exposed to domestic violence (e.g., parents or siblings being mistreated)	
17. Growing up in a violent household (e.g., parents threw things, yelled, threatened)	
18. Having parents who went through a divorce or separation	
19. Being separated from a sibling	
20. Out-of-home placement (e.g., staying in foster care or with other relatives)	
21. Having a parent or caregiver with a mental illness	
22. Living in an unsafe area (e.g., exposure to violence or crime)	
23. Surviving a natural disaster (e.g., tornado, hurricane, earthquake, house fire)	

Traumatic Experiences Inventory for Adults

Trauma can make us feel anxious or unsafe in certain environments, with certain people, or in certain situations. It takes away our feelings of safety and security. It can cause emotions that are overwhelming or difficult to manage. It can change the way we think about ourselves and those around us. Use this worksheet to identify whether any of the following experiences happened to you. Use another sheet of paper if you want to explain any of your answers.

1. Did you feel safe in your home as a child?   Yes   No

2. Did you feel safe with your primary parent/guardian (physically, emotionally, mentally)?   Yes   No

3. Did you feel safe with your other primary parent/guardian (physically, emotionally, mentally)?   Yes   No

4. Did your parents teach you how to cope and calm yourself?   Yes   No

5. Did your parents teach you helpful social skills?   Yes   No

6. Have you ever been in a relationship that felt unsafe?   Yes   No

7. Did you feel safe in your community or neighborhood?   Yes   No

8. Were your needs consistently met as a child?   Yes   No

9. Did you ever go to bed hungry?   Yes   No

10. Did your parents use physical discipline that left a mark?   Yes   No

11. Were your parents responsive to and validating of your emotions? Yes   No

12. Have you ever witnessed violence in your community?   Yes   No

13. Have you ever felt scared for your life?   Yes   No

14. Have you ever experienced a natural disaster?   Yes   No

15. Have you ever had a major medical procedure?   Yes   No

16. Did you have any medical procedures or conditions as a child?   Yes   No

17. Do you currently have a major medical condition?   Yes   No

18. Did you ever witness violence in your family?   Yes   No

19. Was your home ever damaged or destroyed?   Yes   No

20. Have you ever been in a serious accident?   Yes   No

21. Have you ever been the victim of a sexual assault?   Yes   No

22. Have you ever been the victim of a physical assault?   Yes   No

23. Have you ever been the victim of any other crime?   Yes   No

Scoring Key:

Give one point for each of the following item numbers. Any category with a point needs further exploration for possible trauma.

Item numbers	Give one point for each "Yes"	Type of Trauma
4, 5, 6		Attachment
1, 2, 3, 10		Abuse
8, 9, 11		Neglect
15, 16, 17		Medical
14, 19, 20		Natural Disasters
7, 12, 13, 18		Witnessing Violence
21, 22, 23		General

TRAUMA-SPECIFIC QUESTIONNAIRES

The following questionnaires are intended to assess for the presence of specific types of trauma. If you have identified an area where a client may have experienced some trauma, use the following questionnaires to assist you in exploring the specific trauma and the meaning that it has for the client. The questionnaires are labeled numerically so as not to disclose a possible trauma diagnosis while in the process of assessment. Within each questionnaire, the client is asked to identify how they have healed from the trauma. Clients who possess sufficient resiliency factors may not need to resolve anything further, but other clients may identify having healed from the trauma through unhealthy coping strategies. For example, a client who experienced a flood during a hurricane may report that they have resolved this trauma by never going near water, in which case you may want to offer alternative interventions.

The first questionnaire is geared toward trauma in general, including any situations that may have led the client to feel unsafe. Clinicians should focus on how that experience may have changed the client's thoughts and feelings and identify if healing has occurred. If not, this would become a goal of treatment.

The second questionnaire is intended to assess for the presence of attachment trauma. If a client identifies that their mother or father was not present in their life, or if these relationships were abusive in nature, then this would constitute an attachment trauma. Attachment trauma may also be present if the client's parents did not teach them appropriate emotion regulation or social skills, or if their parents modeled unhealthy relationship skills. In these situations, you would want to ask additional clarifying questions about how this impacted the client moving forward in life, including whether the client has been able to develop healthier relationship skills. If not, this would become a goal of treatment.

The third questionnaire can be used to assess for trauma associated with a past history of abuse. If the client is also a parent, then you can also ask questions to assess their relationship with their children and see whether generational abuse is a concern.

The fourth questionnaire is intended to identify any instances of neglect that may have caused the client to begin meeting their own needs before it was developmentally appropriate to do so. Children who begin to meet their own needs early, out of necessity, do not trust adults to meet their needs moving forward. In adulthood, these clients become overly self-sufficient and do not allow others to meet their needs in healthy, attunement-based relationships.

The fifth questionnaire can be used to identify whether a client has experienced a medical trauma, such as being diagnosed with a serious medical condition or undergoing a traumatic medical procedure. Oftentimes, clients who have experienced medical trauma become fixated on trying to control that which they have no control over, which causes frustration and anxiety to multiply. By taking the focus off of what they cannot control and placing it on what they can control, treatment can work to increase their sense of confidence and competence.

The sixth questionnaire is intended to gauge the impact of trauma caused by natural disasters. Individuals who have survived catastrophic events—like earthquakes, floods, fires, and hurricanes—can feel helpless and lose their sense of safety in the world. In addition, since natural disasters impact communities at the mass level, survivors can be plagued by survivor guilt and experience other ongoing symptoms. As the clinician, assess if the client has been able to develop feelings of safety again. If not, this may become a goal of treatment.

Finally, the last questionnaire can assess the extent to which a client has been impacted by vicarious trauma. This type of trauma can include witnessing crime or domestic violence or living in an area characterized by poverty and high crime rates. Clients who live in unsafe environments, such as a war-torn area, a refugee camp, the inner city, or a home with domestic violence, have not had a safe place to go as a refuge. They are constantly in survival mode even when they do enter areas of safety. Assisting them to establish a sense of felt safety is an important goal of treatment.

Worksheet (Adult or Child)

Questionnaire #1

As you reflect on the experiences you have had in your lifetime, please answer these questions and think about how those experiences may have impacted your life moving forward.

1. Have you ever had a time when you were afraid for your safety? Write about it here.

   _____

   _____

   _____

2. How did that experience impact your ability to express or calm your emotions?

   _____

   _____

   _____

3. Have you been able to cope with those feelings? Why or why not? If so, how did you cope?

   _____

   _____

   _____

4. How did that experience change the thoughts you have about yourself, others, or the world?

   _____

   _____

   _____

5. Have you been able to feel safe again and calm any anxious thoughts? Why or why not? If so, how did you return to feeling safe?

   _____

   _____

   _____

6. Did this unsafe incident change your relationships or change your ability to feel safe with others? If so, do your relationships feel safe again now? Why or why not?

   _____

   _____

   _____

Worksheet (Adult or Child)

Questionnaire #2

As you reflect on the experiences you have had in your lifetime, please answer these questions and think about how those experiences may have impacted your life moving forward.

1. How has your relationship with your primary parent/guardian been? Describe it here.

_____

_____

_____

2. How has your relationship with your other primary parent/guardian been? Describe it here.

_____

_____

_____

3. Have your parents taught you coping skills and how to calm yourself? How so?

_____

_____

_____

4. Have you been able to use those coping skills to help you calm your feelings? Why or why not?

_____

_____

_____

5. Have your parents modeled appropriate social skills (i.e., taught you how to act toward others)? If so, have you been able to use those social skills to successfully get along with others? Why or why not?

_____

_____

_____

6. What did your parents teach you about relationships?

_____

_____

_____

7. Has that been helpful in forming your own relationships? Why or why not?

_____

_____

_____

Questionnaire #3

As you reflect on the experiences you have had in your lifetime, please answer these questions and think about how those experiences may have impacted your life moving forward.

1. Have your parents helped you feel safe at home? Why or why not?

_____

_____

_____

2. Have your parents ever used physical discipline that left marks? Describe that here.

_____

_____

_____

3. Have you ever experienced any unwanted sexual touching within your family relationships? Describe that here.

_____

_____

_____

4. How has your relationship with your parents impacted your ability to cope and calm your emotions?

_____

_____

_____

5. How has your relationship with your parents impacted your other relationships?

_____

_____

_____

6. If you have had a difficult relationship with your parents, do you feel like there has been healing in your relationship with your parents? Have you been able to heal? Why or why not?

_____

_____

_____

7. Have you been able to find feelings of safety in your relationship with your parents?

_____

_____

_____

8. For adults: If you have children, what is your relationship with them? Are you able to provide your children a feeling of safety? How so?

_____

_____

_____

Worksheet (Adult or Child)

Questionnaire #4

As you reflect on the experiences you have had in your lifetime, please answer these questions and think about how those experiences may have impacted your life moving forward.

1. Have your parents met your physical needs (e.g., food, shelter, clothing)? Why or why not?

_____

_____

_____

2. Have your parents met your emotional needs (e.g., caring about your feelings)? Why or why not?

_____

_____

_____

3. Have your parents been available to you when you needed them (e.g., to talk to or spend time with)? Why or why not?

_____

_____

_____

4. Have there been any needs that you had to meet for yourself? If so, at what age did you begin to take care of these needs? How do you feel about this?

_____

_____

_____

5. If you could change anything about your parents, what would you change?

_____

_____

_____

6. Has your relationship with your parents impacted how you allow others to meet your needs? Why or why not?

_____

_____

_____

7. Do you feel like you can be vulnerable (i.e., share your emotions and needs) in relationships? Why or why not?

_____

_____

_____

8. Do you experience any difficulty listening to directions from people who are in a position of authority (e.g., at work, school, etc.)?

_____

_____

_____

Worksheet (Adult or Child)

Questionnaire #5

As you reflect on the experiences that you have had in your lifetime, please answer these questions and think about how those experiences may have impacted your life moving forward.

1. Have you undergone any medical procedures that were life-threatening or fear-inducing? If so, describe that here.

   _____

   _____

   _____

2. Were you able to find feelings of safety after the medical procedure? Why or why not?

   _____

   _____

   _____

3. Do you have a medical condition that is ongoing? If so, how does it impact you?

   _____

   _____

   _____

4. Does having this medical condition ever make you feel overwhelmed? Why or why not?

   _____

   _____

   _____

5. What are some aspects of your physical health over which you do and do not have control? How do you feel about this?

   _____

   _____

   _____

6. How do you handle things over which you do not have control?

   _____

   _____

   _____

Questionnaire #6

As you reflect on the experiences you have had in your lifetime, please answer these questions and think about how those experiences may have impacted your life moving forward.

1. Have you ever experienced a natural disaster, such as a flood, tornado, hurricane, earthquake, or fire? If so, describe that here.

_____

_____

_____

2. How did this event make you feel? What emotions did you experience?

_____

_____

_____

3. Do you still experience these emotions now? How do you cope with these feelings?

_____

_____

_____

4. Did this event change the way you think about certain people, places, or things? For example, did it make any of these things feel less safe? How so?

_____

_____

_____

5. Have you been able to feel safe again in these areas of your life? Why or why not?

_____

_____

_____

Questionnaire #7

As you reflect on the experiences you have had in your lifetime, please answer these questions and think about how those experiences may have impacted your life moving forward.

1. Have you witnessed violence, such as crime in your neighborhood, mass violence, or domestic violence in your home? Describe that here.

   _____

   _____

   _____

2. Was it a one-time occurrence or an ongoing situation?

   _____

   _____

   _____

3. How did this event impact your ability to feel safe?

   _____

   _____

   _____

4. Are there still times when you feel unsafe? Times when your heart is racing, you feel on edge, or you feel like you need to protect yourself? Describe that here.

   _____

   _____

   _____

5. Are there any times when you do feel safe? Describe that here.

   _____

   _____

   _____

6. What do you do to help yourself find safety? What do you do to cope when you feel unsafe or to calm yourself?

   _____

   _____

   _____

RESILIENCY QUESTIONNAIRE

When a client has experienced trauma, we know that certain factors—personality characteristics, context, coping skills, and supportive connections—increase a client's chances of being resilient. To assess for resiliency factors, we want to determine whether each of these four factors is present and, if so, the extent to which they are helpful to the client. For example, if a client has access to supportive connections but is not drawing on these connections, we would want to explore what barriers are getting in the way. Does this client value their independence and self-sufficiency at the expense of relationships? If so, a goal of treatment would be to help the client manage the internal conflict they experience between needing help and not wanting to ask for or accept it. We could explore what "independence" means to the client and how they conceptualize those who need help. In removing the barrier that blocks access to supportive connections, we have begun to move the client in the direction of resiliency.

Resiliency Questionnaire

There are several factors that can help you recover from trauma, known as "resiliency factors," which are listed below. Look over these factors and place a check mark by any statement that applies to you. As you complete this questionnaire, it is important to answer honestly. If some of these resiliency factors are not present in your life, this can become a goal of treatment before trauma processing begins. The important point is for you to be as supported as possible during this process.

Personality

_____ 1. I see the glass as half empty.

_____ 2. I see the glass as half full.

_____ 3. I am open to trying new things.

_____ 4. I like everything to be the same all the time.

_____ 5. I like to handle problems by myself.

_____ 6. I am able to ask my loved ones for support.

_____ 7. I feel like bad things always happen to me.

_____ 8. I go with the flow and know that nothing is guaranteed.

Context

_____ 9. I have never experienced a trauma before.

_____ 10. I have experienced a trauma and feel that it has been resolved.

_____ 11. I have experienced several traumas.

_____ 12. I have experienced a trauma and feel that it has *not* been resolved.

Coping Skills

_____ 13. I know what things bring me peace and calm.

_____ 14. I do things that bring me peace and calm every day.

_____ 15. I do things that bring me peace and calm some days.

_____ 16. I do not know what brings me peace and calm.

Supportive Connections

_____ 17. I have loved ones whom I see regularly.

_____ 18. I have loved ones whom I can ask for help.

_____ 19. I have asked for help from my loved ones.

_____ 20. I would not ask my loved ones for help.

_____ 21. I have someone I could call in an emergency.

_____ 22. I have people who understand me.

_____ 23. I have people with whom I enjoy spending time.

_____ 24. I do not feel connected to others.

Scoring Key:

Resiliency is indicated by check marks to the following items:

Personality: 2, 3, 6, 8

Context: 10

Coping Skills: 13, 14, 15

Supportive Connections: 17, 18, 19, 21, 22, 23

Part 2

Healing Interventions
for Trauma

3

Attachment Trauma

Henry was raised in a home with a loving mother and father, two brothers, and a sister. Both of Henry's parents worked, and beginning at age 10, he was responsible for completing his homework on his own and for helping his siblings get a snack when they got home from school. His parents arrived home in the evenings to make dinner, after which they would continue working on whatever project they had brought home from the office. During this time, Henry would watch TV in his room or play video games until he was tired. Although his parents told him that they loved him and took care of his basic needs, they did not spend time with him or connect with him in meaningful ways. As a child, Henry felt alone.

When Henry was 22 years old, he married a woman he had known for only a few months. Shortly after the marriage began, his wife began complaining that they never did anything together, and she described feeling disconnected from Henry and wanting to leave him. Henry began therapy with a desire to save his marriage, but he did not understand what his wife wanted him to do differently or why he should change. While he provided for his portion of the bills and was home in the evenings, he often isolated for hours playing video games. He did not see the need for a relationship beyond the one he currently had, and he did not understand why his wife wanted more than what he was giving. No relationship had ever required more from him, and he was struggling to build a more meaningful connection with her.

Henry's story reflects a movement that began in the 1970s, known as the "Me decade," during which people began pursuing their own wants and needs. Tom Wolfe (1976) described this new attitude in his essay "The 'Me' Decade and the Third Great Awakening." It was during this "Me decade" that people began seeking more independence instead of finding a balance of interdependence. They began to meet their own needs instead of depending on others to do so. Over the decades, this movement toward fierce independence has resulted in a lack of attachment in society as people have increasingly shunned the vulnerability that comes with expressing their needs. However, vulnerability is the foundation of attachment. Vulnerability involves having the emotional openness and willingness to admit that someone cannot do everything for themselves and then allowing someone else to meet their needs.

Although expressing vulnerability is not a sign of weakness, many people harbor this misconception, which keeps them from expressing their needs. Because they equate vulnerability with weakness, they may become frustrated when they are unable to meet their own needs and must rely on others. However, it is critical to reframe this understanding of vulnerability because it holds people to an unrealistic expectation that leaves them frustrated and disappointed. Every person has needs they cannot meet for themselves. That does not mean that there is something wrong with them or that they are less than. It means that they are human.

When someone meets a need, it builds trust. And when we see someone else's need and meet that need, it creates attunement. **Attunement means we are "in tune" with someone else, enough that we see their need and care enough about them to meet that need.** This process begins in infancy when newborn babies cry to let adults know their needs. As parents meet this need over and over again, infants develop trust and begin to understand that when they express their need, someone will come and meet it. This gives the baby confidence to continue expressing needs with the knowledge that someone will be responsive to meet those needs.

In contrast, if children are born to parents who are not responsive to their needs—physically, emotionally, or mentally—then children do not learn to trust others to meet their needs. This impacts children's ability to engage in meaningful, attachment-based relationships moving forward. There are a variety of factors that can cause a parent to be unresponsive to the needs of a child, including the following:

- A parent who is abusing substances may not respond when their baby is crying or hungry.
- A parent with a serious mental illness or postpartum depression may not respond to the cries of their baby or the needs of their older children.
- A single parent who is overwhelmed trying to meet the needs of their child may find that they are routinely unable to do so.
- Parents who are preoccupied with technology may unintentionally ignore their child or their child's expressed needs.
- A parent's own trauma or abuse history may make them unable to parent in a way that was different than what was modeled for them.

Ultimately, **attachment requires an emotional connection to another person, which begins with vulnerability.** That person allows themselves the vulnerability to show their emotions, and we connect with them because we recognize their emotional vulnerability and understand it. However, we can only recognize and understand another person's emotions if we have the insight to understand our own. We use our own understanding of our emotions to recognize and understand those same emotions in others.

Being able to exhibit this level of empathy and insight requires appropriate emotion regulation skills, which is the ability to recognize your own emotions, to express them appropriately, and to use coping skills to manage them effectively. Children learn how to regulate their emotions in childhood through attachment-based relationships with adults. For example, when an infant is fussy, the parent soothes the baby by rocking, bouncing, or swaying the baby. They may also shake a rattle or make silly faces to change the baby's mood. However, if this kind of attachment-based relationship is missing, then the child may not learn how to regulate their emotions. Children need adults to help them co-regulate because they have not yet learned how to soothe themselves. Without any insight or understanding of their own emotions, children who lack attachment-based relationships will develop into adults who struggle to recognize and understand the emotions of others.

Struggles related to emotion regulation may be particularly salient for children raised in the wake of the "Me decade." Following this movement, the desire for increased independence led many families to become dual-income families, and single parents emerged on a larger scale. As a result, children were placed in daycare at increasing rates, and latchkey children, or kids spending unsupervised time at home alone, became common. Many of these latchkey kids are now parents today, and they may struggle in helping their children develop emotion regulation skills or attachment-based relationships because they themselves didn't learn how to parent in an attachment-based way.

In today's society, many parents want their children to be independent, even at young ages. However, this is not developmentally appropriate, as children are not able to function independently, and they experience anxiety and depression when pressured to do so. For example, a parent attending an individualized education program (IEP) meeting for their elementary-age child may express a desire for their child to independently complete homework. However, what that child needs is for their parent to sit with them, explain new concepts, and help them problem solve. This is part of an attachment-based, parent-child relationship. It strengthens the relationship and allows the child to feel more secure.

The parent-child relationship is so important because it is the first relationship anyone has. It becomes the template on which a child bases all future relationships. What children know about relationships is what their parents have modeled to them. If a parent does not model attunement, emotion regulation, or trust-based attachment, then their child will not know the way to meaningful relationships as they transition into adulthood. They may struggle to form meaningful, attachment-based relationships in life, leaving them feeling alone and disconnected. There are many symptoms that can serve as an indicator that someone may have experienced this type of attachment trauma, including:

- Difficulty maintaining relationships
- Complaints from partners that the person is disconnected
- Complaints from partners that the person is not responsive to their needs
- Difficulty expressing their needs
- Inability to admit vulnerability or fear of vulnerability
- Extreme value placed on independence
- Dissatisfaction with relationships
- Belief that relationships are "too much work"
- Belief that there is no value in allowing others to meet their needs
- Lack of trust in relationships
- Lack of emotional insight or empathy

How does this trauma heal? How can parents be more strongly attached to their children? How can adults heal this trauma for themselves to have more fulfilling relationships? **Relational trauma is healed through healthy relationships that meet our needs and that are attachment-based.** Presenting the brain with information about relationships that is new and that challenges the person's belief system about how relationships work is how we create and reinforce new neural pathways.

Start at the beginning. Teach adults and parents how to attach so they can teach their children how to do so. Encourage healthy attachment in families. Teach what should have been taught in the family context. Attachment-based relationships are the foundation for healing all other traumas. When there is a secure relationship between a parent and child, or between two adults, this creates an environment of safety where healing can begin. The nurturing and comfort within this relationship is essential for recovery and resilience. There are several phases involved in this process of healing attachment trauma, which can be taught to children and adults alike:

- **Phase 1: Teach Emotion Regulation Skills.** Without insight into their own emotions, clients will be unable to have empathy and to recognize those emotions in someone else, even their own child. Teaching clients about emotions and how to effectively express and cope with those emotions is the foundation of emotion regulation. Validate the emotions that clients do express, and encourage them to mindfully explore the emotions they have not had the vulnerability to share.

- **Phase 2: Teach Relationship-Building Skills.** Once clients have developed an understanding of their own emotions, encourage them to practice being vulnerable by sharing those newfound emotions with others. They can start by sharing their emotions with the clinician in session and, as they become empowered, move to sharing those emotions with others to whom they feel close. Ask them to choose a safe relationship to exhibit vulnerability. Teach and practice listening skills so they can begin to hear the needs and unspoken emotions of others.

- **Phase 3: Teach Attunement.** As clients begin to meet the needs of others, encourage them to do so without the expectation that others will meet their needs in return. They should instead invite their partner or friend to the dance of attunement without attempting to force or control it. Process how it feels for the client to meet another's needs and how it feels when the other person meets their needs in turn. Emphasize the foundations of trust: how to build it, keep it, and repair it.

- **Phase 4: Teach Attachment.** Everyone wants to feel connected to another person, to feel that they are not alone in the world. Clients can build relationships by spending quality time with others. By finding things that they share in common or by learning new things together. By helping one another with tasks or through difficult times. By exhibiting empathy and attunement on a daily basis. By meeting needs (physically, emotionally, mentally) consistently. And by working to repair relationships instead of leaving them when they become difficult.

When a client has learned these four phases, they have the foundation needed for healthy relationships. The following interventions will give support in teaching these four phases to heal attachment trauma and will provide a foundation to heal all other traumas.

EMOTION REGULATION INTERVENTIONS

Helping clients identify the emotions they are currently feeling can tell us where we need to begin teaching based on what clients are already experiencing. Use the **My Feelings Chart** to have clients identify any feelings they experienced throughout the week, how they expressed it, and how they coped with it. Adult clients should complete the worksheet each day for a week. For child clients, you can simplify the exercise by asking them to simply think about all the feelings they have had on that particular day. When reviewing the worksheet in session, identify any emotions they are not consistently reporting.

You can use the **Which One?** worksheet to help children identify what emotions might be elicited across different scenarios. Have them read each scenario and then match it with the corresponding emotion. Clinicians can use this as a teachable moment if clients identify the wrong emotion. This exercise can also serve as a useful homework assignment for a parent and child to complete together.

The **Learning About Emotions Together** worksheet is intended to be used with a child and their parent. This worksheet asks clients to identify a time they experienced a particular emotion, including how they expressed it and calmed it. It is important to normalize that even positive emotions need to be calmed sometimes. For example, an adult who just received good news about a promotion while at work may need to take a few deep breaths to calm themselves and wait until they get home to dance around the kitchen and celebrate with their spouse. Likewise, a child who is excited at school because it is their birthday will still need to sit quietly in class and follow directions. Being able to calm both positive and negative emotions allows individuals to function without becoming overwhelmed.

Therefore, this worksheet is useful in teaching children and adults alike about emotion regulation, especially if parents have not learned how to regulate their own emotions. It allows parents to assess how they have expressed and modeled emotions for their child, and it also allows the child to see that emotions are a normal part of everyone's experience. The parent and child can complete this worksheet together in session or as homework. It will strengthen the attachment-based relationship between the parent and child, allowing the parent to be the leader. You can repeat the worksheet, processing one emotion per week over the course of several weeks.

Clinicians can also use the **My Inner World** worksheet with adult clients by asking them to review the emotions they experienced over the past week and to think about whether or not they actually expressed the felt emotion. This exercise will help identify any feelings that clients are not reporting or expressing. Look for themes with regard to emotions or experiences that cause repeated triggers.

Once clients begin to recognize their own emotions, the next step is to help them develop the capacity to recognize emotions in others. Using **The World Around Me** worksheet as a guide, ask adult clients to identify emotions that other people have experienced over the past week. They can focus on a spouse, significant other, friend, or coworker. This exercise can begin to strengthen that relationship as the client focuses on the feelings of their identified loved one and begins to develop empathy for that person's experience.

Part of teaching emotion regulation skills involves helping clients identify the coping and calming skills that work for them. Different coping skills work for different people. Identifying activities that relax a person and then being intentional about incorporating them into their daily routine can assist them in staying at emotional baseline. For example, a child can visit a calm-down area in a classroom or at home every two hours to help them proactively de-stress. Incorporating this calm-down routine into their schedule at regular intervals can prevent instances of emotional escalation that then require a reactive response.

Similarly, adults can think about things that relax them and that bring them happiness and joy. If they have difficulty identifying activities, ask about their daily routine, and see if certain parts of this routine may work to calm them. For example, if they identify going to the gym each day but don't acknowledge it as a coping mechanism, point out the physical benefits of exercise, including increased dopamine and endorphins (and decreased adrenaline), and emphasize the importance of self-care in regulating emotions.

The two **Coping and Calming** interventions are intended to provide ideas for different activities that clients can use to self-soothe and promote emotional stability. A different version of the handout is included for adults versus children. By proactively using coping skills at regular intervals—instead of waiting for their emotions to overwhelm them—clients can more effectively keep themselves at baseline.

In teaching clients about their emotions, it can help to include movement and laughter because when clients are laughing and having fun, their defenses are low and they are engaged in learning new concepts. In addition, by incorporating body movement and having clients act out the appropriate expression of emotion, we are creating muscle memory, which allows their body to remember how to respond to similar situations in the future. The **Feeling Charades** activity can be used with children, with adults, or in a family session to teach clients about healthy emotional expression and to build the bonds of attachment. Clients are asked to pick an emotion and to act out how they can express that emotion in an appropriate and inappropriate manner. When they act out the emotion inappropriately, we are reinforcing that this is not a healthy way to react. We then contrast that with their being able to successfully act out the emotion appropriately, which reinforces this new way of responding.

The **Teaching Your Child Emotion Regulation** handout is a helpful tool for processing with parents the importance of teaching emotion regulation skills to their child. Oftentimes, parents will tell their child to "calm down" when the child is escalating, but doing so is not helpful or nurturing. Rather, it is important for parents to model how to manage emotions and how to express them in a healthy manner. The process of learning emotion regulation occurs across three phases—(1) parent-assisted regulation, (2) co-regulation, and (3) self-regulation—and unless children learn all three steps, they will be unable to tolerate or manage their emotions as they develop into adulthood. Share this handout with parents, and use it as a way to give gentle direction and education about what children need from their parents.

My Feelings Chart

We have lots of feelings every day. These feelings can feel big or small. They can also last a long time or a short time—sometimes even changing every few minutes. When our feelings are big, they can become overwhelming and take control over us. Even happy feelings like excitement can feel big and overwhelming at times. For example, many children feel very excited the last week of school and have a hard time controlling themselves, resulting in consequences for talking out of turn, running around the classroom, or not listening—even though excitement is a positive emotion. Think about the feelings you have already had today, and answer the following three questions about each feeling.

	What caused the feeling?	How did you express the feeling?	How did you calm the feeling (if it was overwhelming)?
Feeling 1			
Feeling 2			
Feeling 3			

Which One?

Below are several different scenarios that might cause people to feel certain ways. See if you can identify what emotion each person was feeling in each scenario. Then try to think of a time during the past week when you felt each emotion.

Sad   **Angry**   **Happy**   **Scared**   **Disappointed**   **Frustrated**

1. Bill was waiting for his grandmother to come take him out to lunch. Bill's mom told him that his grandmother had just called and said she couldn't come to visit him because she was sick. Bill is feeling _____.

2. Susan is getting an award at her soccer practice for scoring the most points in the last game. She is excited and looking forward to this special honor. Susan is feeling _____.

3. Antonio has been learning about multiplication in math class, and it is so hard! He has to keep trying again when he gets an incorrect answer, and sometimes he just wants to give up. Antonio is feeling _____.

4. Darius heard a noise outside and doesn't know what it is. His father just went next door to ask the neighbor a question, and Darius is alone at home. Darius is feeling _____.

5. Karis just heard that Uncle Tommy is sick and in the hospital. The family is getting ready to go visit him, and Karis feels low and like she might cry. Karis is feeling _____.

6. Kyle's little sister just broke his favorite toy, the one he got for his birthday last week. Kyle feels himself getting hot and his hands clench into fists. Kyle is feeling _____.

Answer Key:
1. Disappointed
2. Happy
3. Frustrated
4. Scared
5. Sad
6. Angry

Learning About Emotions Together

Emotions can be overwhelming. Pick an emotion that can be intense for you and answer the following questions together.

	Parent	**Child**
I feel _____ when…		
I express my _____ feelings by…		
I calm my _____ feelings by…		

Worksheet (Adult)

My Inner World

We all experience a variety of emotions every single day. Our emotions can change quickly, and we are often unaware of them. Think back to the last week, and see if you can remember any intense emotions that stand out—emotions that were elicited by events that happened during this time. Note those emotions on the chart below, and describe how you expressed them. Then go back and think about less intense emotions you may have felt. Add those to the chart too, including how you expressed those emotions.

	My Emotion	How I Expressed It	My Emotion	How I Expressed It	My Emotion	How I Expressed It
Monday						
Tuesday						
Wednesday						
Thursday						
Friday						
Saturday						
Sunday						

The World Around Me

Every day, people all around you experience emotions just like you. Think about your social interactions over the last week, and see if you can remember any times when someone expressed an emotion, whether big or small. It may have been a coworker, friend, neighbor, spouse, partner, or someone at the grocery store. What did you see? What did you hear? What did you notice that may have contributed to that feeling? Being mindful, explore the experience and think about how that person was feeling.

Emotion I Witnessed	How They Expressed the Emotion	What May Have Caused the Emotion?

Coping and Calming

The following are a variety of soothing activities that children can use to remain calm and cool. These activities can be used at home or at school. You can introduce the activities by placing several coping stations around the room and encouraging the child to visit each station as they try out various coping skills. Given that we use our senses to gather information about the world around us, ask children to think about engaging their sense of sight, sound, touch, taste, and smell as they move through each station. In addition, some activities are intended to tap into children's proprioceptive (awareness of one's body in space) and vestibular (sense of movement and balance) systems, which can help children with sensory processing issues learn how to feel more in control of their bodies.

Encourage children to visit the coping stations at regular intervals throughout the day to help them remain emotionally grounded, especially if it appears that a child is emotionally escalating. The following are a variety of items that you can include at these coping stations:

- Kinetic sand
- Play-Doh®
- Modeling clay
- Coloring utensils
- Stretch toys
- Cotton balls with different essential oil scents on them
- Peppermints
- Sound machine with various options (e.g., ocean, white noise, jungle)
- Mandalas
- Containers of uncooked pasta, beans, rice, or popcorn with toys or figurines mixed in
- Weighted blanket
- Exercise station (five jumping jacks, four toe touches, three sit ups, two push-ups, one turn around)
- Texture box with pieces of felt, Velcro, silk, and flannel inside

Coping and Calming

Incorporating self-care activities into your everyday life is an important way to maintain emotional consistency. For example, taking a run every morning can help you de-stress before starting the day, while watching a funny television program when you get home from work can help you de-stress as you head into the evening. In addition, reading for 30 minutes before bed can clear your mind and help you get a good night's sleep.

Implementing self-care at regular intervals throughout the day can be easy. It doesn't take extensive planning or require you to build in extra time. It can be as simple as:

6 a.m.:   Going for a run

8 a.m.:   Drinking coffee or tea

10 a.m.: Calling a friend while on break at work

12 p.m.: Eating a nutritious lunch

2 p.m.:   Spending two minutes gazing at a calming picture (e.g., one's family, a beloved pet)

4 p.m.:   Listening to relaxing music in the car on the way home from work

6 p.m.:   Talking to one's spouse or significant other about the day

8 p.m.:   Watching a lighthearted TV show

10 p.m.: Reading a book for 30 minutes before bed

In this manner, you can calm yourself every two hours by simply being mindful and intentional about enjoying the moment and taking time for yourself. On the following page, think about different coping and calming activities you might be able to incorporate into your schedule throughout the day.

Coping and Calming Schedule

	Mon	Tues	Wed	Thurs	Fri	Sat	Sun
6 a.m.							
8 a.m.							
10 a.m.							
12 p.m.							
2 p.m.							
4 p.m.							
6 p.m.							
8 p.m.							
10 p.m.							

Feeling Charades

Look at the list of emotions and choose one to act out. Begin by acting out the emotion inappropriately. For example, if you choose to act out pride, you might brag about your accomplishments or put others down. Or if you choose to act out anger, you might stomp and throw imaginary things. Then act out the emotion a second time, this time role-playing how you would express that emotion in an appropriate and healthy manner. The goal is for the other players to guess what emotion you are acting out. Feel free to exaggerate and have fun! Channel your inner actor! If you find it difficult to think of an appropriate way to express an emotion, pause the game and brainstorm together how you could express that emotion without causing harm to yourself or others.

Happy

Frustrated

Silly

Angry

Proud

Disappointed

Shy

Sad

Jealous

Scared

Teaching Your Child Emotion Regulation

Being able to effectively manage and respond to our emotions is known as *emotion regulation*. This is a skill that develops across the lifespan, and it is a skill that children do not yet possess. Children's brains are still developing, so they are not able to manage their emotions or control their impulses the same way an adult would. It is a life skill they need to learn, just like walking and talking. And they cannot learn how to regulate their emotions if their parents do not teach them. So how do you teach your child how to take care of their emotions?

As a parent, you need to be able to regulate your own emotions before you teach your child how to do so. However, if no one ever taught you how to calm your emotions, then the concept of emotion regulation may seem foreign to you. It is important to be honest with yourself about whether you have what is needed to successfully teach this skill to your child. Do you have coping skills? Do they work to calm you? Are you able to calm yourself when you are getting upset? You are a role model for your child, and they learn about emotion regulation from you, whether you realize it or not.

Children learn what their parents model for them, so if you yell or scream when you become upset, then you can expect your child to do so as well. If you throw things when you are angry, then you can expect your child to mimic this behavior too. In contrast, if you take deep breaths to calm yourself during times of distress, then your child will follow your lead. Your child is watching you, following you, repeating you, and learning from you. They will do what you do, not what you say. Here are the three steps involved in the process of helping your child learn emotion regulation skills:

1. **Parent-Assisted Regulation:** You teach your child what emotions are, how to express their emotions appropriately, and how to use coping skills to calm themselves down. This means giving your child a vocabulary of emotions so they can come to you when upset and say, "I feel frustrated" or "I feel angry." They need to know the difference between emotions so they can express how they are feeling. In addition, parent-assisted regulation involves letting them know that it is okay to have emotions and teaching them how to express those emotions without getting into trouble. For example, we can feel angry and express that anger with our words instead of doing something that will result in consequences. Finally, it involves teaching them coping skills they can use to calm down, such as taking a few deep breaths or asking to take a break and walk outside for a few minutes. We have to teach them and practice *with* them so they can learn.

2. **Co-Regulation:** At this next step, you provide supportive and warm interactions that help your child calm down when they are escalating. In these moments, you respond with empathy and support by remaining emotionally regulated (cool, calm, and collected) to help your child manage their arousal. These interactions model your own ability to self-regulate and form the template from which children eventually learn to do so on their own. You validate the child's feelings (e.g., "I can see that you are really sad right now") and offer comfort. Then you may offer a coping skill to calm them. For a baby, it may be a rattle; for an older child, it may be a special stuffed animal; and for a teen, it may be putting on their favorite song. You practice these coping skills with the child until they can use them independently. This step can take a little longer as your child learns how and when to use coping skills. It will take a lot of investment to support your child and to comfort them before they will be able to comfort themselves. It is important to be patient throughout this process as they are learning.

3. **Self-Regulation:** The goal is for children to eventually be able to self-regulate and use coping skills independently. Instead of melting down, your child will now be able to come to you for support and to use their words to tell you how they are feeling. Instead of screaming when they are angry or frustrated, your teenager may be able to say, "I feel angry, and I need a time out," and then take a break before returning to the conversation. They will begin to notice when they are starting to feel upset and will use coping skills early to avoid escalation. Although self-regulation is the goal, it does not happen unless we follow steps 1 and 2 first.

As you think about your ability to handle your own emotions, take a few minutes to think about your readiness to teach this skill to your child and whether you would benefit from working on your own emotion regulation skills first.

RELATIONSHIP-BUILDING INTERVENTIONS

Once clients have developed greater emotional awareness, they can work toward developing more attachment-based relationships. Use the child version of the **Relationship Inventory** worksheet to help young clients take inventory of their current relationships and to determine their level of comfort and safety in those relationships. This worksheet can be repeated several times, one for each significant relationship in the child's life.

Work with the child to determine if they feel safe in this relationship, to identify activities they like to do with this person, and to uncover what role that person plays in the child's life. If the child completes several worksheets for different people, compare and contrast how different people fill different roles. Doing so reinforces the notion that different relationships have different boundaries. In addition, begin to identify if some relationships are not healthy. For instance, if a child reports that they do not feel comfortable sharing their feelings in a given relationship, ask clarifying questions to determine whether or not this is a safe relationship where they can exhibit vulnerability.

In addition, you can use the adult version of the **Relationship Inventory** worksheet to help adult clients identify the various roles that people play in their lives. Sometimes clients have relationships they don't recognize or acknowledge. This worksheet can help them think more broadly about their relationships and begin to recognize that they may have more relationships than they realize.

The **Roles in Relationships** worksheet is a helpful tool for adult clients to assess their relationships and the roles that other people play in their life. The range of these relationships can vary from minor contacts and associates to best friends and family members. Ask clarifying questions about how clients decide what relationship category people fall into. Talk about how people move in and out of categories depending on the qualities that each person brings to the relationship. For example, if a close friend or family member serves in a major relationship role—but that person continues to be untrustworthy or continuously hurts the client—then it may be appropriate for that person to move to a less important category. In these cases, discuss how the client can work to develop appropriate boundaries that protect their emotions.

Healthy relationships involve a mutual degree of give and take. Everyone is important, and no one's rights are more important than someone else's. While people may differ in terms of education, social status, or wealth, no one's thoughts or feelings are more important than another's. As humans, everyone is equal and important. The **Everyone Is Important** worksheet can help children develop this realization as they navigate relationships and find balance in these relationships. Ultimately, building healthy connections with others involves teaching children to be respectful of others and to be equally respectful of themselves.

In addition, use the **Relationship Likes and Dislikes** worksheet to help children explore their relationship preferences. Asking children to think about things they like and don't like in the context of relationships can increase their insight into personal preferences and help them develop healthy boundaries. Once they have come up with a list of relationship likes and dislikes, encourage them to respectfully share these preferences with the people they are close to. Teaching them to express their needs and wants in relationships is a lifelong skill. Help them find their voice and use it appropriately to get their needs met. You can also role-play with them so they can practice using their voice until they have the confidence to use it independently.

In order to build healthy relationships, it is important for children to distinguish between the relationships they have with adults versus those they have with their peers. The **Relationship Differences** worksheet can help children explore their relationships and see the different characteristics of each, depending on the role the person plays in their lives. Although children may feel that all relationships are the same, this worksheet can help them recognize that different people have different responsibilities. For example, adults have responsibilities to keep children safe and to teach them new things. Peer relationships do not have the same characteristics. Once the child has identified these relationship differences, ask clarifying questions about the roles that people play in their life. For example, if a child identifies that their parents do not set rules, ask them more questions about the structure at home.

In addition, the **My Relationships with Adults** worksheet can be helpful in further clarifying the difference between peer and adult relationships. When a child feels like they are equal with adults, this is often a symptom of an attachment trauma in which the child has been put in a position where they were required to meet their own needs. As a result, this child often does not trust adults to be in a position of authority or to meet their needs. To bring healing to this child, they need to learn to see adults as safe people who protect them. One important way that adults keep children safe is by enacting rules and consequences. However, children who have experienced an attachment trauma often do not recognize that rules and consequences are intended for their own well-being. Helping a child come to this realization can allow them to more easily accept when adults are in charge and hold them accountable. When they can feel safe with adults, they can begin to move forward in healing.

In the context of relationships, there are things we can control (ourselves) and things we cannot control (other people). And it is the things that are out of our control that can become the most frustrating. When clients try to control another person's words, behaviors, or choices, this can destroy the relationship. Focusing on that which they cannot control is exhausting and eternally frustrating because no matter how hard they try to change someone else's behavior, they will never be able to do so.

In order to bring stability to an unstable relationship, clients must learn to accept the things they cannot change, which most often involve the choices the other person makes. Instead, they can shift their focus to what they can control: their own choices, behaviors, and words. Encourage adult and child clients to use the **Reacting and Responding** worksheet to identify more effective ways to handle frustration and to take ownership over how they respond in their relationships. Doing so will relieve frustration and can empower them to take accountability for their own actions.

In addition to teaching clients how to effectively respond to conflict, it is equally important to teach them how to repair relationships that have already been ruptured. Knowing how to apologize is not a skill we are born with, and just like emotion regulation skills, children can only learn this relationship skill if someone models it for them and prompts them to apologize at the correct times. Use the **Anatomy of an Apology** worksheet to help children begin to think about how they can heal broken relationships and reconcile attachments. Teaching this important social skill will help children learn how to repair damaged relationships.

Cultivating healthy relationships requires the ability to compromise, share with others, treat others with kindness, accept differences in opinion, respect personal space, and use active listening skills. Use the **Relationships Skills Role-Play** activity to encourage children to act out these various skills with another person. Engaging children in this playful activity can create muscle memory of appropriate social skills and allow these relationship skills to develop more quickly. Clinicians can complete this activity with a child in individual therapy or with a parent and child in family therapy. Including the parent in the activity will strengthen the attachment-based relationship and allow the parent to be the leader, reinforcing that they are modeling skills for their child. You can also have the parent role-play the skill incorrectly so the child can see what inappropriate skill use looks like in practice, and then have the child act it out correctly to reinforce appropriate relationship skills in their mind and body.

When introducing this activity, it is important to note that parents will differ in their own ability to exhibit effective social skills. Some parents are able to model appropriate relationship skills and can teach children how to interact with kindness, while others struggle with these skills. This can be a good time to educate parents about relationship effectiveness and to redirect them to think about what they are modeling to their children and why their child may be having a hard time in various environments (e.g., school, neighborhood, home life). The clinician may also need to act out the skills to provide modeling to the parent. Remind parents that even if they do not sit down and explicitly talk about social skills, their child is always watching them. They are constantly modeling how to treat other people, and children are learning from the example they are setting. Use the **Essential Social Skills** handout to help parents assess their ability to use various social skills, which will inform treatment and create insight into any skills that need attention.

When working with adults to assess their relationships, it can be helpful to develop a better understanding of what they value in relationships. Oftentimes, a person's level of satisfaction or dissatisfaction in their relationships is dependent on what they are looking for in another person and whether or not that person meets those needs. Sometimes a client may be seeking out something that is unrealistic. For example, a client may identify a list of 22 attributes they want in a relationship, and it is not realistic that they will find someone who meets all of those criteria. No perfect person exists. Everyone has pros and cons, and in healthy relationships, we appreciate the other person's strengths and have grace for their weaknesses.

Use the **Relationship Values** worksheet to help adult clients take stock of the qualities they are looking for in a relationship. This worksheet can assess how realistic your client's expectations are, allowing you to redirect them if you find that the list of values they require is long or unrealistic. Oftentimes, individuals who have experienced attachment trauma struggle to accept other people's imperfections, or they expect others to meet all of their needs. Process having grace for another's weaknesses, and help clients identify some of their own weaknesses for which others need to extend grace. This normalizes the healthy expectation that we all have strengths and weaknesses.

Challenges in relationships often have two outcomes: Either the relationship becomes stronger or it breaks apart. When relationships break apart, this is often because each partner grieves differently or has a different approach to overcoming hard things. **One way to overcome this conflict is to help clients understand that people don't need to handle challenges in the same way**. They can respect the other person's way of coping and provide the support this person needs regardless if it is the same support they themselves need.

Relationship challenges can also arise when clients feel overwhelmed by their own emotions. When two people are both going through the same grief or crisis, it can be challenging for both parties to comfort each other when they are struggling to comfort themselves. In these situations, it is important for clients to focus on their own self-care needs before attempting to meet the needs of their partner. They must also be willing to express vulnerability and to allow their partner to support them in meeting their needs. In doing so, clients put themselves in a position to better meet the needs of their loved one in return. This dance of attunement strengthens the attachment bond, and a closer relationship results. Use the **Overcoming Relationship Challenges** worksheet to help adult clients work through these steps in navigating any current relationship difficulties.

It is normal for conflict to happen in relationships. No two people think the same, and individuals will frequently disagree on what to do in a given situation. When people believe that relationship "perfection" is the goal—for example, hoping they will never argue or never disagree—they set themselves up to fail. They feel less than because they will never be able to achieve this unattainable goal. In contrast, when people come to the understanding that disagreements are a normal aspect of relationships, they can begin to talk about how to handle those disagreements and to move forward from them. Not arguing is not the goal. Rather, the goal is to argue well by being respectful, listening, and finding a compromise. Use the **Conflict in Relationships** worksheet to explore how adults manage conflict in their significant relationships.

Once you have identified how adult clients typically navigate conflict, you can use the **Listening for Emotion** worksheet to help them practice their reflective listening skills. Being able to listen to what other people have to say and to recognize how they are feeling can help clients work through disagreements more effectively. Ask clients to read each scenario on the worksheet and to list any unspoken emotions they heard in the dialogue. Then have them brainstorm how they could respond to that person in a way that validates these identified emotions. Based on clients' answers, see if there are any emotions they are repeatedly missing or denying, as this may serve as an indicator of an emotion they have more difficulty experiencing themselves.

Worksheet (Child)

Relationship Inventory

Relationships are important. They help us feel connected and valued. If a relationship is healthy, it makes us feel good about ourselves. In healthy relationships, we feel comfortable sharing and opening up. When you have a relationship with someone, here are some things you may want to ask yourself:

1. How long have I known this person?

_____

_____

_____

2. What role do they play in my life?

_____

_____

_____

3. Do I feel safe with this person? Why or why not?

_____

_____

_____

4. Does this person listen to me? Why or why not?

_____

_____

_____

5. Does this person care about my feelings? Why or why not?

_____

_____

_____

6. What feelings do I feel safe sharing with this person?

_____

_____

_____

7. What feelings do I not feel safe sharing with this person?

_____

_____

_____

8. Does this person meet any of my needs? Which ones?

_____

_____

_____

9. What things do we like to do together?

_____

_____

_____

Relationship Inventory

We have relationships in every aspect of our lives, including those that are a part of our daily routines. Although we often don't pay attention to seemingly minor relationships—instead choosing to focus on our major relationships—these more minor relationships can sometimes impact us in ways we do not recognize. For example, perhaps there is someone at work who asks how your day is and who genuinely appears to care. Although this may seem like an insignificant relationship, you see this person every day, for several hours a day, and this relationship may be more significant than you realize.

Use this worksheet to take inventory of your relationships. List out people you have relationships with at home, at work, and in the community—no matter how insignificant the relationship seems—and think about how well that person knows you.

	What do they know about my loved ones?	What do they know about the work I do or how I spend my day?	What do they know about my likes and dislikes?
At Home			
At Work or During My Day			
In the Community			

Now that you have taken a few moments to take inventory of your relationships, ask yourself whether there is a relationship that was more significant than you thought it was. What do you want to do with this realization? Is there a relationship that is less significant than you thought it was? How will that knowledge change your interactions with that person?

_____

_____

_____

_____

Roles in Relationships

There are several different categories of relationships, ranging from people we see in passing every day to very close friends who know our deepest secrets. These people all fulfill different roles in our lives, and what we share with them depends on the major or minor role they play. Look at the relationship categories listed here, and identify people in your life who fit each description. As you complete the worksheet, take time to consider whether certain people do not meet the criteria for the category in which you currently have them, and consider any relationships that may have different characteristics than you originally thought. For example, perhaps a close friend has repeatedly hurt you in the past, but you still allow them to fulfill a best friend role. Or perhaps you are getting to know someone better at work and would enjoy spending more time with them. Relationship categories are not set in stone, and it's possible for people to change relationship roles as the circumstances of your life change.

Minor Contacts
People whom you regularly interact with in everyday life, like grocery clerks or workmen. You may or may not know them by name.

_____

_____

_____

Associates
People whom you see in everyday life and who know you on a small scale. You make small talk but don't talk about important life events.

_____

_____

_____

Work/Daily Relationships

People who know some of your personal information and whom you talk to every day about superficial and sometimes deeper topics.

_____

_____

_____

Friends

People who know you and whom you can depend on for some support.

_____

_____

_____

Best Friends

A small group of people who know you very well, who have seen your life evolve, and who have supported you along the way. These are people you put your trust in.

_____

_____

_____

Family

The people who know you the best. Family is sometimes biological (e.g., parents, siblings, grandparents) and sometimes of our choosing (e.g., friends who become family). Family can also happen via commitment (e.g., spouses).

_____

_____

_____

Everyone Is Important

In healthy relationships, people treat one another as equals. That means everybody in the relationship is important. You are important, and so are your friends. Think about a friendship you have with someone and answer these questions:

1. Who do you feel is more important in this relationship? Or are you equals?

_____

_____

_____

2. Think about the last five times you and your friend had to make a choice about an activity. How many times did you do what *you* wanted to do? How many times did you do what *your friend* wanted to do?

_____

_____

_____

3. What are three things your friend likes to do?

_____

_____

_____

4. What are three things you like to do? Does your friend know what these are?

_____

_____

_____

5. What are three interesting things about your friend?

_____

_____

_____

6. What are three interesting things about you? Does your friend know what these are?

_____

_____

_____

7. Is there anything you want to tell your friend but feel that you can't? What stops you from sharing this?

_____

_____

_____

Relationship Likes and Dislikes

Taking time to think about what we like and don't like in relationships can help us make better decisions about how our relationships work. When we know our likes and dislikes, we can talk about the relationship and make sure everyone is comfortable with and getting what they need from the relationship. If something in a relationship makes you uncomfortable or you need something to change, make sure to use your voice to let the other person know. It is also important to listen to the other person if they say they don't like something about the relationship the two of you have.

1. My most favorite relationship is/was with _____

   because _____.

2. My least favorite relationship is/was with _____

   because _____.

3. These are the things I like about relationships:

   _____

   _____

   _____

4. These are the things I do not like about relationships:

   _____

   _____

   _____

5. I felt happy in a relationship when this happened:

_____

_____

_____

6. I felt sad in a relationship when this happened:

_____

_____

_____

7. I felt scared in a relationship when this happened:

_____

_____

_____

8. I felt mad in a relationship when this happened:

_____

_____

_____

Relationship Differences

We all have many different types of relationships, each of which is unique. For example, the relationship we have with our parents is not the same as the relationship we have with our grandparents, friends, or neighbors. Think about the different relationships you have and what makes them the same and different. Read each statement in the chart below, and place a check mark in each box if the statement is true for that relationship.

	Parents	Grandparents	Siblings	Friends	Teachers
They have rules I have to follow.					
They give me consequences.					
They teach me new things.					
They have fun with me.					
They make me feel safe.					
They are responsible for me.					
They care about my feelings.					
They listen when I talk.					
They help me when I don't understand something.					

My Relationships with Adults

The relationships you have with adults are different than the friendships you have with friends your own age. In a friendship, you are equals. But in a relationship with an adult, the adult is in charge. The adult leads while you follow their directions, as long as those directions are safe. Adults are leaders because they know more than kids do. They have experience and have learned many important things they want to share with you. You can learn a lot from adults if you listen and follow directions.

Think about adults who are in your life—your parents, grandparents, aunts, uncles, or teachers—and fill in these blanks as you think about your relationships with these adults.

1. These are safe directions an adult may give me:

   _____

   _____

   _____

2. These are unsafe directions an adult may give me—ones that I will need to think about before deciding if I will follow them:

   _____

   _____

   _____

3. When an adult is leading, I feel _____ because

   _____

4. I have a hard time following adult directions when

   _____

   _____

   _____

5. When an adult is _____, it makes it easier for me to follow directions.

6. I have a hard time letting adults be in charge because

_____

_____

_____

7. I think adults can teach me about

_____

_____

_____

8. I feel safe with adults when

_____

_____

_____

Worksheet (Adult or Child)

Reacting and Responding

In relationships, there will always be things you can control and things you cannot control. You always have control over yourself: your choices, your words, and your behaviors. You never have control over another person: their choices, their words, and their behaviors. It can be hard when another person makes a choice you do not like, but when that happens, you also have a choice you get to make: how you respond with your words and behaviors. Although you cannot control the other person, you can control whether you react or respond.

When you **react**, you make a choice without thinking it through, which can get you into trouble or damage the relationship. When you **respond**, you think about your choice before acting on it, and you determine how to best handle the situation. When you respond instead of reacting, you are more likely to get your needs met and to maintain a strong relationship, but it takes practice. Think about a relationship you have with someone, and write down something they said or did recently that upset you. Then think about how you typically react, and brainstorm different ways to respond more effectively.

1. I do not like it when you

   _____

   When you do this, I react by

   _____

   Instead, I will respond by

   _____

2. I do not like it when you say

   _____

   When you say this, I react by

   _____

   Instead, I will respond by

   _____

Anatomy of an Apology

When you have said unkind words or hurt someone's feelings, you can heal the relationship by apologizing. Here are the three parts that make up an apology:

1. Recognize what you did that was hurtful, and say you are sorry for that particular act.
2. Make an effort to avoid making the same mistake again.
3. Identify what you will do differently next time.

Although no one is perfect and you may mess up again, apologizing involves making a commitment to change. Otherwise, you are bound to repeat the same mistake over and over again. In order to practice apologizing, think back over the past week and see if you can remember any incidents where you may have said or done something that was hurtful. Think about the person you may have hurt, whether intentionally or unintentionally, and then answer the following questions.

1. What did you do that hurt this person?

_____

_____

_____

2. Can you promise that you will try to avoid repeating these hurtful words or behaviors? Why or why not?

_____

_____

_____

3. What will you do differently next time?

_____

_____

_____

Relationship Skills Role-Play

There are certain ways we can act to help our relationships be healthy and strong. For example, we can take turns sharing and use kind words when we speak to others. With the help of a parent or trusted adult, talk about each of the skills below, defining them and making sure you understand them. Then take turns acting out each skill. Remember to have lots of fun!

- **Compromise:** When two people want different things, it isn't fair for one person to always get their way. You have to take turns. When you compromise, it often means that each person gets some of what they want but not all of what they want.

- **Sharing:** This means allowing someone else to use or borrow something that is yours. It also means being respectful of someone else's things when they share with you.

- **Good Words:** *What* you say (your words) is as important as *how* you say it (your attitude). Use kind and respectful words, even when you don't agree with the other person, and don't raise your voice or yell. Using good words helps others feel safe in the relationship.

- **Accepting No:** When someone says no, you have to respect that you can't always have everything you want and that other people get to make choices too. When someone says no, you can accept their decision and say, "Okay!"

- **Personal Space:** Everyone has a personal space that is all their own. Most of the time, you need to ask permission before entering someone else's space. Although it may be okay to run and give your parent a hug, someone else may not be comfortable with a hug. You can find out whether someone is comfortable with you entering their personal space by simply asking them. To find your personal space, stretch your arms out on either side of your body and turn in a circle with your arms extended. This is your personal space!

- **Listening:** We like it when people listen to us and hear what we have to say. That means we also have to listen when other people talk and give them a chance to share what's on their mind.

Essential Social Skills

There are several foundational social skills that make all relationships work, whether at home, at work, or in the community. Take some time to think about each skill listed here, how well you use that skill, and if you need more practice. Circle any skills you may need to focus on more.

- **Compromise:** No one can have everything their own way all the time. When we are in a relationship with another person, their thoughts and feelings are as important as ours. We must consider their wants and needs if we want them to consider ours. Compromise means that each person states what they want or need in a given situation, and then both individuals work together to find a solution. When you compromise, the solution will involve some of what you want and some of what the other person wants. If you find that frustrating, then this would be a great time to practice coping skills to calm yourself, like taking a few deep breaths or going for a short walk outside.

- **Sharing:** When you share with others, you allow them to access a part of you for a period of time. But you still hold ownership over that part of you. It still belongs to you. How willing are you to share? Not only with regard to material goods but also when it comes to thoughts and feelings. If you find it difficult to share, think about why this may be the case. For example, do you feel like other people don't value your thoughts or emotions, or do you have difficulty valuing your own thoughts or emotions? What may be the reason for that? Do others validate your emotions and offer support when you share how you are feeling? How do you feel when others share their emotions with you? Think about these questions as you reflect on the factors that may impact your ability to share with others.

- **Respect:** You exhibit respect for others by allowing them to share their thoughts and feelings, by validating their feelings, and by offering support when necessary. Speaking with respect also involves being mindful of your tone of voice and body language. Think about how you compose yourself when you interact with others. Do you keep your voice calm, use a soft speaking volume, and use respectful language? When you have a disagreement, do you express your thoughts and feelings without becoming upset, or do you call people names? If you find it difficult to be respectful, especially when you are angry, you might benefit from learning some skills to make your relationships more effective.

- **Problem Solving:** When you problem solve with someone else, you work together to define a problem and to brainstorm possible solutions. You then consider the pros and cons of each option and choose one to try. And if your chosen solution does not work, you come back and pick another option to try. If it is difficult for you to problem solve with others when there is a dilemma, then you may need to practice this skill independently before you are ready to try it with someone else.

- **Active Listening:** When you practice active listening, you mindfully stay in the moment with the person as they talk, listen to their tone of voice, and watch their facial expressions and body language. Then you repeat back what you heard them say to make sure you didn't misinterpret their meaning. For example, if your friend says, "I can't believe my boss threw this file on my desk as I was leaving today and told me it had to be finished first thing in the morning," you may say, "It sounds like you are upset that you have to work late tonight to get that file finished." Active listening lets the other person know you hear what they're saying.

Relationship Values

What are the things you look for in a relationship? What do you value in another person? Use this worksheet to identify what qualities are important to you in a relationship. When you have a better understanding of what you are looking for in relationships, you can make better choices and increase the health of your relationships.

Put a check mark by any values that you expect your relationships to embody:

_____   Honesty

_____   Independence

_____   Work ethic

_____   Compassion

_____   Thoughtfulness

_____   Empathy

_____   Punctuality

_____   Spirituality

_____   Trustworthiness

_____   Athleticism

_____   Musical ability

_____   Humor

_____   Intelligence

_____   Other: _____

_____   Other: _____

_____   Other: _____

Now reflect on the items you chose, and explore what makes those values important to you. Think about how you would respond if you met someone who embodied most of these values but not all of them. It is important to remember that we all have strengths and weakness. When entering into relationships, you need to assess the other person's weaknesses and determine if this is something you can live with and extend grace to. Keep in mind that the other person will also be assessing your qualities and determining whether or not they can extend grace to your weaknesses as well. Sometimes the values we search for in relationships reflect healthy or unhealthy relationship priorities that were modeled for us in childhood, and these expectations may be helping or hurting us now in adulthood.

Overcoming Relationship Challenges

Relationships sometimes face challenges that test the strength of the relationship. For example, you may be coping with the loss of a family member, experiencing financial struggles, dealing with the aftermath of a natural disaster, or going through another type of difficulty that impacts the relationship. You and your partner may not process or overcome challenges in the same way, but you can still recognize and respect the way your partner is coping and provide them with support. In order to strengthen your connection with loved ones through these struggles instead of allowing it to divide you, you can follow these four steps:

- **Step 1:** Take care of your own feelings first. Self-care is important so you can be there for your loved one. This may involve taking 20–30 minutes a day to do yoga, meditate, go for a run, read, or quietly drink a cup of coffee. You need to prioritize yourself because if you do not fill your own cup, then you will have nothing left to pour for others. As the common airline announcement goes, place your own oxygen mask on before helping the person beside you.

- **Step 2:** See the needs of your loved one and meet those needs. If they need comfort, comfort them. If they need support, offer support. If they need self-care, help them find it. Remember: Your loved one may not need the same type of support you do. Listen to them and watch them to see what they actually need help with. For example, if your spouse is doing well in terms of handling the kids, doing laundry, and running errands but is struggling with meal preparation, then support them in that area. Take the time to see their need and then meet that need, whatever it is. This reflects attunement, which allows individuals to feel connected and to know they are not alone in times of challenge.

- **Step 3:** Allow your loved one to meet your needs. This means being vulnerable enough to express what you need. No one can meet all of their own needs, so lean into your loved one in those challenging times and accept the support they provide. Just as you provide support for others, allow others to do the same for you. This mutual meeting of needs strengthens and deepens the relationship as you both show your vulnerability and find fulfillment and comfort on meaningful levels.

- **Step 4:** Problem solve together, if appropriate. Define the problem and think about options. Then choose one solution and move forward together. For example, if you are experiencing a job loss, a house foreclosure, or a serious health diagnosis, create a plan together for how you will face the challenge. Doing so will unite the two of you against the challenge instead of against each other. When you problem solve together and brainstorm solutions, you work together as a team. Knowing that neither of you is alone in facing this challenge can bring peace and comfort.

How do you feel you handle challenges in your relationships? Do you follow these four steps? Why or why not?

_____

_____

_____

Is there one step that is more difficult for you? In what ways?

_____

_____

_____

How could you work on this step?

_____

_____

_____

Conflict in Relationships

It is normal for *all* relationships to have conflict. When two or more people come together—each with their own personality and perspectives—they will not agree on everything. Conflict is inevitable, but how you handle that conflict has more of an impact on your relationship than the conflict itself. You have control over how you respond to disagreements and whether you do so in a way that strengthens the relationship.

1. When you have a disagreement, do you stay calm and state your thoughts and feelings? Or do you escalate in frustration and anger?

   _____

   _____

   _____

2. Do you use kind words, or do you name-call and speak disrespectfully?

   _____

   _____

   _____

3. Are you able to listen to the other person's thoughts and feelings? Why or why not?

   _____

   _____

   _____

4. Are you open to a compromise? Why or why not?

   _____

   _____

   _____

5. Are you able to consider the other person's needs? Why or why not?

   _____

   _____

   _____

Listening for Emotion

When people talk, they express emotions through their voice and words. Being able to identify these emotions can assist you in connecting on a deeper level with your loved ones. One way to do so is to practice something called reflective listening, which involves repeating back what you think you heard the other person say. For example, if someone is discussing a divorce, then you might say, "I think I hear you saying that this is hard for you because you miss your family."

When you practice reflective listening, you should always end by checking in and giving the other person a chance to confirm or deny your observations. You can simply ask them, "Do I have that right?" and then allow them to correct anything you may have misunderstood. In addition, you should never tell someone else that what they are feeling is "wrong" or that their feelings are not worthy of respect. All feelings are valid, even if you don't happen to agree with them.

To practice reflective listening, read the scenarios here and see if you can identify what emotions the person might be experiencing. Then come up with a reflective listening response for each scenario.

1. Peter tells his wife, "You never listen to me. I told you I'd be home late tonight because I had to go over some contracts with our senior partner. I told you that this morning, and you nodded your head like you understood. Now you are yelling at me because I am late? I can't do anything that makes you happy."

   Emotions:

   _____

   Reflective Listening Response:

   _____

   _____

2. Sarah tells her boss, "My husband just called to let me know that my mother has been rushed to the hospital with chest pain, and I need to leave work right now. I don't know how long it will take me to get to the hospital, and I don't know how bad things are with my mother."

   Emotions:

   _____

   Reflective Listening Response:

   _____

   _____

3. Amy tells her husband, "Tomorrow night I am going to receive an award at the annual company dinner. It would mean so much to me if you would be there. I worked so hard on that project, and it feels so good to have recognition. Can you please be there?"

Emotions:

_____

Reflective Listening Response:

_____

_____

4. Mel tells his friend, "I gave you $100 last week for that home repair, and now I really need it back. You said you'd have it for me this week, and I have bills to pay. I don't mind helping you out sometimes, but I need you to honor what you said because I am counting on it and want to be able to trust you."

Emotions:

_____

Reflective Listening Response:

_____

_____

Answer Key:

1. Frustration, disappointment, sadness

   Sample Reflective Listening Response: "I hear you saying that you feel frustrated when I don't listen to you and disappointed that you can't make me happy. Is that right?"

2. Fear, anxiety, sadness

   Sample Reflective Listening Response: "I hear you saying that you are worried about your mother because she was just taken to the hospital and that you would like to leave now but you're not sure when you can return. Is that right?"

3. Pride, excitement, longing

   Sample Reflective Listening Response: "I hear you saying that you are really proud of yourself because this is a big accomplishment and that you would like me to go to the dinner with you tomorrow. I would love to go because I am proud of you too!"

4. Frustration, anxiety, anger

   Sample Reflective Listening Response: "I hear you saying that you do not mind helping me sometimes but that you need me to be responsible to pay you back on time. Is that right?"

ATTUNEMENT INTERVENTIONS

As clients work to build their relationship skills, teaching the importance of attunement can assist them in meeting the needs of others and getting their own needs met in return. Part of this process involves helping clients distinguish wants from needs. Children in particular will need some guidance with this distinction, but it is an important one for them to understand. Not only can it reduce entitlement and acting-out behaviors, but it also gives you an opportunity to make sure that a child's needs are actually being met.

Use the **What Are Your Needs?** worksheet to help children learn the difference between wants and needs. If there appear to be any unmet needs, ask clarifying questions to see if these needs are, in fact, not being met or if the child simply has difficulty identifying their needs. In addition, review this worksheet with the parent after the child has completed it to have a conversation about the parent's ability to meet their child's needs versus wants. Some parents do a great job of meeting their child's wants but struggle to meet their child's need for love and attention. For example, a parent may buy their child video games but then leave them alone to play them. That child's need for love and connection is not being met, and inappropriate and dysfunctional behaviors may emerge as that child tries to meet their own needs. This worksheet gives clinicians an opportunity to have that conversation with a parent.

Once children have a better understanding of wants versus needs, use the **Three P's of Parenting** worksheet to help them identify the extent to which their parents are meeting their needs. This worksheet can be particularly helpful when working with foster and adoptive families, as it allows them to explore how the child's past family may not have fulfilled each of the child's needs. It can help the current family understand why it may be difficult for the child to accept current rules that keep them safe or chores that prepare them for life. It is important to remind children and parents that nurture and love are the foundation of the three P's of parenting. A parent provides for, protects, and prepares their child because they love and care for them.

The **Meeting My Child's Needs** worksheet can help frame parenting responsibilities and allow the parent to develop insight into areas they may need to work on. This can be especially useful when a parent has been unable to parent effectively (e.g., a parent with a history of substance abuse who is now sober) and is now trying to establish themselves as a healthy parent. It can help parents understand why their child may be having a hard time accepting parenting in a certain area, especially if the parent has not been parenting consistently in that area. Being able to process these worksheets can bring change to family relationships. When the parent has completed the worksheet, the clinician can send it home as an action plan or objective for the parent to implement.

A child's relationship with their primary caregiver forms the template from which they view the world, themselves, and others. It is a cognitive template that guides an individual's future behaviors and expectations. Therefore, an individual's ability to exhibit attunement in the context of relationships is largely dependent on whether their childhood experiences involved attunement. Clinicians can use the **My Experience of Attunement** worksheet to help adult clients explore their past experience of having their needs met, which may inform their understanding of their current beliefs about attunement and their ability to meet the needs of others.

In addition, the **When Someone Meets My Needs** worksheet can help adults explore their feelings about having others meet their needs. If a client feels like their childhood needs were met out of duty or responsibility instead of love, then they may have difficulty allowing others to meet their needs now. In contrast, if they feel like their needs were met with love and compassion, then they may be more willing to exhibit vulnerability and to allow others to meet their needs. Therefore, if a client exhibits difficulty in allowing other people to meet their needs, explore their past experiences of attunement and whether or not their past relationships were characterized by a healthy connection. Everyone has needs they cannot meet for themselves. No one can meet their own need for connection independently.

We learn to trust other people when we express vulnerability and allow our needs to be known and when those needs are then met. We feel cared for, seen, and heard. We feel like we are important to someone, like we matter. The **Building Trust** worksheet can help adult clients think about whom they trust and how they came to trust these people. Maybe they trust different people in different areas. It's important to understand that attunement is the building block to trust. We don't trust other people if we feel like we can't depend or rely on them. When people continuously let us down, they lose our trust. However, when people are faithful and follow through, it allows us to develop relationships with them that are based in trust.

If clients have broken relationships or have lost the trust of friends or partners, knowing how to repair those relationships and regain trust is key. The **Repairing Trust** worksheet can help adult clients think through what they did to lose trust and what they can do to repair the relationship. When trust is lost, it is often a result of some harmful action, like lying, stealing, or failing to meet someone else's needs. The remedy is to change that behavior. For example, if a spouse lied about having an affair, they can attempt to repair the relationship by exhibiting open and honest communication instead of harboring secrets. Or if a friendship fell apart because a client wasn't meeting their friend's emotional needs, then the client can work to be more emotionally present and involved. Use this worksheet to walk clients through the process of repairing a relationship by reestablishing trust.

When it comes to attunement, healthy relationships are characterized by a mutual degree of give and take in which an individual meets someone else's needs, and that person meets their needs in return. These relationships are characterized by healthy interdependence. However, some relationships are skewed too heavily in the direction of dependence or independence such that attunement becomes imbalanced. One person is always giving, or one person is always taking. Although there are times when these disproportionate relationships are appropriate—like in the case of a dependent relationship between a parent and a young child, or between an adult child and their elderly parent—most healthy relationships fall in the middle of the spectrum.

Use the **Relationship Scale** worksheet to help adult clients think about their relationships along a continuum, as this can assist them in identifying healthy versus unhealthy relationship patterns. Notice if the client describes having a large number of relationships in which the other person depends on them, such as a mother with three young children. If this mother does not have others who can even out the emotional investment she is making when it comes to her children, she can become burned out or emotionally exhausted. In these situations, it is important to help clients find balance, which may involve spending time with people who invest in them or teaching them to invest in themselves through daily self-care. These strategies can help clients manage any periods of time when they have several people depending on them.

You can also use the **When I Meet the Needs of Someone I Care About** worksheet to gauge the extent to which adult clients are (or are not) attuning to the needs of others. This can allow you to identify whether they are actively meeting the needs of others and what their beliefs are about independence versus interdependence.

Oftentimes, clients have difficulty sharing their emotional needs with others because doing so requires exhibiting a certain level of vulnerability, which many try to avoid. They may be unsure with whom they can safely share their emotions and may struggle to build attunement in relationships. As a result, they may either withhold their emotions from everyone or indiscriminately share all of themselves with everyone (and then exhibit surprise when others do not reciprocate).

When this occurs, the **Sharing My Emotions** worksheet can help adult clients think about how they can be vulnerable with an emotionally safe person. Encourage them to start by sharing a small feeling with that person, as opposed to a large feeling that could cause emotional pain. Sharing emotions and building trust is a process. By sharing small parts of themselves, they can gradually build relationships as they learn whether or not the other person is responsive and caring. The healthy way to build emotional attunement is to take baby steps. This worksheet can help clients understand this.

Once adult clients work to identify emotionally safe people with whom they can share smaller emotions, use the **Expressing My Needs** worksheet to help them think about what their specific needs are, who can meet those needs, and how they can ask for those needs to be met. Sometimes the largest barrier to getting needs met is not knowing how to express needs in a way that others will understand. The best way for clients to do so is to simply verbalize their desires in specific, observable terms. Once a client has identified their needs and whom they can ask for help, role-play appropriate ways to verbalize those needs.

Finally, the **You Need to Be Attuned** handout can solidify adult clients' understanding of the importance of being "in tune" with others. Review what it means to meet the emotional needs of others and to allow others to meet their own needs. Ask for examples of each need to assess whether clients need to talk through a specific area of need in more detail.

What Are Your Needs?

We all have needs in life, which help us feel safe and keep us alive. That is why needs are so important. Using this worksheet, make a list of your needs and wants. Next to your needs, write the name of the person who meets that need. When someone meets your needs, that creates a relationship. For example, when your parents meet your needs for food and shelter, that strengthens your relationship with them. But if someone doesn't meet that need, then we can have a hard time trusting them to take care of us, and we may start trying to take care of ourselves.

My Needs	Who Meets This Need	My Wants
Example: Shoes	Mom and Dad	Brand name shoes

Three P's of Parenting

Do you know what a parent is or what a parent does? A parent is someone whose job in life is to provide for you, to protect you, and to prepare you to be successful in the world. They do this because they love and care about you. Use this worksheet to think about how your parents take care of you in each of these three areas.

Parents **provide** for you. This means they make sure your needs are met. They are responsible for making sure you have enough food, clothing, and love, as well as proper shelter and safety. How do your parents take care of your needs in these areas?

Food: _____

Shelter: _____

Clothing: _____

Safety: _____

Love: _____

Parents **protect** you. It is their job to keep you safe. Sometimes parents keep you safe by setting rules. You may not like these rules or want to follow them, but these rules keep you from getting hurt or getting into trouble. How do your parents set rules to protect you?

Rules I like and understand:

_____

_____

_____

Rules I don't like or don't understand:

_____

_____

_____

Parents **prepare** you for life. It is their job to make sure you know how to take care of yourself when you become an adult and go out into the world on your own. They have a lot of things to teach you, including how to cook, clean, shop, and manage money in a responsible way. In order to prepare you, your parents may ask you to do chores, but these chores are meant to teach you how to take care of yourself. How do your parents prepare you to be a successful adult?

_____

_____

_____

Now think about how much you trust your parents in each of these areas. On a scale of 0 to 10, with 0 being "don't trust at all" and 10 being "trust completely," how much do you trust your parents to:

Provide for you: _____

Protect you: _____

Prepare you: _____

Is there anything they can do differently to increase these ratings?

_____

_____

_____

Meeting My Child's Needs

Children have a lot of needs. They are not independent and cannot take care of themselves, which is why parents are responsible for meeting these needs. As a parent, you have various responsibilities and roles in your child's life. You teach them life skills and lessons, keep them safe, and help them cultivate the characteristics needed to become a competent adult. Answer the following questions and think about the ways you meet each of your child's needs.

1. What are your child's needs? How do you meet those needs?

   _____

   _____

   _____

2. Children need to be taught a variety of social skills, life skills, and emotion regulation skills. How do you teach your child something new each day?

   Social skills: _____

   _____

   Life skills: _____

   _____

   Emotion regulation skills: _____

   _____

3. Children need to feel safe. How do you help your child feel safe?

   _____

   _____

   _____

4. Children need to feel connected through a warm and loving relationship. How do you invest in your relationship with your child every day?

_____

_____

_____

5. What is the difference between your child's needs and their wants? Remember, needs keep your child alive, whereas wants are optional.

_____

_____

_____

6. What message do you send your child when you meet all their wants? Does anyone else do this for them?

_____

_____

_____

7. As your child matures, do you feel like they will become responsible to meet their own needs *and* wants? Why or why not?

_____

_____

_____

My Experience of Attunement

When you were a child, your parents were responsible for meeting your needs. Understanding how your parents did or did not meet your needs can help you better understand the way you react in relationships now when you're asked to meet the needs of others. If your parents set a positive example for you in which they met your needs, then that is the model you learned to follow. You learned how to be "in tune" with other people in a way that allows you to meet their needs. This is a process called *attunement*. Take a few minutes to think about these questions in regard to your own childhood.

1. How did your parents keep you safe? Did they have rules that kept you safe? What did they do to ensure your safety?

   _____

   _____

   _____

2. How did your parents provide for you? Did you have enough food and clothing, as well as proper shelter? Did you feel loved? How did your parents express their love for you?

   _____

   _____

   _____

3. How did your parents prepare you for life? Do you feel like they taught you the skills needed to become an independent adult? Why or why not?

   _____

   _____

   _____

4. How did you feel about the way your parents did (or didn't) meet your needs?

   _____

   _____

   _____

When Someone Meets My Needs

Attunement is a part of healthy relationships. It involves being willing to meet the needs of others and allowing them to meet your needs in return. Do you allow others to meet your needs? Do you allow others to see your needs? Sometimes allowing others to meet our needs can make us feel vulnerable. If you feel anxious or uncomfortable allowing people to meet your needs, use this worksheet to explain why that may be the case.

1. Do you have needs you can't meet for yourself? Why or why not? If so, what are they?

   _____

   _____

   _____

2. Do you allow others to see your needs? Why or why not? Are there certain needs you have that you do not allow anyone to see?

   _____

   _____

   _____

3. When others see your needs, how do they respond? How does this make you feel?

   _____

   _____

   _____

4. Are you able to be vulnerable with others? Why or why not? What is the hardest part of being vulnerable? What does vulnerability feel like to you?

   _____

   _____

   _____

Building Trust

Relationships are based in trust. Most of us don't form (or maintain) relationships with people we don't trust. But how is trust built? It is built by the mutual meeting of needs: When other people meet our needs, we learn to trust them. And when we meet their needs in return, they develop trust in us. There is an equality in meeting each other's needs. Although we all go through times when this scale tips out of balance—for instance, if a spouse is ill or loses their job—eventually the scale tips back and we return to mutually meeting each other's needs. Think about your relationships and explore the balance in each by identifying the ways that you meet each other's needs.

My Relationships	How They Meet My Needs	How I Meet Their Needs
1.		
2.		
3.		
4.		
5.		
6.		
7.		

If you find that one of your relationships isn't characterized by a mutual degree of give and take, what could this mean for that relationship? How do you feel about this inequality? Is there something that can be done to bring balance?

_____

_____

_____

What would happen if you expressed your needs, including your need for the relationship to be more balanced? If you find that your needs are being met but the other person's needs are not, how could you become more aware of their needs and begin to meet them to bring balance?

_____

_____

_____

Repairing Trust

Many relationships face difficult times or come to an end when there is a loss of trust. When this occurs, it can be helpful to explore what you did that resulted in a loss of trust, as well as what steps you can take to repair the relationship and rebuild people's confidence in you. You can regain trust if you are willing to engage in the repair process. However, the road to repair is long and hard, as trust is rebuilt over a period of time while you prove that your behaviors are different. The chart here provides you with a road map you can use to rebuild a healthy relationship with your loved one.

My Relationship	What I Did That Lost Trust (Make sure to list specific, observable behaviors)	To Repair Trust, I Need to Take These Steps (Make sure to list concrete steps to change)
Example: With my child	I embarrassed them in front of their friends by running up to give them a hug and kiss.	I have to respect their space when they are with their friends by developing a secret hand signal that sends them love instead.

Relationship Scale

Our relationships fall along a continuum. At one end are **dependent** relationships. These are relationships where we depend wholly on another person or they depend on us. In certain relationships, like a parent-child relationship, this is developmentally appropriate. In the middle of the spectrum are **interdependent** relationships, where both parties depend on each other equally. They lean into each other for support, comfort, and companionship. Finally, **independent** relationships are those where people do not depend on each other. Each person in the relationship is independent.

Use this worksheet to place your current relationships on a continuum. Notice if your relationships tend to tip to one side of the scale or the other. For most relationships, a healthy balance is in the middle. Notice if there are any patterns among family relationships versus friendships. Notice if other people depend on you more than you depend on them or vice versa.

_____

Dependence   **Interdependence**   **Independence**

When I Meet the Needs of Someone I Care About

We all have needs. Just like you need others to help you sometimes, others need you too! Think about your relationships and how you meet the needs of others. Maybe you already help people without even thinking about it. Or maybe it's been a long time since you met someone else's needs. Take some time to reflect on your relationships and your ability to attune with others. Are you in tune with their needs?

1. What are the needs of three people you interact with daily?

    a. _____

    b. _____

    c. _____

2. When was the last time you met the needs of a loved one? What did that look like? What was the need, and how did you meet that need?

    _____

    _____

    _____

3. What was that experience like for you? How did it feel?

    _____

    _____

    _____

4. If you have not met the needs of a loved one recently, why not? What is holding you back? Is there a barrier?

    _____

    _____

    _____

Sharing My Emotions

Sharing emotions is a part of developing attuned relationships. When two people meet each other's needs for emotional support, this builds trust in the relationship. Take a few minutes and think about a person in your life with whom you may or may not share your emotions. Perhaps you already share some of your feelings with this person and would like to share more. Or perhaps you haven't yet opened up to them but are considering doing so in the future. As you think about the type of relationship you have with this person, reflect on whether they have been trustworthy, as a trust-based relationship is one in which you may feel more comfortable sharing larger emotions.

1. How do you know whether you can consider someone an emotionally safe person?

_____

_____

_____

2. Is there anyone in your life you can trust and share your emotions with? How long have you known this person?

_____

_____

_____

3. How do they react when you share about your day or talk about smaller events that have impacted you?

_____

_____

_____

4. How do they offer support as you share smaller emotions?

_____

_____

_____

5. How could you share a little bit more without sharing everything?

_____

_____

_____

6. What would you look for in their response that lets you know they care and will meet your emotional needs?

_____

_____

_____

Expressing My Needs

Everyone has needs. You have needs that you cannot meet by yourself, in which case you need others to help you. In the same way, others have needs that they cannot meet by themselves, in which case you have gifts and talents you can offer. The point is: We all need one another! Think about the needs you have that you cannot meet for yourself. Then think about the people who could help you with those needs and how you could ask for their support.

My Need	Whom I Want to Share This Need With	How I Can Ask for Support
Example: *I'm working late tonight and need help making dinner.*	My spouse	*"Honey, I need to work late tonight and won't be home in time to make dinner. Would you get it started or pick something up on the way home?"*

You Need to Be Attuned

Attunement involves meeting the needs of others while also allowing others to meet your own needs. These needs can be emotional, physical, or mental. Attunement is a building block to trust, which leads to attachment and healthy relationships. When we meet each other's needs, we build trust in our relationships. We stay in relationships with people we trust. If we don't trust someone, then that relationship normally doesn't last very long.

When we are attuned to others, we see their needs and meet those needs because we care about them. We listen to what they say and express, and we then find ways to meet their needs. We choose to meet other people's needs not because they cannot do so for themselves but because we care about them. For example, if you wake up in the morning and your spouse offers to bring you a cup of coffee in bed, it is not because you cannot get it yourself. It's because your spouse cares about you and wants to meet your need for affection. And when they bring you that cup of coffee, you feel seen, heard, and cared for. That makes you feel like you are important and of value—because you are! That reflects attunement in an attachment-based relationship.

Attunement requires that we exhibit a certain level of vulnerability in sharing our needs with others, which can be difficult. But if we don't make our needs known, then we will never know if anyone will step up to meet them. Therefore, while being vulnerable involves taking a risk, it is a risk that has the potential for an amazing reward when you find someone who cares about you.

As you think about what it means to be attuned, ask yourself whether you're "in tune" with the people in your life. Do you see their needs and meet them? Do you allow them to see your needs and meet them? If not, think about what steps you could take to allow yourself the emotional vulnerability needed to build attunement in these relationships.

ATTACHMENT INTERVENTIONS

As clients increase their capacity to "tune in" and engage in the reciprocal meeting of needs, they begin to develop relationships characterized by healthy attachment. For children, though, the process of building attachment-based relationships is largely dependent on the parent. Children do not yet have the necessary skills or understanding needed to form healthy and secure relationships. Therefore, it is necessary for parents to take the lead by modeling appropriate ways to connect and by inviting their child into the comfort and security of an attachment-based relationship. Ultimately, the goal is for children to recognize what it means to attach so they can do so in future relationships. Use the **Connecting to My Parent** worksheet to help children identify when their parent is connecting with them, as well as the **I'm Leading the Way** worksheet to remind parents that it is their responsibility to lead the dance of attachment.

When working with a child who does not live with their biological parents, it is important to keep in mind that some sort of trauma is always the cause. That child has been separated from their parents as a result of parental divorce, illness, death, substance use, or a myriad of other traumatic causes. Children who are in foster care may also have been separated from their biological siblings, and that is a relational trauma for that child, as well as all of the children involved.

Regardless of the specific type of trauma involved, the loss of a family member impacts a child's beliefs about relationships moving forward. Young children in particular—who are concrete thinkers and cannot rationalize the reasons for their family member's absence—will have a difficult time understanding and accepting why that person is no longer present in their life. Young children are very "me" focused and see everything in their world in relation to themselves. As a result, they may erroneously believe that they somehow are to blame for their family member's absence.

To help young clients work through this attachment trauma, use the **Life Without My Loved One** worksheet. This worksheet focuses on a child's loved ones. Use this worksheet to process with children how it feels to not have that person present in their life.

When they are completing the worksheet, pay attention to how clients answer the question "What caused that to happen?" so you can gauge whether the child is blaming themselves or taking responsibility for the loss. Once clients have completed the worksheet, encourage them to draw a picture for their family member, to write them a letter, or to engage in some other form of creative expression. Even if that family member is no longer a part of their life, expressing their emotions can allow the child to better cope with the loss.

When clinicians are working with a child who has an attachment trauma, or an adult who had an attachment trauma in childhood, they can use the **My Role in Attachment** worksheet to assist clients in thinking through their relationship with their parents. Separate versions of this worksheet are provided for adults and children. When the client is answering questions about the role their parents played, clinicians should always frame for the client that their parents may have been doing the best they could given the understanding of relationships that they had. Emphasizing an attitude of compassion and empathy can bring healing to the attachment trauma and to the child's (or adult child's) relationship with their parents. It can also allow the client to develop a different perspective of their parents.

Clinicians can also use the **My Attachment Style in Parenting** worksheet, either alone or in conjunction with the previous worksheet, to have parents explore how their attachment style may be impacting their relationship with their child. The worksheet asks parents to read through various descriptions of attachment styles and to pick the description that best matches how they parent their child. The first description reflects secure attachment, the second reflects anxious-preoccupied attachment, the third reflects dismissive-avoidant attachment, and the fourth reflects fearful-avoidant attachment. If a parent chooses any attachment style other than secure attachment, explore their thoughts about their relationship with their child based on the description they chose. Gently explore any unhealthy relationship characteristics and the impact this is having on their child's developing attachment style.

Intergenerational attachment trauma can be a cycle that a family gets stuck in. This is because parents model how to build relationships for their children, and those children then grow into adults who repeat those same patterns and who parent the way that they were parented. What they learned in childhood becomes their internal working model for what relationships are and how relationships work. But if an individual's parents modeled unhealthy relationship building, how does the next generation change? The **Intergenerational Attachment** worksheet can help adult clients identify their beliefs about relationships and whether they are healthy or not. Clinicians can also recommend that clients read *Parenting from the Inside Out* (Siegel & Hartzell, 2003), which addresses intergenerational attachment.

Clinicians can also use the **Relationship Messages** worksheet to help adult clients evaluate the relationship messages they received from their parents and determine whether they want to embrace or discard those messages. Having them think about what a healthy relationship looks like can motivate them to change some aspects of their adult relationships. When using this exercise, be respectful and encourage clients to be respectful of their parents. It is important to remember to extend grace to parents, who may have been doing the best they could with their given circumstances. In addition, clinicians may need to reframe relationship skills if clients endorse unhealthy relationship patterns on the worksheet. For example, if clients embrace the message that everyone should be independent and meet their own needs, then the clinician may want to have a conversation about interdependence and attunement.

Attachment extends beyond the parent-child relationship. Therefore, it is also necessary for clinicians to work with adult clients to examine how their attachment style may be impacting their relationships as a whole. Unhealthy attachment styles can develop into personality disorders given that these patterns of interaction reflect learned ways of treating others in relationships and reflect beliefs about what relationships should be. To help clients identify the ways they connect with others in relationships, clinicians can use the **My Attachment Style** worksheet. The worksheet asks clients to identify which attachment style describes their overall manner of interacting, with the first description corresponding with secure attachment, the second with anxious-preoccupied attachment, the third with dismissive-avoidant attachment, and the fourth with fearful-avoidant attachment.

Once clients have identified an attachment style that characterizes their relationships, they can use the next series of worksheets to explore the healthy and unhealthy characteristics of each insecure attachment style. For example, clients with an anxious-preoccupied attachment style may worry about the longevity of relationships, worry about the other person leaving the relationship, or have anxiety about their partner finding someone better. As a result, they hold their relationships close, too close, which often creates a self-fulfilling prophecy when the other person does not get the space they need, feels smothered, and leaves. This increases the individual's anxiety in relationships and perpetuates a never-ending cycle. The **Anxiety in Relationships** worksheet challenges clients to think about how their anxious behaviors in relationships impact those relationships.

Another insecure attachment style that can impact the health of a person's relationships is a dismissive-avoidant attachment style. Clients with this attachment style are emotionally unavailable and hold others at a distance. Because they come across as aloof and independent, they have difficulty forming or maintaining close relationships. Clients who have described their attachment style in these terms can use the **Avoidance in Relationships** worksheet to explore the ways their behaviors are helping or hurting their relationship.

Finally, clients who exhibit a fearful-avoidant attachment style may struggle connecting with others because of their propensity for mixed reactions in relationships. While they desire intimacy, they also experience discomfort with closeness due to fears of rejection and abandonment. Because of this ambivalence, they struggle with commitment and withdraw when others get too close, resulting in a variety of short-lived relationships. The **Ambivalence in Relationships** worksheet can help clients with this insecure attachment style examine how their ways of interacting may be affecting the relationship.

Once clients have identified the specific insecure attachment style that best describes them, the next series of worksheets will challenge them to think about their way of attaching to others, what may and may not be working for them, and how to move toward healthier attachment. Secure attachment can be earned. It is earned through working hard to change the way that the client views relationships and interacts with others. Using the **Anxious-Preoccupied Attachment**, **Dismissive-Avoidant Attachment**, and **Fearful-Avoidant Attachment** worksheets, help clients identify what needs to change in their relationships, and work with them to create action steps based on those identified changes.

Attachment style is closely connected to personality because our personality is rooted in the way that we connect to others and see the world around us. When it comes to trauma, our personality can either promote resiliency or cause us to experience challenges in the face of recovery. For example, a client with a dismissive-avoidant attachment style may have a more introverted personality, making them reluctant to ask for or accept help from others. In this situation, their personality is a barrier that prevents them from drawing on their social supports. Similarly, a client with an anxious-preoccupied attachment style is more likely to exhibit personality traits associated with emotional instability, making it more difficult for them to tolerate and regulate uncomfortable emotions when working through the trauma. The **Personality in Resiliency** worksheet can help clients understand how their personality traits influence trauma recovery and challenge them to think about how they could draw on their strengths or work to remove barriers related to personality.

Connecting to My Parent

Parents have a lot of different ways to show love to their kids. See if you can think of all the ways your parents love you!

1. List five ways your parents show they love you.

   _____

   _____

   _____

   _____

   _____

2. List four ways your parents meet your needs.

   _____

   _____

   _____

   _____

3. List three ways you show your parents that you love them.

   _____

   _____

   _____

4. List two ways you and your parents spend time together.

   _____

   _____

5. List one thing your parents could do differently to show their love to you.

   _____

I'm Leading the Way

In building an attachment-based relationship with your child, it is contingent upon you—as the parent—to do most of the work. Your child may respond to you and engage with you, but you need to lead the way. Children don't know how to develop relationships, especially healthy ones, unless someone shows them. They learn how to connect with others based on what you teach them. Reflect on the following questions and brainstorm ways to connect with your child.

1. Spending quality time with your child is essential to build a healthy relationship. Quality time means face-to-face time with no distractions. How much quality time do you spend with your child? What types of activities do you do? Is there anything you could rearrange in your schedule to spend more quality time with your child?

   _____

   _____

   _____

   _____

2. Being playful with your child is a quick way to build connection. How often do you smile at your child? Laugh together and have fun? Sometimes building your connection may involve doing things you don't necessarily enjoy in order to strengthen the relationship. For example, you may not enjoy playing a board game, but perhaps that is something your child loves. Can you put your feelings aside to meet the need of your child? Can you play pretend as dinosaurs or princesses? What other ways can you bring playfulness and laughter into your relationship with your child?

   _____

   _____

   _____

   _____

3. Teaching your child something new is a great way to build attachment. What kinds of things do you teach your child? Do you have them help you when you make dinner? Mow the lawn? Do laundry? Repair things around the house? Showing them how to do new things builds a strong relationship, and they get the added benefit of more quality time with you.

_____

_____

_____

_____

4. Supporting your child or helping them with something difficult helps build attachment. For example, if your child is struggling with homework or reading, explaining it to them or problem solving with them helps them feel like they are not alone in their struggle. It also establishes you as someone who is knowledgeable and willing to teach them. Moving forward, your child will also feel comfortable going to you when they are faced with bigger issues. What are things you can help your child with this week? Even helping them complete a chore can be a bonding activity.

_____

_____

_____

_____

Life Without My Loved One

If one of your loved ones is not a part of your everyday life, it is normal to really miss them. There are things you may want to show them and tell them. You may wonder what they would think or how they would feel if they could see you now. Take a few minutes to think about them as you answer the questions here. When you are done, you can draw a picture or write a letter to let them know how you feel.

1. What happened that your loved one is not a part of your everyday life?

_____

_____

_____

2. What caused that to happen?

_____

_____

_____

3. How do you feel about them not being there every day?

_____

_____

_____

4. What is something you want to know about them? Is there someone you can ask?

_____

_____

_____

5. Are there things you want to tell them? If so, what?

_____

_____

_____

6. Are there things you want to be able to do with them? If so, what?

_____

_____

_____

7. What do you miss the most?

_____

_____

_____

8. What do you do when you start to miss them?

_____

_____

_____

My Role in Attachment

Attachment is how you build a relationship with another person. Each person has their own way of building relationships, which they learn about from their parents. Your parents show you how to have relationships with other people through the ways in which they form a relationship with you. Think about your relationship with your parents as you answer these questions.

1. What have your parents taught you about having relationships with others?

   _____

   _____

   _____

2. In most homes, the parents are the leaders. That's their job! If your parents are leading you to learn about relationships, what is your role or job?

   _____

   _____

   _____

3. Your parents know about relationships because they learned from their parents. How are your parents the same as your grandparents, and how are they different from your grandparents, when it comes to relationships?

   _____

   _____

   _____

4. Think about other adults in your life. Do they build relationships in different ways? What are some things you see in these relationships that you want (or don't want) to be part of your relationships?

   _____

   _____

   _____

My Role in Attachment

As a child, your responsibility was to follow your parents in the dance of attachment. Your parents led the way in developing a relationship with you. It was like a dance where your parents led you around the dance floor and you followed them. Understanding the various roles in this dance can help you understand the responsibility that each person held in teaching you about relationships.

1. As a child, how did you learn how to have relationships with others?

   _____

   _____

2. How did your parents invite (or not invite) you to an attachment-based relationship?

   _____

   _____

3. What do you know about your parents' relationships with their parents? What did your parents learn about relationships from your grandparents?

   _____

   _____

4. How will you change your relationships moving forward? What will you do differently?

   _____

   _____

5. What do you hope your children will say one day about what you taught them about relationships?

   _____

   _____

My Attachment Style in Parenting

When you are a parent, you serve as a model to your child of how relationships work. Every day you show them how to have relationships with other people, and they learn about making connections with others by watching you and by mimicking the ways you connect to them. This is how they learn. Think about the relationship you have with your child. Put a check mark by the description that best describes that relationship.

_____ 1. You want your child to come to you for help if they are having a hard time. Your child seeks you out for comfort or to problem solve. You help them understand the world around them and then send them back out into the world to try out the new skills you have taught them. You allow your child to make age-appropriate decisions and to make mistakes, and then you help them learn from their mistakes. You give them age-appropriate space, allowing them to play independently but also engaging them in play to strengthen your relationship. You take care of your own emotions, not depending on your child to help you with them. You stay calm when your child is not and help them calm themselves, taking care of your own emotions at a later time.

_____ 2. You like to keep your child close and feel uncomfortable with them going to a friend's house—preferring that the friend come to your house instead. You help your child with everything, often doing things for them to make their life easier. You worry that bad things could happen to your child, so you protect them all the time, even with things they may be able to safely do for themselves. Your child depends on you for everything, and while that may feel like a large responsibility at times, in the end you enjoy being needed by your child. Sometimes you even share your emotions with your child because you need your child too.

_____ 3. You value your child being independent and self-sufficient, so you teach them how to do things on their own. You want them to be able to take care of themselves, and this includes taking care of their own emotions. When they are upset, you tell them to calm down, not wanting to engage in a conversation about why they are upset. You believe that the quicker they can calm themselves down, the faster you both can get back to your day. You are busy with your obligations and responsibilities, and you need your child to be independent in taking care of themselves. You rarely share your emotions with your child, choosing to take care of your own emotions independently.

_____ 4. You struggle to feel connected to your child. You want to have a better relationship but are not sure how. You find that your child constantly irritates you with their behavior. There are happy times too, but overwhelmingly you feel frustrated by your child. Your child often melts down or is difficult to calm down. When your child is upset, you get upset too. When you feel angry, you yell and explode at them, and then you feel bad and want to hug them and apologize. Sometimes it is easier to take a break from your child than it is to work on your relationship with them. You love your child, but you're not sure how to show it.

Intergenerational Attachment

We often parent the same way we were parented. We build relationships with our children based on the ways our parents built relationships with us. Were your relationships in childhood grounded in healthy attachment? Take the next few moments to consider how you were parented as a child, what was communicated to you about relationships, and if that helped or hurt your relationship skills.

1. What were your parents' beliefs about nurturing? Did they display affection? Were they emotionally available? How did you feel about this?

   _____

   _____

2. What were your parents' beliefs about discipline, correction, or limit setting? How did you feel about this?

   _____

   _____

3. What were your parents' beliefs about attunement? Did they model how to meet other people's needs? Did they model how to express your needs (and then meet these needs in return)? How did you feel about this?

   _____

   _____

4. Did your parents create a space that felt safe—physically, mentally, and emotionally? Why or why not? How did you feel about this?

   _____

   _____

Worssheet (Adult)

Relationship Messages

We all receive relationship messages from our parents. They are our first teachers about relationships. Sometimes they teach us things that are helpful. Sometimes they teach us unhealthy messages, in which case we want to evaluate whether that is something we want to embrace or discard. Write down some relationship messages that your parents taught you, and place a check mark to indicate whether you want to embrace or discard that message. Thinking about these relationship messages can help you make some changes that move you toward healthier relationships.

Relationship Message	Embrace	Discard
Example: *My way is always the right way.*		X

My Attachment Style

Attachment has to do with how we connect to others in relationships. We all have an attachment style, which defines how we act and react in our relationships. Read the following descriptions, and put a check mark by the one that best describes the way your relationships work.

_____ 1. In relationships, you value trust and taking care of each other. You seek balance in your connections and give people space when needed. You do things independently but also enjoy returning to your significant relationships for support and comfort. You can depend on the people you have relationships with to help you problem solve when necessary, and you have fun together but also enjoy doing things alone. You have two or three close relationships, and those people know you very well. You enjoy your relationships and are able to relax in them. It is easy to make new relationships with people and to feel close, but you are also willing to put work into making relationships more satisfying.

_____ 2. You value finding people who need you and who you need. You become anxious when you feel like someone no longer needs you. You want your relationships to be closer and more engaged, even when the other person is satisfied with the way it is. Other people often tell you that they want space or that you can be "clingy." You just want to stay closely connected and do everything together to make the relationship stronger. No relationship feels like it is close enough.

_____ 3. You value independence in relationships. Each person meets their own needs, and you expect others to be self-sufficient. You form relationships with people because you want to be with them, not because you need them. You tend to cut off relationships when you no longer enjoy someone's company. You are busy with tasks and have relationships that are mostly light and easy. When a relationship becomes difficult or too much work, it can often end as well. You don't mind not being in a relationship and feel comfortable being alone. You don't necessarily need to be emotionally vulnerable or to share your emotions for a relationship to be successful.

_____ 4. You value people who are there for you. You want to be more closely connected and to share your emotions with others, but you worry that others won't care about your feelings. You may have had experiences where others were not respectful or caring when you shared your emotions, so you find it hard to trust others on this deeper level. This holds you back from finding the intimate connection you long for. You are uncomfortable expressing love for others and feel that your expressions of love may not be returned because you are not worthy of the love of others.

Anxiety in Relationships

When we are in relationships, we can experience a significant amount of anxiety that can make us uncomfortable. This anxiety may impact our choices and behaviors, which then impacts our loved ones. Take a few minutes to think about the following questions in regard to your relationships.

1. What makes you feel most anxious in your relationships?

_____

_____

_____

2. How do you express your anxiety? What does it look like in your relationships?

_____

_____

_____

3. How do loved ones respond to these behaviors?

_____

_____

_____

4. Does this help or hurt your relationships? How so?

_____

_____

_____

5. If you could manage your anxiety, how would that change your relationships?

_____

_____

_____

6. Are there ways you could better cope with your anxiety in relationships? How so?

_____

_____

_____

7. Is there anything stopping you from doing this? If so, describe that here.

_____

_____

_____

Avoidance in Relationships

Relationships can be hard work! When they require a lot of us, it can sometimes feel like it would be easier to end the relationship or to become more independent so we don't need to rely on others. This can cause us to have many relationships but none that are long-lasting and fulfilling. Take a few minutes to think about the ways you interact in relationships and whether this helps or hurts your relationships.

1. When a relationship becomes a lot of work, how do you typically react?

   _____

   _____

   _____

2. Is there value in investing in a long-term relationship? Why or why not?

   _____

   _____

   _____

3. When you emotionally withdraw from a relationship, what impact does that have on the relationship?

   _____

   _____

   _____

4. When was the last time you noticed a loved one's needs and met those needs? How did the other person react?

   _____

   _____

   _____

5. Do you want others to care about your needs and to take care of you? Why or why not?

_____

_____

_____

6. What would it feel like to have someone meet your needs because they care about you?

_____

_____

_____

7. When was the last time you experienced that care?

_____

_____

_____

8. How would your relationships change if you were cared for and if you cared for others in those ways?

_____

_____

_____

Ambivalence in Relationships

Relationships can be very fulfilling, and although you desire to get closer to other people, trusting another person with your feelings requires more vulnerability than you feel able to share right now. Take a few minutes to think about the ways you interact with others and whether this helps or hurts your relationships.

1. If you could imagine a fulfilling relationship, what would it be like?

   _____

   _____

2. How is your imagined relationship different than your present relationships?

   _____

   _____

3. What is your greatest fear related to emotional intimacy?

   _____

   _____

4. How does that fear keep you from getting closer to others? Does that keep you from developing the fulfilling relationship you imagined?

   _____

   _____

5. What would help you move past that fear?

   _____

   _____

6. How would you feel if you could find a fulfilling relationship?

   _____

   _____

Anxious-Preoccupied Attachment

If this attachment style best describes your relationships, you may not find complete satisfaction in relationships. However, relationships can be very satisfying and can meet our needs for emotional connection and fulfillment. Answer the questions below, and then think about what action steps you could take to move toward healthy and secure attachment.

1. What is your largest worry in your relationships?

_____

_____

_____

2. When do you think this anxiety in relationships began? What could have caused you to feel insecure in your relationships?

_____

_____

_____

3. What things do you do to keep people close to you in relationships? How do they respond?

_____

_____

_____

4. What activities do you ask people to do with you that you could do on your own?

_____

_____

_____

5. What would it mean for you to do activities on your own?

_____

_____

_____

6. When you ask others to help you manage your emotions or anxiety, what is their response? Does this help or hurt your relationship?

_____

_____

_____

7. Think about how your anxiety in relationships could make your biggest worries come true. Describe that here.

_____

_____

_____

Action Steps:

1. What are three things you can do on your own that are fulfilling and fun? Now make a plan to do those activities.

_____

_____

_____

2. Think of three benefits of doing activities on your own.

_____

_____

_____

3. What are five personality characteristics you have to offer in a relationship?

_____

_____

_____

4. What are three things loved ones have said to you about your talents? Things that they liked about you or that they thought you were good at?

_____

_____

_____

5. What do you do to take care of your own emotions? How do you cope independently? If you can't think of anything, brainstorm new ideas to try this week.

_____

_____

_____

6. Can you think of one person who has the type of relationship you want to have? Someone who is emotionally connected and fulfilled in a healthy relationship? Ask them to coffee or lunch, and interview them about what makes their relationship work. Write down some of their responses here.

_____

_____

_____

Dismissive-Avoidant Attachment

If this attachment style best describes your relationships, you may not find complete satisfaction in relationships. However, relationships can be very satisfying and can meet our needs for emotional connection and fulfillment. Answer the questions below, and then think about what action steps you could take to move toward healthy and secure attachment.

1. What does "independence" in relationships mean to you?

_____

_____

2. How did you learn about being "independent" in relationships? How does that work (or not work) in developing depth and intimacy in relationships?

_____

_____

3. How do you feel about being emotionally intimate in relationships?

_____

_____

4. What would vulnerability in a relationship mean to you?

_____

_____

5. How do you allow others to meet your needs? Who meets your needs?

_____

_____

6. How do you meet the needs of others? Whose needs do you meet?

_____

_____

7. What takes the most work to maintain a relationship? Do you think putting work into a relationship is a good use of your time? Why or why not?

_____

_____

Action Steps:

1. What are three ways you can depend on others? What are three things you need from others?

_____

_____

2. Think of one relationship in which you do not currently share your emotions but would like to. What is holding you back? What would be one action step toward sharing your emotions with that person?

_____

_____

3. How do you determine with whom you can safely share your emotions? How do you know whom to trust? How do you develop trust in relationships?

_____

_____

4. Think of one person whose needs you can meet. Find a way to meet one need this week, and write about how it feels to meet that person's need.

_____

_____

5. What is one thing you could do to make one of your current relationships better? How can you plan to work on that one thing over the next few weeks?

_____

_____

6. Can you think of one person who has the type of relationship you want to have? Someone who is emotionally connected and fulfilled in a healthy relationship? Ask them to coffee or lunch, and interview them about what makes their relationship work. Write down some of their responses here.

_____

_____

Fearful-Avoidant Attachment

If this attachment style best describes your relationships, you may not find complete satisfaction in relationships. However, relationships can be very satisfying and can meet our needs for emotional connection and fulfillment. Answer the questions below, and then think about what action steps you could take to move toward healthy and secure attachment.

1. What makes you uncomfortable or hesitant to engage in a relationship on an emotional level?

   _____

   _____

2. What have been your past experiences with intimate relationships that may have caused you to feel this way?

   _____

   _____

3. How do you express emotions in your relationships? Does this help or hurt your relationships?

   _____

   _____

4. What do you think others will do if you share your emotions? Will they be supportive? Dismissive? Judgmental?

   _____

   _____

5. How do you feel when others share their emotions? Does it make you feel uncomfortable? Do you offer support? Why or why not?

   _____

   _____

6. Do you feel you are unworthy of love or support? If so, why?

   _____

   _____

Action Steps:

1. What are three ways you can express emotions in relationships that will allow you to feel closer and more connected with others?

   _____

   _____

2. Think of one person you trust whom you want to share your emotions with. Make a plan this week to share a small emotion with them and note their reaction. If you cannot think of someone, what would it take for someone to earn this level of trust?

   _____

   _____

3. Think of one person you care for. Think back to a time when they shared their emotions with you. How did you respond? If you didn't respond with support, what are some ways you could have been supportive? Once you come up with some ideas, go back to that person and offer support—even if some time has passed.

   _____

   _____

4. What are three reasons why your emotions are important and deserve support?

   _____

   _____

5. What is one reason why you deserve to be loved and accepted?

   _____

   _____

6. Can you think of one person who has the type of relationship you want to have? Someone who is emotionally connected and fulfilled in a healthy relationship? Ask them to coffee or lunch, and interview them about what makes their relationship work. Write down some of their responses here.

   _____

   _____

Personality in Resiliency

When you have experienced trauma, there are several factors that can increase your likelihood of overcoming the trauma and finding healing. One of these factors is personality, which influences how you see and interact with the world around you. As you think about the questions below, consider whether your personality traits help you heal or are a barrier to your healing. If your personality traits promote resiliency, how can you draw on those strengths and use them in your healing process? If they interfere with your recovery, how can you overcome those barriers so you can adapt in the face of adversity?

1. Are you an extrovert (like being around people) or an introvert (like being by yourself)? How does that help or hinder your healing?

   _____

   _____

   _____

2. Are you open to new things (like new interventions and ways of coping), or do you prefer to stick with what you know and are comfortable with? How does that help or hinder your healing?

   _____

   _____

   _____

3. Do you see the positives and negatives in each situation, or do you believe that life "should" be a certain way and that if it is not, then life is unfair? How does that help or hinder your healing?

   _____

   _____

   _____

4. Do you feel anxious about things going wrong, or do you look for growing points in life that develop your character? How does that help or hinder your healing?

   _____

   _____

   _____

4

Abuse

Kenny was raised in a home where his parents fought constantly and had great difficulty managing their feelings. When they felt angry or frustrated, they would strike each other and Kenny, often leaving him physically injured as a result. His parents were also verbally and emotionally abusive, telling Kenny that they wished he hadn't been born, that he ruined their life, and that he was a bad child. Because his parents had modeled ineffective ways to manage anger, Kenny soon began to express his anger the same way. Even as a small child, Kenny was often in trouble at school for hitting others—children and teachers alike—when he became angry. Due to these difficulties with aggression, he had few friends. As Kenny grew older, his father continued to hit him until, one day, Kenny struck his father back and broke his father's nose. At that point, the physical assaults against Kenny stopped, but the emotional and verbal abuse continued.

When Kenny was in his twenties, he met Sarah. They had both come from dysfunctional homes and married after only three months of dating. When Sarah became pregnant shortly thereafter, Kenny became angry because they were already having a hard time paying bills, and he couldn't imagine having another mouth to feed. He knocked Sarah to the floor, and although he felt guilty for doing so, that didn't help him control his anger any better in the months to come. Sarah experienced intense anxiety and fear, causing her body to release high levels of adrenaline and cortisol. These stress hormones, in turn, were introduced into the developing child's environment during a critical period of brain and nervous system growth.

The physical and verbal abuse continued throughout Sarah's pregnancy until their first child, Katie, was born. Katie was one year old when Kenny began having difficulty managing his anger toward her. She had been crying for an hour, and Kenny felt his anger rising with each minute. He slapped Katie, and when Sarah screamed at him to stop, he hit her too. The abuse continued for five more years, with weekly physical, emotional, and verbal attacks on Sarah and Katie. At that point, Katie began school, and her teacher noticed that Katie was covered in bruises and often cowered when adults raised their voices. After a call to Child Protective Services, Katie was removed from the care of her biological parents and placed in her first foster home.

When she arrived at her first foster placement, Katie was frozen with fear. Although she was initially quiet—following all directions and staying in her room most of the time—she soon became jealous when she saw her foster parents interacting with their biological children and wished she could have the same relationship. She began expressing her jealousy and sadness through destructive behaviors that caused her to be removed from the foster home. Over the next three years, Katie was moved to seven different foster homes and was hospitalized several times due to her inability to manage her emotions. In therapy, Katie focused on increasing her ability to build relationships with her current foster parents so she could maintain that placement. She made a "containment box" where she placed her worries and angers on strips of paper whenever they began to overwhelm her. Each night she processed one item with her foster parents, and they partnered with her to problem solve or provide support. She also brought the box to therapy each week and processed the items together with her therapist.

As Kenny and Katie's story illustrates, abuse experienced during childhood can follow that individual into adulthood, impacting all of their future relationships and their relationship with their own children. This generational cycle can be difficult to break because children learn how to relate to others based on what their parents model for them. What a child learns through this early modeling about relationships becomes a template for how they interact with others and the world. That is why abuse during childhood is so impactful. Prior to school age, parents serve as the primary models for their children. Children do not yet have other experiences or context to which they can compare what their parents model for them, so everything that happens in their life during this time becomes foundational to their belief system. If parents model verbal abuse and disrespect as a way of communicating, then children will believe this is how they are supposed to interact with others. This dysfunctional framework becomes normative for them.

Unfortunately, abuse often goes unrecognized until children reach school age and other adults begin interacting with them. By this time, the abuse has often been occurring for years, during the developmental period when a child's most critical beliefs about the world have been forming. These beliefs are foundational, so individuals who experience abuse during childhood often grow into adults who have difficulty trusting other people, especially authority figures. This can impact their ability to function successfully in society or to hold a job because they react to authority with resistance.

The repercussions of childhood abuse can be likened to a train that has become derailed. If the child is the train, then abuse derails that train off the tracks. Once that child develops into an adult, the train has been derailed for so long that they may not remember how it feels to be on the tracks. In these cases, it's only possible to get back on the tracks with help from an adult the individual views as safe. As humans, we typically do not follow the directions of someone we don't trust or see as safe, which creates a challenge for mental health professionals. If we present ourselves as experts on the topic of mental health, this can feel intimidating and unsafe for individuals who do not trust those in authority positions. Instead, we need to present ourselves as safe people who can be trusted. In order to help survivors of childhood abuse get their trains back on track, we have to build a trust-based relationship with them before they will listen to us when we attempt to process their experiences or teach them how to more effectively manage their emotions and behaviors.

What does this look like in a professional setting? It could involve playing a game with a child to build rapport before talking about hard things. It could involve offering an adult a cup of coffee or tea—and having one yourself as you sit across from the client. It could involve engaging a child and parent in a playful interaction of blowing bubbles or playing with musical instruments to begin a family session. Building the relationship first will allow you to teach emotion regulation and social skills more quickly once the client accepts you as a safe person they can trust. Until that relationship develops, expect resistance and opposition to learning new things.

One of the things that we, as adults, can do to help survivors of childhood abuse feel safe again is to ensure that we are emotionally regulated. When we are emotionally regulated, we are in control of our emotions instead of allowing our emotions to control us. We are cool, calm, and collected at all times, which helps individuals who have been traumatized feel safe as they co-regulate with us. This may sound like an unrealistic expectation, but it can be achieved. We simply need to make sure that we are aware of our emotions, express them appropriately, and know how to calm those emotions. If we can do this for ourselves, then we can teach others how to do it.

One aspect of emotion regulation involves the concept of containment, in which we place a lid on any emotions that we cannot cope with in the current moment and take the lid off at a later time when we can safely and appropriately experience them. Containment is not the same thing as pushing emotions away or ignoring them. It is about putting them somewhere for safe keeping until we have the time to give them the attention they deserve. Containment is an important concept for clients who have experienced trauma because their emotions can feel large and out of control at times. When we teach them to contain those emotions—to temporarily put a lid on them—this allows them to function and to get through the demands of their daily lives, like going to work or sitting in class. It prevents them from being overwhelmed by their emotions so they can focus on other tasks.

When working with children who have experienced abuse, it is particularly important that we take the time to develop our own skills when it comes to emotion regulation and containment. Doing so allows us to keep our feelings under control so we can focus on the needs of the child. Focusing on the child's needs and meeting those needs is the basis of attunement, which is a building block to trust. Children need to be able to trust that adults will be cool, calm, and collected—even if they are not. Maintaining this level of emotional consistency is vital for children who have experienced abuse because they often have the belief system that *all* adults are unsafe, which can influence the way they interact with adults. For example, they may begin to "push buttons" as a means of testing limits and seeing if there is a certain threshold when a new adult in their life will become an unsafe person.

This is a typical trauma response: Trauma makes people feel out of control, so they try to cope by engaging in behaviors that give them some semblance of control. Children who have been abused often do so by "pushing buttons" that trigger the other person to engage in unsafe behavior, such as yelling or threatening. When the other person reacts in this manner, it gives the child the illusion that they were in control of that reaction. But the reality is, everyone has buttons—things that irritate us, annoy us, or cause us to become dysregulated—and almost always, these buttons have to do with our own unresolved issues. As adults, we must take a look at our issues and work on resolving them instead of engaging in a power struggle with the child.

Safe adults never engage in a power struggle with children because doing so gives the impression that the power is up for grabs and that the child can take the power from the adult. However, the truth is that the adult has the power and is in control. Therefore, instead of power struggling, it is important to *power share*, which involves giving the child appropriate choices. This gives the child some semblance of control and allows the child to feel safe with adults. When adults are responsible with their power and do not misuse it, it can result in a powerful change in the brain of a child who does not trust adults as safe people. It presents their brain with new information about adults that challenges the information they already have. It challenges their belief system that all adults are unsafe people, which allows for the development of a trust-based relationship where they view the adult as someone who is safe, who can meet their needs, and who can take care of them.

The following interventions will help build that trust-based relationship. These interventions focus on helping clients learn how to differentiate safe people from unsafe people, how to contain their thoughts and feelings, and how to express themselves appropriately to receive validation and support. With these interventions, clients can increase feelings of felt safety and healthy control.

INTERVENTIONS FOR HEALING

Oftentimes, children and adults who have experienced abuse have difficulty telling the difference between safe and unsafe people. As a result, they can become hypervigilant and feel unsafe in all relationships. They can also begin to seek out people who are unsafe if that is all they have known and are comfortable with, which can then lead to increased vulnerability and victimization. In order to help clients differentiate between safe and unsafe people, clinicians can use the following two worksheets. The **Safe or Unsafe** worksheet is geared toward younger children, who may need more guidance and redirection to identify the difference between safe and unsafe people, whereas the **Who's a Safe Person?** worksheet is intended for adults. These worksheets can allow clients to make informed choices about healthy relationships moving forward.

As clients complete each worksheet, observe what they categorize as safe versus unsafe characteristics because this will inform possible areas that you need to work on in treatment. For example, if a client is used to being around individuals who are controlling, they may believe it is normal for their partner to isolate them from their family and friends. In this case, it may be necessary to use gentle reframing and additional psychoeducation to help clients learn the difference.

Oftentimes, individuals who have experienced abuse during childhood hold themselves responsible for the abuse instead of recognizing that they were a helpless victim. Blaming themselves for the abuse gives them the illusion that the situation was somehow in their control. However, this blame results in feelings of guilt and shame that follow children into adulthood, leading them to take responsibility for things for which they are not responsible. This can leave the individual confused about responsibility, about a child's power over an adult, and about an adult's responsibility in the life of a child. It is important to help children (or adults who were abused in childhood) understand who was responsible. Clinicians can use the **Whose Control?** worksheet with adults and children as they explore who was in control when the abuse occurred. Helping clients understand what they could and could not control about the abuse can assist them as they move forward in recognizing the circumstances of their life over which they do have control. For example, they are in complete control of their recovery. When clients are able to establish that they do have control over something in their life that feels out of control, this can be very empowering.

Individuals who have been traumatized by abuse are in a perpetual state of nervous system activation and are easily triggered into fight, flight, or freeze reactions when something in their environment elicits feelings of unsafety. Clinicians can use the **Feeling Safe Again** worksheet with children or adult clients to assist them in identifying what caused them to lose their feelings of safety and how they can feel safe again. When the client can identify the impact that the abuse had on them, healing can begin by implementing relationship or structural changes that allow the person to feel safe again. For example, if hugging is a trigger for a client—because a client associates hugging with sexual abuse— then working in current relationships to define and experience healthy hugging may allow the client to feel safe again. They may not be able to feel safe in all environments, but if at least one environment— the most impactful being the home environment—feels safe, then it can provide the space for healing to begin. Healing cannot begin until a person feels safe.

In order for clients to heal from abuse, we need to help them move through the three stages of recovery as defined by Judith Herman (1992). First, we must help clients establish or reestablish feelings of safety and stability so they can begin the healing process. Once we have begun that process, we move on to the second stage by helping clients find ways to express the pain and loss associated with the abuse. Remembering and mourning are important steps in the healing process that should not be rushed. The client needs time to experience these emotions and thoughts so they don't continue to block future growth. Finally, we move to the third stage where we help clients reconnect to others in their life and integrate the experiences into their understanding of themselves and their narrative. Doing so is important for self-acceptance and recovery.

When a person has experienced childhood abuse, their emotions can feel large and overwhelming. As a result, their emotional responses can be larger than the situation warrants as the individual struggles to manage and contain out-of-control emotions. For example, someone who has been physically abused may be hypervigilant about being touched, causing them to flinch or to respond with verbal or even physical aggression in response to physical contact. In order to reduce this emotional reactivity and better assist individuals in dealing with overwhelming feelings, clinicians can use the following three interventions with both children and adults.

First, we want clients to understand the role that adrenaline plays in the escalation process. The **Getting Your Train Back on the Track** handout explains how the brain's alert system triggers the release of adrenaline when it senses danger, causing the body to escalate into fight, flight, or freeze mode even when no actual threat is present. Next, the **Coping with Big Emotions** handout gives examples of various coping strategies clients can use to manage overwhelming feelings and to mitigate the effects of adrenaline triggered by stress. Finally, the **Emotions Scale** worksheet is intended to help clients process their emotional responses to various events and to evaluate more effective ways to cope with the situation. In particular, this worksheet asks clients to identify when their reaction to an event may not match the severity of the situation.

Part of a trauma diagnosis is intrusive thoughts and flashbacks. When clients are able to contain these feelings, thoughts, or memories, they regain some control back over a symptom that feels out of control. To do so, adult or child clients can use the **Containment Circles** worksheet in which they temporarily place any overwhelming thoughts or feelings inside the circle. The circle, with no beginning and no end, provides containment and control. When clients place items in the circle, it allows them to hold those items until a later time when they can unpack the thought or feeling more fully. Clients can also use this worksheet as a "brain dump." They can simply empty their mind by writing everything they are thinking about in the circle. This can be especially helpful at bedtime so clients can release any difficult thoughts or feelings before falling asleep. If clients complete several circles during the week and bring them to session, look for recurring themes and topics to discern what the client is most affected by.

The **Containment Box** activity is a similar intervention that adults and children can use to temporarily contain difficult feelings. Clients can write their overwhelming thoughts and feelings on strips of paper and place them in a box (or jar) with a lid. The box represents a safe place where clients can store their thoughts and feelings until they are ready to further explore them. After placing the strips of paper in the box, the client can also decorate the box with drawings, positive affirmations, or inspiring quotes.

Both of these exercises are intended to make overwhelming thoughts and feelings seem more tangible and real. It allows other people to "see" the client's difficulties and to provide validation and support. Overwhelming thoughts and feelings start to lose their power when they are no longer secret or hidden. And in being validated, clients no longer have to worry about what others will think of them for having these thoughts, feelings, or experiences.

Clients who have experienced abuse often feel numb and disconnected from their body, or they may struggle to find ease in their body because they are constantly holding on to tension. Clinicians can use the **Body Scan** exercise with children or adults to promote muscle relaxation and stress reduction, as well as to mindfully anchor clients in the present moment. This exercise improves the mind-body connection as clients think about how their body feels, identify areas of tension, and then work to relax and release it. The focus on the body also provides a welcome distraction from racing thoughts that may be contributing to tension and hypervigilance.

Although clinicians should guide clients through the script first, clients can complete the exercise on their own once they become familiar with the directives. Once they develop this familiarity, encourage them to complete the body scan on their own whenever they need to take inventory of their body. This is also a useful exercise that clients can complete in the morning and evening as a form of relaxation and mindfulness.

Given that abuse can come in many forms, the next series of worksheets is intended to address specific types of abuse, including physical, sexual, and emotional abuse, for both child and adult clients. You may use multiple worksheets with the same client if they experienced several different types of abuse, which is often the case. Each worksheet provides a specific healing intervention that may need repeated application to bring healing. To facilitate recovery, encourage clients to keep practicing the exercises on a regular basis.

Physical abuse causes harm to a person's body, which can lead individuals to hold physical memories of the trauma in their body, in addition to their mind. They may have physical symptoms of trauma in their body, such as tension or pain, that trigger them to feel unsafe or to experience anxiety. The **Healing from Physical Abuse** worksheet helps clients identify how their body continues to respond to trauma and allows them find healing as they honor and connect with the parts of themselves that were hurt.

When clients have been violated sexually, they may struggle to experience intimacy and connection in their relationships. These individuals no longer feel safe being vulnerable, which makes it challenging for them to find comfort and fulfillment in sexuality. Use the adult version of the **Healing from Sexual Abuse** worksheet to explore the impact of sexual abuse on a client's thinking about sexuality and to move them toward healing as they find ways to reclaim their body. In addition, a child version of this worksheet is provided to help children recognize the ways in which their boundaries have been affected by sexual abuse and how they can create healthier ones.

Emotional and verbal abuse are two common forms of abuse that are often intertwined and that can severely damage a client's self-view. If the mind is like a recorder, then emotional abuse is like a song that plays in a feedback loop over and over again through the years. For example, when a child is told that they are "never going to be anything good" or called degrading names, these words stay in that child's head for life. Similarly, an adult in an emotionally abusive relationship—who has, for years, been told that they are "no good," "a mess," or "a disappointment"—begins to believe these things about themselves. To help clients change the words running through their minds, use the **Healing from Emotional Abuse** worksheet so clients can learn to differentiate the lies they were told from the truth about themselves.

When clients have experienced abuse, an important component of recovery involves understanding the difference between abusive relationships and healthy relationships. Use the **Relationship Comparison** worksheet to help adult clients determine whether they are making choices to keep themselves safe and healthy or whether they are repeating the same patterns by entering into abusive relationships. If clients continue to gravitate toward unhealthy relationships, work with them to build a healthy perspective regarding attachment, which is foundational for healing relationship trauma. The worksheets in chapter 3, specifically those focused on relationship building, attunement, and attachment, would also be helpful.

In addition, given that many people with abuse histories struggle with self-esteem, the **Growing Self-Esteem** worksheet can assist adult and child clients in identifying their strengths and positive characteristics. Shame is a natural outgrowth of abuse, especially when a victim takes responsibility for some or all of the abuse. Clients can move toward healing by identifying the strengths they possess as a result of surviving the abuse.

When children have experienced abuse, the stability and security of their family relationships is the largest predictor of that child being able to recover from trauma. Helping parents provide this felt safety in the home environment can be the most effective intervention in allowing a child to heal. To help parents facilitate a healing environment for their child, clinicians can give parents the **Creating Felt Safety** handout, which explains how parents can best support their child in recovering from trauma.

One of the key components of felt safety is an atmosphere characterized by nurturing care. In contrast to instrumental care—which has to do with ensuring that a child's basic needs are met (e.g., food and shelter)—nurturing care is a more encompassing concept that involves five components: adequate nutrition, safety and security, responsive caregiving, opportunities for early learning, and good health (Black et al., 2017). Oftentimes, when there is a breakdown in attachment, instrumental care is present but nurturing care is not. This is especially the case if parents have not experienced nurture in their own relationships. They may think that meeting a child's basic needs for food, clothing, and shelter is an expression of love, when the reality is that children also need affection, affirmation, and encouragement.

Clinicians can use the **Nurturing Care** worksheet to help parents conceptualize what nurturing care looks like and to challenge themselves to think of ways to nurture their child. The **My Child's Needs** worksheet can assist parents in further developing nurturing care skills as they find ways to recognize and meet their child's needs. When parents are attuned to their child's needs, this facilitates healing. If a child has lost trust in a parent's ability to meet their needs, the **Trust-Based Parenting** worksheet is a useful resource parents can use to regain this trust. Finally, the **Parenting with Attachment** worksheet asks parents to brainstorm ways they can again engage in relationship-focused activities to foster a nurturing environment.

Safe or Unsafe

Sometimes it can be hard to know who is safe and who is unsafe. But it's important to know the difference so you can stay happy and healthy. If you are ever around someone who is unsafe, make sure to let a trusted adult know so they can help you. For each statement listed here, put an "S" if you think it's an example of a safe person and a "U" if you think it's an example of an unsafe person.

_____ A person who gives you things after your parents say it is okay.

_____ A person who touches you without asking.

_____ A person who offers you candy without asking your parents for permission.

_____ A person who gives you money for no reason.

_____ A person who asks before they give you a hug.

_____ A person who yells and screams.

_____ A person who asks your parents before taking you on an outing.

_____ A person who asks you to help them find a lost dog.

_____ A person who talks to your parents and gets permission before asking you private questions.

Who's a Safe Person?

It's important to be able to tell safe and unsafe people apart. If we have relationships with unsafe people, this can cause us to be harmed in a variety of ways. To keep ourselves safe, we have to be able to find safe people. Think about what qualities make a person safe and what makes them unsafe. Look at the characteristics below, and circle the examples that appear safe and cross out the ones that appear unsafe.

1. Only wants me to spend time with them
2. Listens to what I think/express
3. Wants us to have the same thoughts
4. Respects my body
5. Is nice to me all the time
6. Hurts or scares me when they are mad
7. Never calls me names
8. Takes a break when they are angry
9. Breaks rules
10. Makes me feel uncomfortable

11. Has different interests than I do
12. Values my strengths
13. Pushes my boundaries
14. Belittles me
15. Tries to change my mind
16. Only wants to do things they like
17. Sometimes calls me names
18. Offers me substances/alcohol
19. Makes me feel accepted
20. Encourages me to follow rules

Answer Key:
Safe: 2, 4, 5, 7, 8, 11, 12, 19, 20
Unsafe: 1, 3, 6, 9, 10, 13, 14, 15, 16, 17, 18

Whose Control?

When something hard or hurtful happens in our life, it is common for us to think about how those events have molded and shaped us into who we are today. This allows us to develop insight, which can help us to make different choices in the future, to avoid hurtful or harmful situations, and to protect ourselves. Part of thinking about these events involves determining who was in control at the time. Oftentimes, individuals who experience abuse as children will come to believe that they had control of the abuse and that they are therefore to blame. Moving forward, this can lead them to experience confusion about the circumstances for which they are (and are not) responsible. If you experienced abuse as a child, it is important to realize that the abuse was not your fault, and there are many things over which you *do* have control now. Focusing on what you can control in your present-day life and letting go of that which you cannot control can help you heal and find balance.

1. When you think about times in your childhood that felt out of control, what is most upsetting or brings the strongest feelings to mind?

   _____

   _____

   _____

2. As a child, did you have control over any of these upsetting situations? Do you feel like you were responsible for what happened? Why or why not?

   _____

   _____

   _____

3. If you were not in control, who was? Who was responsible? How does it make you feel as you reflect on this?

   _____

   _____

   _____

4. When you think about your present-day life, what are some things you *do* have control over?

_____

_____

_____

5. What are you doing with that control? How are you using it?

_____

_____

_____

6. What are some things you do *not* have control over in your present-day life?

_____

_____

_____

7. When you cannot control certain aspects of your daily life, what kinds of feelings arise? What do you do to cope with those feelings?

_____

_____

_____

Worksheet (Adult or Child)

Feeling Safe Again

When we have experienced something that causes us to feel unsafe and insecure, something that scares us and takes away our control, we can begin to feel unsafe in more places and with more people. Take a few minutes to think about things that have happened in your life and what could help you to feel safe again.

1. What happened that caused you to feel unsafe?

_____

_____

_____

2. What about that event(s) felt unsafe?

_____

_____

_____

3. What people, places, or things feel unsafe now? Are there certain places, people, or things you attempt to avoid as a result? What about them feels unsafe?

_____

_____

_____

136

Copyright © 2021 Christina Reese. *Trauma and Attachment Workbook*. All rights reserved.

4. To move past our fears, we sometimes need to confront the very thing we are afraid of. We expose ourselves to it slowly, with small steps. If we are in an environment where we feel safe and are with safe people, being exposed to whatever it is that we're afraid of may not feel as scary. Can you think about what a good first step would be to expose yourself in a small way to your fear?

_____

_____

_____

5. Do you think it is realistic or unrealistic to make these changes? How so? What will be the hardest part?

_____

_____

_____

6. How can you ask people in your life for help with these changes?

_____

_____

_____

Getting Your Train Back on the Track

Imagine yourself as a train, rumbling down the tracks of life. Everything is going along just fine when something happens that alerts the conductor that there is danger ahead. The conductor sends a message to the coal car to start loading tons of coal into the furnace so the train can speed up and quickly pass through the dangerous area up ahead. The train starts to move too fast and quickly derails! What just happened?

This is what happens inside your body every time you experience anxiety. Your life (train) may be rumbling along just fine. Then something happens that gets your attention. Maybe your senses tell you something is wrong—you see, hear, smell, taste, or touch something that does not feel safe. Maybe someone bumps into you or looks at you in a way that you perceive as threatening. When this happens, you have an alert system in your brain (the conductor) that activates and sends messages to your adrenal gland (the coal car) to release adrenaline (load more coal!). Adrenaline is a hormone in your body that helps you in an emergency. When the alert system says there is danger, adrenaline comes to the rescue. Adrenaline does several things in your body to get you ready to face the danger:

- Speeds up your heartbeat
- Constricts your lungs
- Raises your blood pressure
- Tightens your muscles

Some of those bodily changes may look familiar to you because you may remember feeling that way when you were getting upset about something. When those things happen inside your body, it can also cause a stomachache or headache. Your adrenaline is moving too fast, which can cause you (the train) to derail. It does not feel good when these things are happening inside of us, and we can begin to feel grumpy or angry.

How do we get the train back on the track? How do we get *you* back on track? By getting rid of all that extra adrenaline through physical activity. Adrenaline does not just go away; it has to be burned off. Therefore, when you feel like your train is derailing, start moving. You can take a walk, do a few jumping jacks or yoga poses, or do some wall push-ups. Any kind of activity will calm your body so you can stop the emotional escalation and quickly get your train back on the track.

Coping with Big Emotions

When your feelings are BIG and overwhelming, you can reduce them in size by using coping skills. Coping skills are simply tools and techniques that calm down your feelings, helping your mind and body to be calm too. Below are some examples of coping skills that you can try out. Coping skills are very personal—everyone has different things that help them feel calm—so take some time to see which ones work best for you. After you have tried a few, or all, of the coping skills listed here, try to brainstorm some more!

1. **Practice deep breathing:** When your emotions feel out of control, your heart rate speeds up and your respiration rate increases. Given that your heart rate changes with your breath, one way to calm your body and mind is to practice deep breathing. Take four deep breaths, breathing in through your nose and out through your mouth.

2. **Take a walk:** Get moving outside to burn off the excess adrenaline that is moving through your body.

3. **Do a few yoga poses:** Not only does yoga stretch and relax your muscles, which helps your body to feel less tension, but it can also burn off adrenaline.

4. **Say a positive affirmation:** When you are having a negative thought, try saying a positive affirmation to counteract that thought. For example, if you are thinking, *I can't do this*, try telling yourself, *I've done harder things than this! I can handle it!* When you repeatedly confront negative thoughts with positive ones, it actually changes the way your brain thinks! You can control your thoughts and change them.

5. **Talk to someone in your support system:** Connect with someone who cares about you, and work together to problem solve or brainstorm solutions as to what is troubling you. Sometimes it just feels good to talk the trouble out! Relationships help us feel validated and valued, which can help us in moments of sadness or frustration.

6. **Take a mindful moment:** For a few minutes, just sit quietly and be "in the moment." If you find yourself getting caught up in worries, triggers, or negative thoughts and feelings, imagine placing them on clouds that are passing by in the sky. Then take a few deep breaths while you take a moment to tune in and listen to your body. How does it feel? What do you see, hear, smell, taste, or touch? If any parts of your body are holding tension, try to relax them. Paying attention to your body and your senses, instead of getting caught up in negative thoughts and worries, can provide you with a sense of grounding, meaning that it helps you to stay focused and centered in the moment instead of being swept away by emotion.

7. **Draw for five minutes:** Just pick up a pencil and start drawing. See what the end result is after a few minutes. This sort of creative expression frees our emotions by making visible what was once invisible, and it also calms our souls. Once we express our emotions in this manner, they can often become quieter.

8. **Journal for five minutes:** Just pick up a pen and start writing. Let your thoughts and feelings flow out of you onto the page. When you release everything that was intangible out of your mind, you no longer feel obligated to carry it around with you. Having these thoughts and feelings in front of you, on the page, can also help you problem solve as you see things from a different perspective.

9. **Listen to music:** What's your favorite song right now? Put it on repeat and dance and sing along. Not only does this use up extra adrenaline through physical movement, but singing can be very freeing and can lift our mood.

10. **Watch a video:** Watch a funny or cute video that makes you smile or laugh. Even just a two-minute video can distract you from overwhelming feelings and release endorphins (our "feel-good" hormones).

Emotions Scale

At times, our emotions can feel large and overwhelming. Even when the event that triggered these big emotions is small, it can still feel very important to us. For example, if someone were to bump into us in the hallway, this may cause us to feel very upset or unsafe, when someone else in the same situation might be surprised and just keep walking. Our feelings can get really big really fast without a lot of warning. When this happens, we can use coping skills, like taking deep breaths or going on a walk, to reduce our emotions in size and to make them more manageable. This can avoid a larger problem or consequence. Coping skills don't remove feelings—they just help us deal with them. Use the scale below to compare the seriousness of an event you are experiencing to the emotional response you are having. Then describe what coping skills you can use to more effectively manage the situation. A few examples are provided for you first.

Scale:

Seriousness of Event		Emotional Response
A good day	0	Cool, calm, and collected
Someone bumps into me	2	Uncomfortable, feeling hot
I drop a bag of groceries	4	Irritated, grumpy
Someone calls me a name	6	Angry, upset
Someone hits me	8	Very angry and distraught, like I could lose control
I lose something/someone I love	10	Completely overwhelmed, cannot function

The Event	The Seriousness of the Event	My Emotional Reaction	What I Need to Do
Someone called me a name	2	9	Take three deep breaths to calm my feelings down to a 2
My favorite pet ran away	7	7	Talk to my friend about what happened so my feelings do not reach an 8
My plans for this Saturday were cancelled	3	5	Take a walk outside to calm my feelings down to a 3
Someone I love is very sick	9	9	Make a card to tell that person how much I love them so my feelings do not reach a 10

Containment Circles

When we are holding difficult thoughts and feelings inside of us, it can be helpful to get them out on paper. Doing so allows us to see the thought or feeling more objectively and to begin to problem solve or cope with it. It can provide a release to no longer have it inside of us. In the circle here, place any thought or feeling that is overwhelming. You can do this as often as needed to release thoughts and feelings that are intrusive or that you do not have time to fully explore. Whatever you put in the circle will remain in the circle. It will be contained and held until you are ready to think about it at a later time. When you are able to spend more time, look at the items in the circle and explore the meaning they have for you.

Containment Box

When unwanted thoughts or feelings enter our mind, it can be distracting and upsetting. In order to contain these thoughts and feelings until a later time, we can place them in a container that has a lid. We can then decide when we want to take the lid off and spend time with those thoughts and feelings. We can take control back by putting these thoughts and feelings where they belong until we are ready to tackle them. Here are the steps to make your containment box:

1. Get a box or a jar with a lid.
2. Cut pieces of paper into strips.
3. On each strip of paper, write down thoughts and feelings that come into your mind and distract you.
4. Place the strips into the box or jar and place the lid on. The lid will keep them safe and contained until the next time you want to visit them.
5. If you'd like, decorate the box or jar. You can write positive affirmations or find quotes in a magazine to cut out and paste on the container. You can also use beads or stickers to decorate the container and make it your own.

After you finish making your container, think about when would be a good time to take the lid off and spend time with these thoughts and feelings, as well as who you want to share these thoughts and feelings with. It should be someone you trust to help you to manage them, such as a parent, friend, therapist, or spouse.

Remember that you are in control of when the lid comes off and when you choose to think about these things. You do not have to feel flooded by these thoughts or feelings anymore. One day, you may not need this box or jar because your mind will be able to contain them more easily. But for now, this is a good reminder that you are in control!

Body Scan

You can complete this body scan exercise whenever you are feeling tense, worried, angry, or escalated, or just as a daily check-in as you become more familiar with your body. At times, especially if we have experienced abuse, we may lose touch with certain parts of our body that can become "numb," or we may experience certain areas of our body as triggering, causing us to rarely experience relaxation. When we come to peace with our body—when we awaken the numb parts and calm the triggered parts—we can lessen our emotional reactivity and increase our mental balance. Use this exercise whenever you are feeling tense or tight, or practice it every day to proactively train your body to relax.

Find a place that is comfortable, restful, and quiet. You can lie flat on the ground, a mat, or a bed. You can also sit in a chair with both feet on the floor and your hands resting gently in your lap. Close your eyes or gaze softly at a fixed spot on the wall. Spend the next 15 to 20 minutes becoming aware of your body and responding to the following prompts, pausing to allow your body and mind to connect between each one:

- Take five deep breaths, becoming aware of your breathing and the rising and falling of your chest as you feel your lungs inflate with air.

- Become aware of your five senses. If your eyes are open, think about what you can see. Think about what you can smell as you take a deep breath. Think about what you can hear. Think about what you can taste. Think about what you can feel. Focus on what your hands are touching, what your body is resting on. Pause for a count of 10.

- Now turn your attention to the top of your head. Become aware of your scalp and facial expression. Just notice how your head feels. Notice if you are holding any tension in your head or face. Pause for a count of 10.

- Move your focus down to your neck and shoulders. Focus on whether your shoulders are hunched up around your ears or if they are relaxed away from your ears. Pause for a count of 10.

- Continuing to move down, focus on your arms. Notice how they are positioned and if they are relaxed or tense. Pause for a count of 10.

- Now think about your hands. Are they folded over each other or resting side by side? Are they tense or relaxed? Pause for a count of 10.

- Move down to your trunk. Focus on your breathing and listen for your heartbeat. Notice your stomach and intestines. Is your stomach full or comfortable? Are you hungry? What does your back feel like sitting in your chair or laying on the ground? Listen to what your body is telling you. Pause for a count of 10.

- Now move your attention down to your legs. Are your muscles tense or relaxed? Is there tension anywhere in your legs? Notice if your knees are bent or straight. Pause for a count of 10.

- Finally, move to your feet. Are your toes relaxed or curled? Wiggle them and feel the sensation of them moving. Pause for a count of 10.

- Take a moment and allow your whole body to rest, and melt into the floor or chair.

- After a few moments, bring your attention back to your body. Beginning at the bottom and working your way back up, focus on your feet. Curl your toes and tense all the muscles in your feet for five seconds. Then relax them. Feel the floor beneath you, grounding you to the moment. Pause for a count of 10.

- Moving back up into your legs, repeat this same pattern of tensing for five seconds and then relaxing. Tighten and relax the muscles in your calves and then in your thighs. Notice how your legs feel as they relax and fall against the floor or chair. Pause for a count of 10.

- Coming back up into your trunk, tighten your chest and back muscles for five seconds. Then release them and feel them all relax. Focus again on your breathing, and take a few minutes here to breathe in and out.

- Now tense your hands into fists, hold for five seconds, and then relax them. Focus on the feelings in your fingers as they loosen and relax. Pause for a count of 10.

- Moving back into your arms, tighten your forearms and then your upper arms for five seconds, and then relax. Feel the tension leaving your body as you release those muscles. Pause for a count of 10.

- Focusing on your shoulders and your neck, tense your shoulders—bringing them up to your ears and holding for five seconds—and then relax them, pushing them back down as far as they can go. Elongate your neck and feel the stretch. Pause for a count of 10.

- Finally, move back up into your scalp and face. Tense and tighten all the muscles in your face for five seconds, and then release and relax. Let your face fall as you lose all expression. Feel your scalp relax. Pause for a count of 10.

- Take five deep breaths as you return to the room. Open your eyes and slowly get up as you become aware of your surroundings.

Healing from Physical Abuse

When physical abuse has been a part of your story, your body remembers the trauma. You may have parts of your body that are numb—that you cannot feel—because you have separated from them to avoid painful reminders of the abuse. Other times, parts of your body will remember the pain and cause you to feel unsafe, even if you are safe now. It is important to take care of your body to find healing. Your body deserves respect and care because it has survived hard things.

1. What part(s) of your body experienced the pain of the abuse?

   _____

   _____

2. Are there times when you can still feel the pain? When?

   _____

   _____

3. Take a few minutes and think about the parts of your body that you identified above. As you visit each body part in your mind, tighten and then release that body part. Now in your mind or out loud, talk to that body part—acknowledging the pain it has experienced and thanking it for fighting hard to survive. Then think of a way to take care of that body part, to honor it, and to strengthen it.

   For example, if your leg has a burn scar on it, then think about that leg, focusing your attention on it and feeling it. Then tighten and relax that muscle, feeling the tension release. Do this several times. Talk to that leg, acknowledging its pain: "I know you have been through a lot. You took a lot of pain, and you had to work hard to recover." Then thank your leg for the way it supports your body: "Thank you for walking me around every day, for holding me up when I stand, and for being there for my child to sit on." Finally, think about a way to honor your leg, to care for it. Maybe you put lotion or cream on it. Maybe you take a bubble bath to soothe your muscles. Be creative.

Do this for each body part that you identified. You may want to set aside some time each week to spend with your body, repeating this exercise over and over again until you feel connected to and at peace with every part.

Healing from Sexual Abuse

When your body has been sexually violated, this can create discomfort and anxiety about situations that require intimacy and vulnerability. Some people who have lost control of their body may attempt to reclaim control in other ways—for example, by choosing to express themselves or dress their body in particular ways—which may provide fulfillment but leave peace and comfort lacking in relationships. Think about your body as you answer these next few questions.

1. In what ways did you lose control of your body when you were violated?

   _____

   _____

   _____

2. How have you attempted to reclaim your body? Have these efforts been successful or fulfilling?

   _____

   _____

   _____

3. If your virginity was taken, as opposed to you giving it willingly, is it possible to give it to someone else? Can you hold a ceremony or special ritual to mark that you are making a choice and having control in this instance? What would that look like?

   _____

   _____

   _____

4. If sexual activity no longer feels safe or comfortable for you, how has this affected your current romantic relationship?

_____

_____

_____

5. Do you think it would be possible to take small steps toward intimacy—with a respectful partner who understands when you need to stop or take a break—to feel close and connected in a sexual relationship again? What would those small steps look like for you? There are no wrong answers, and everybody needs to move at a different pace depending on what they are comfortable with.

_____

_____

_____

6. Are you comfortable with your own body? Or are there parts of your body that you don't want to look at, touch, or feel because they remind you of the abuse? Those parts of your body were dishonored but deserve honor, especially because of the pain and misuse they experienced. Think about a small ceremony you could perform to honor those parts of yourself. They have survived hard things and still hold value. Perhaps you write them a letter using the space here, letting those parts know that you appreciate them, acknowledging the abuse they experienced, telling them that they were not at fault, and comforting them for the pain they experienced. In this way you will be honoring, even restoring honor, to a special part of yourself.

_____

_____

_____

_____

_____

_____

Healing from Sexual Abuse

When someone has touched you inappropriately or made you feel uncomfortable by the way they talk to you about personal and private things, you may come to believe that it's normal for others to touch you or talk to you in those ways. However, there are rules about how people can touch and talk to you, which are called *boundaries*. Boundaries are like fences around you that let others know what they can and cannot do. When those fences have been moved by abuse, it is important to put them back. In the space below, draw a picture of yourself. Then add fences around you, and label them with the boundaries listed below. Think about how you'd like your fences to look. Would you want them made of wood or stone? How tall would you want them to be? Would they have any special designs to keep anyone unwanted out? When someone comes to a fence and tries to move it or get inside, remember that you can say NO and that your fence is there to help keep you safe.

Fence #1: It's not okay for others to touch me without my permission.

Fence #2: It's not okay for others to touch the personal and private areas of my body.

Fence #3: It's not okay for others to talk to me about the personal and private areas of my bodies.

Fence #4: It's not okay for others to ask me to touch them or their personal and private areas.

Healing from Emotional Abuse

When someone abuses you with their words, what they say stays inside your mind, negatively impacting your thoughts and self-concept. Your brain records those words and begins to repeat them until you begin to believe that those hurtful words actually describe you. So how can you stop the recording? By changing it. When a negative thought enters your mind, you can invite it to stay and become stuck in it, or you can confront it, call it a liar, and replace it with the truth. On the lines below, write the negative lies that are running through your mind. These are hurtful things that others have said to you or about you. Then write the opposite—the truth about you—as a positive affirmation.

The Lie

"You can't do anything right."

The Truth

"I can sing beautifully."

Now take those truths and write them on strips of paper. Place a few around your house where you will see them: on the bathroom mirror, the refrigerator, and the frame around the television screen. Read them every day to change the recording in your head. You can also make an actual audio recording of those positive truths in your own voice (or you can ask a friend to read them) and play it in the car or when you are falling asleep at night. The more you hear these positive affirmations, the more they will become your new thoughts.

Relationship Comparison

When you have been abused by someone close to you, it can be difficult to recognize what a safe and healthy relationship looks like. You may find yourself in one unsafe relationship after another. That is because you are more familiar with abusive relationships and have learned how to adapt to and respond within them. When you meet someone who exhibits hurtful and unsafe behaviors toward you, you recognize it as something you have dealt with before, and it can become normal for you to function in that type of an environment. In healing your trauma, it is important to be able to recognize abusive relationships and to separate yourself from them.

Look at the following chart. For each category, think about the qualities of a past abusive relationship, and then think about the qualities of a safe and healthy relationship. Perhaps you have a healthy relationship now that you can think about when answering these questions. If you get stuck, ask your therapist for help in defining the characteristics of a safe relationship.

	What an Abusive Relationship Looks Like	What a Safe and Healthy Relationship Looks Like
The way we talk to each other		
The way we touch each other		
The way we support each other		
The way we spend time together		
The way we make decisions		
The way we respect each other		

Now think about your answers. If you find that your current relationships look similar to past abusive relationships, what would you like to change about that? It is possible to change the way we interact in relationships, but it takes hard work and determination. Ask your therapist to help you create goals around learning about healthy and safe relationships.

Growing Self-Esteem

When you have experienced abuse, one of the things that becomes hard is growing your self-esteem. Abuse can hurt you to the very core by taking away your feelings of personal respect and value. It touches your deepest parts and changes how you view yourself. In healing abuse and reclaiming your value and respect, you have to be able to identify your strengths before you can believe that you are of value. This can be hard because you may have spent a long time, maybe many years, thinking that you are not capable or good enough. But as a survivor, you have strength inside you, as evidenced by the fact that you are here. You are standing, and you are proof that you are strong. Read the following paragraph and recognize the survivor in you!

Anyone who has survived abuse is a powerful person. You had to be courageous to face hard things. You persevered and did not give up. You were determined to find a better life. You are strong physically because your body overcame the abuse. You are strong mentally because you were able to problem solve your survival. You are strong emotionally because you did not collapse under that abusive situation. You are here and you are standing tall. You are a survivor! You are an overcomer! And these characteristics are in you, a part of you, so that whatever you face in the future, you will survive because you have these qualities to help you. That is just who you are, and you are amazing!

Now go back through that paragraph and circle all the strength-based words you can find. They describe you! List those words on the lines here, and then ask five friends or family members for two more positive words that describe you. Add those to the list as well. Now think of five more things about you that are special. What are your strengths? What are you good at? What are your talents? Read this list daily until you start to believe that this is who you are—because it is!

_____   _____   _____

_____   _____   _____

_____   _____   _____

_____   _____   _____

_____   _____   _____

_____   _____   _____

Creating Felt Safety

When a child has experienced abuse, their feelings of safety and security have been taken from them. Healing from this trauma requires restoring a felt sense of safety, and as a parent, you play the most important role in facilitating this healing. Your child may *be* safe, but it is also important for your child to *feel* safe. Here are ways you can provide felt safety at home to help your child feel safe again:

- **Stability:** This means that everything about the family life remains the same each day. The same people are at home every day, and the family relationships are safe and supportive. With stability, the child knows what to expect within the family and knows that their needs will be taken care of consistently.

- **Structure:** Your child thrives when there is a predictable schedule or routine in place. There is a scheduled time when everyone sits down to eat dinner, an established bedtime routine, and a specific time for doing homework versus having fun.

- **Nurturing care:** Your child needs to have love from you—all day, every day. They need affection, which can come in the form of giving hugs and kisses, snuggling on the couch to read, baking cookies together, or connecting at bedtime to talk about their day.

- **Safety in relationships:** Children need to be around calm adults who do not yell or lose their tempers. Rather than being punitive, you can provide corrective and supportive experiences when you want to teach your child a new way to do things. Give them chances to try again when they do something incorrectly. Although your child may have large emotions that seem out of control, they need you to teach them how to cope and calm those emotions.

Nurturing Care

When a child has experienced abuse, it is essential for parents to provide nurturing care so their child can heal and learn to feel safe again. Nurturing care is a stable environment where parents provide health and nutrition, protect and maintain safety for their children, teach their children new concepts, and are emotionally supportive and responsive. Below are some questions to help you think through how to provide this type of care to your child. If you are having a hard time brainstorming ideas, talk to your child's therapist, who can assist you in identifying nurturing care.

1. How are you providing a stable environment for your child? What are some things your child expects and depends on you for every day?

   _____

   _____

2. Children typically need to hydrate and eat (either a snack or meal) every two hours. How are you providing hydration and nutrition? What kinds of healthy choices do you offer?

   _____

   _____

3. How do you protect your child and help them feel safe in your care?

   _____

   _____

4. What do you teach your child every day? This can involve more abstract concepts (like emotion regulation and social skills), as well as more basic life skills (like helping you make dinner or folding laundry).

   _____

   _____

5. How do you emotionally support your child? Can they talk to you about their feelings? Do they feel like you support and accept them?

   _____

   _____

My Child's Needs

When a child has experienced abuse, it is crucial for adults to be responsive to that child's needs. If children cannot trust adults to meet their needs for safety or care, then they will attempt to do so themselves, most likely in a dysfunctional and inappropriate manner that involves acting out. In order to heal, children need to feel like adults will keep them safe and take care of them. Consider the following questions and think about ways you can consistently meet your child's needs.

1. What can you do to meet your child's need for safety? What things can you do to help your child feel safe at home? In the community? At school?

_____

_____

_____

2. What can you do to meet your child's need for love? How do you express your love for your child? How does your child respond to your expressions of love?

_____

_____

_____

3. What other needs does your child have? Are these needs being met? If not, how can you meet them? Do you need to ask for help in meeting your child's needs? Who could you ask?

_____

_____

_____

Trust-Based Parenting

Children who have experienced abuse often lose trust in adults' ability to take care of them and to keep them safe. Think about how much trust your child has in you and if there are ways you can earn more trust in your child's eyes. Are there things you can do to increase trust?

1. Have there been times when you felt like you let your child down? Times when you were not able to meet their needs for safety or other basic needs? Describe that here.

    _____

    _____

    _____

2. How did it make you feel when you weren't able to meet your child's needs? In what ways did it impact you?

    _____

    _____

    _____

3. How did your child feel? How did they respond?

    _____

    _____

    _____

4. Were you able to re-earn your child's trust? Why or why not?

    _____

    _____

    _____

5. How much do you think your child trusts you on a scale of 0 to 10?

_____

_____

_____

6. One way to increase your child's trust is to consistently meet their needs. What can you do to better meet their needs?

_____

_____

_____

7. What does a safe person look like? Are you that person to your child? If not, how can you present yourself as a safe person to your child?

_____

_____

_____

Parenting with Attachment

Connecting with your child is crucial in helping them heal from experiences of trauma and abuse. Your relationship predicts their ability to recover from trauma above all else. Your support is essential to your child's recovery. Use this worksheet to think about how you can be more attachment-minded in your everyday activities with your child.

1. What are five ways you can spend quality time with your child this week?

_____

_____

_____

2. What are four things they do well that you could praise them for?

_____

_____

_____

3. What are three activities you can help them with this week (e.g., homework, chores)?

_____

_____

_____

4. What are two ways you can physically connect with your child each day using loving and healthy touch?

_____

_____

_____

5. What is one thing you can do every day to play with your child or to make them laugh?

_____

_____

_____

5

Neglect

Sam was raised in a single-parent family. His father left shortly after Sam was born, and his mother struggled to provide for Sam and his three siblings. Sam's mother worked three jobs to pay the bills, often coming home after 8 p.m. each night and working all weekend. Sam's oldest sister helped raise him and his siblings—cooking the children dinner and shuffling them to various appointments—but she was a teenager and resented having to take care of them. She believed her responsibility was to keep her siblings alive while they were in her care and nothing more.

Because of their limited resources, there was seldom enough food in the house. Sam and his siblings would split food that should only have fed two mouths, but they had to stretch it to feed all four. He went to school hungry most days and could often be seen taking food from other children. When he was caught, he received detention for bullying other students, but these consequences did not deter his behaviors because he was simply trying to meet a basic need. The school frequently called in his mother for meetings to address the issue, which took her away from one of her jobs. Sam didn't get to see his mother very often, and the few times a week he did, she was angry with him for all the meetings she had to attend for his behaviors. Feeling disconnected from his primary attachment figure, Sam began exhibiting attention-seeking behaviors in the classroom, such as being the class clown or having loud outbursts that required frequent intervention. He was stuck in a negative cycle that led to more consequences.

Like Sam, children experience neglect when the adults in their lives are unable to meet their needs. Neglect can be intentional or unintentional in nature, depending on the circumstances of the situation. Intentional neglect occurs when parents deliberately choose not to meet the needs of their child, which often happens when parents are not connected to their children in an attachment-based relationship. For example, parents may be intentionally neglectful if they abuse substances or have a severe mental illness. Other parents may have been neglected themselves as children and are continuing the cycle because they never had healthy parenting modeled for them.

In contrast, unintentional neglect involves the failure to meet a child's needs as a result of stress or limited resources (e.g., lack of time or physical resources). Many parents, especially in areas of poverty, work several jobs to make ends meet and still have difficulty putting food on the table. Particularly in low-income, single-parent families, unintentional neglect can occur when the oldest child begins co-parenting out of necessity. As illustrated in Sam's case, the oldest child is often expected to fulfill an adult role by caring for their siblings. In these cases, parentification can happen because the child has been given a caretaking role that is outside of their developmental capacity.

Parentification is a role reversal that occurs when a child is required to assume a caretaking role in the family. When this occurs, a child can begin to see themselves as equal to adults, which impacts their ability to work with other adults, to take directions from them, and to recognize them as authority figures. When children are placed in an adult role with adult responsibilities, they have difficulty switching out of this role and into the role of a child because their brains have not yet developed the ability to change roles and "hats" repeatedly throughout the day.

For example, consider a child whose mother leaves for work early in the morning and who is expected to make sure his siblings are dressed, fed, and on the bus on time. When that child walks into school later that morning, he still has his adult "hat" on. He sees himself as equal to the other adults in the building and has difficulty taking directions. He struggles all day at school as adults attempt to put him back into a child role. However, when the bell rings and he returns home, he is again in the adult role: helping his younger siblings with homework, feeding them a snack, and starting dinner before his mother gets home. He cannot abstractly understand that in different environments he has different roles. The capacity for abstract thinking does not fully develop until about age 25, so to that child, he is the same person in all environments.

Whether neglect happens intentionally or unintentionally, the impact is the same. Children's needs are not being met—physically, mentally, or emotionally—which undermines their ability to trust adults to take care of them. In turn, children will attempt to meet their own needs in inappropriate ways, not because they want to be difficult or have challenging behaviors but because they are doing the best they can in the given situation. For example, a child who arrives to school hungry may bully others into giving them food, or a child who does not receive enough affection may act out in the classroom as a means of getting the attention they crave. When children do not have their basic needs met, they will struggle to regulate their emotions and will have difficulty controlling themselves, resulting in a variety of acting-out behaviors. These dysfunctional behaviors will not be deterred regardless of the consequences because the need is a stronger motivator than the resulting consequence.

The way to extinguish these behaviors is to meet the need. For example, if a child arrives to school hungry because there is a lack of food in the home, adults can meet the need proactively by putting out a communal snack tray or by putting any leftover breakfasts in a basket for anyone who is hungry. This will derail the behavior because the need has been met. It doesn't exist anymore. Teachers can also have a "need" box in the classroom where children can put in notes about what they need. A child may ask for a coat or shoes, and the teacher may be able to find a way to meet that need.

Similarly, adults can meet a child's emotional need for affection by providing them with enough attention. Attention is a form of love, and by giving a child positive attention, adults can fulfill the need for affection before that child acts out in an attempt to meet this need themselves. For example, a teacher can give the child the responsibility of "dry-erase marker holder" for an hour each morning so the child gets sufficient connection time with the teacher at the beginning of the day. When adults are proactive about meeting a child's needs, it can extinguish behaviors without the use of consequences, which are ineffective and inappropriate in these situations.

This may sound counterintuitive. Often, interventions attempt to correct attention-seeking behavior by sending children to time out, denying them what they are seeking, or engaging in "planned ignoring" of the child. Although these consequences are implemented in an effort to extinguish the behavior, they are largely ineffective because the need still exists. **Consequences do not deter need-based behaviors because the need is always greater than the consequence.** Needs do not respond to consequences, which is why adults must give children what it is they are seeking. The idea of "giving in" to a child who has been manipulative in trying to secure their needs may elicit some pause. However, this is where thinking must change. Adults are not giving in to what a child *wants*. Adults are meeting the child's *needs*. There is a difference between wants and needs, and knowing the difference is the first step to helping children find effective ways to meet their needs.

In addition, we must encourage children to express their needs with their words instead of their behaviors. As humans, we have a natural instinct to use our voice to make ourselves heard. As babies, we cry when we are hungry, when our diaper is wet, or when we are tired. When a baby expresses those needs in a healthy environment, the parent meets those needs in a timely manner. The parent meets those needs anywhere between 15 and 20 thousand times within the first two years of life, which provides overwhelming positive reinforcement to the child that they will get their needs met when they use their voice. In turn, the child continues to use their voice to ask for their needs to be met. The positive reinforcement of having their needs met also provides a firm foundation for the development of healthy self-esteem, which follows children as they continue to grow.

In contrast, when a child's voice is not heard and their needs are not met, they stop using their voice. For example, research in Eastern European orphanages has found that babies who were deprived of basic human needs—who sat in soiled diapers for hours, were deprived of human touch, and suffered from malnutrition—eventually stopped crying because they learned that no one would respond to their cries (Weir, 2014). Within 48 hours of their voice not being heard and their needs not being met, they simply stopped using their voice. They became silent, and the deafening silence of those rooms, filled with babies lying awake in their cribs, is the horrific truth about what happens when a child's needs are not met.

In order to restore a child's voice, we must encourage them to use their words again. To do so, it is crucial for adults to be connected to children—watching and listening for expressed, as well as unexpressed, needs. When you recognize and meet a need, even before the child expresses it, this communicates to the child that they are important. It lets them know that you are watching and listening and that you care about what is important to them.

For example, if you notice that a child is coming to school every day in tattered clothing and you bring them some clothing options—whether new or secondhand—this communicates to the child that they are not invisible and that someone cares to meet the need. In turn, this child may use their voice to let you know about other needs they have. For example, they may tell you that there isn't enough food at their house on the weekends. Many schools have bags of food that they send home with certain students over the weekend because they know there is a need—whether the child has voiced it or not.

When we meet needs before a child even expresses that need, it reinforces the notion that we see the child and that what they need is important to us. It encourages them to continue expressing their needs as we listen for and meet those expressed needs. They have their voice back and can use it appropriately. This returns us to the importance of attunement: meeting one another's needs to build trust and attachment.

For an adult who did not have their needs met in childhood as a result of neglect, the same principles apply. That adult may have mastered using manipulation and attention-seeking behaviors over the decades to meet their own needs, leading to a diagnosis of a personality disorder. For example, someone with borderline personality disorder may not have had their needs for attention or love met as a child, causing them to rely on manipulative tactics to get their emotional needs met in adulthood. Similarly, someone with histrionic personality disorder may exhibit overly dramatic behavior (no matter how dysfunctional it may be) in an attempt to meet their needs for attention. Or someone with antisocial personality disorder, who grew up in a disconnected family where their rights were not regarded, may now attempt to independently meet their own needs at the cost of others. Finally, someone with narcissistic personality disorder may have grown up in an emotionally invalidating family where empathy was not modeled or taught, leading them to have difficulties valuing and respecting others.

Adults will need to invest more work in changing these behaviors, thoughts, and beliefs because they have become ingrained over the years. First, we need to challenge the belief that others will not meet their expressed needs. We may ask clients to think about the relationships in their life and to consider if those people care for them. Explore what "care" means for the client and what they believe about this relationship. At the foundation of this relationship should be the notion of trust. Do they trust this person to meet their needs if they express themselves openly and honestly? If they don't, clients will feel like they have to use manipulation to get their needs met. Learning to trust others is foundational to healthy attachment and relationships.

Once we have addressed these underlying beliefs, we focus on behaviors by having clients use their words to get their needs met. Doing so requires that they take a risk by giving someone else an opportunity to meet their needs. You can facilitate this process by asking clients to voice their needs in the context of a secure relationship where they already have some confidence. This may initially involve identifying a smaller need: "I need help picking up the kids from soccer practice on Friday because I have a doctor's appointment." We want to ask clarifying questions to make sure the request is reasonable because this is not meant to be a large test of the partner; it is meant to be a situation that gives our client a successful experience.

Next, we process what the experience was like: How did it feel to ask for help, and how did it feel to be supported in having the need met? Then we move slowly toward identifying larger needs that clients can ask others to meet. We may initially encourage dozens of small requests to build into this experience, and with each successful interaction, the client's confidence grows. We present their brain with new information that challenges long-held beliefs about attunement, which changes their brain and the way they think about needs and relationships.

The following worksheets and interventions can be useful in assisting clients with a history of neglect to explore using their voice and to trust others to meet their needs. In particular, these exercises are intended to help clients understand the different roles held by adults versus children in meeting needs. Children and adults alike need to find their voice and to use words instead of relying on dysfunctional behaviors to have their needs met. This can be difficult if they have not had positive experiences with this before. These interventions will challenge them to consider how a history of neglect has impacted their relationships and will teach them new ways to begin using their voice to express their needs.

INTERVENTIONS FOR HEALING

When a person has experienced neglect of any kind, they have lost the ability to trust others to meet their needs. Even though histories of neglect are rooted in childhood, when children could not take care of themselves, the experience often carries into adulthood, causing adults to have difficulty trusting others to take care of them. In turn, they may experience high stress or anxiety as they try to independently meet all of their own needs. They may also struggle to form attuned, trust-based relationships and often experience relationship dissatisfaction as they attempt to meet their own needs but ignore the needs of their partner. Their partner may even want to end the relationship. To heal from childhood neglect, it is important to recognize how this trauma continues to impact the client today. Use the **Feeling Taken Care of Again** worksheet with adult clients to explore these concepts and to identify areas where they are not trusting others.

Children who have experienced neglect can struggle to differentiate between adult and child roles. In order to help them understand the roles held by children versus adults, clinicians can use the **Roles and Relationships** worksheet. When a parent places a child in an adult role, this can be confusing for the child. This worksheet gives the child and the parent clarification. Based on the child's answers, ask follow-up questions about the roles they play at home. In addition, encourage the child to share their answers with parents in the context of a family session, as doing so reinforces the notion that there are roles that children and adults need to fill.

In addition, the **Roles and Places** worksheet can help children understand the different roles that may be required of them at home versus at school (or in the community). There may be different rules or expectations in each setting, and this worksheet can assist them in coming to the realization that they can act different ways in different environments. For example, if a parent allows a child to curse at home, but they are not allowed to do so at school, then it is important to help that child recognize these different rules and expectations. The specific "environment" columns are intentionally left blank on the worksheet so the child can compare a variety of environments (e.g., home versus school, home versus summer camp, school versus summer camp, one parent's home versus the other). It may be helpful to have a few different hats in your office that children can alternate wearing as they talk about their different roles in different places. This provides children with a visual and concrete representation of a more abstract concept. As children go through their day, they may be able to visualize themselves changing "hats" as they did in your office.

The **I Am a Survivor** worksheet is intended to help adults process their own experience of neglect. It uses a strength-based approach to help them think about how the trauma changed their personality, and it may allow them to find meaning in the experience as they examine the strengths and skills they may have developed as a result. For example, an adult who experienced neglect in childhood and had to take care of themselves may have developed character qualities of determination and perseverance that serve them well at work but may cause challenges in their relationships. This worksheet can allow clients to consider how they can draw on their strengths in certain environments but not others.

In order to decrease manipulative and attention-seeking behaviors, it is necessary to see the need behind the behavior and to meet that need proactively. However, in order to find their voice, children also need to believe that they are being listened to, that they are heard, and that they matter. Use the **Finding My Voice** worksheet to encourage children to share their thoughts and feelings. You can also allow children to carry a dry-erase board and marker or a pad of paper and pencil with them so they can write their needs instead of saying them out loud. For children with selective mutism, this type of compromise allows the child to express themselves without the fear that they will not be heard, while also increasing the chance that adults will "hear" the request because it is in a more concrete format. With repeated practice, this intervention reinforces the notion that you want to hear what the child is thinking, which builds their confidence in expressing themselves.

For children who continue to have difficulty expressing themselves with words, give them the choice to draw instead. Asking them to draw can be less intimidating than having them express their needs with written (and eventually spoken) words, which is the ultimate goal. Oftentimes, artistic expression helps clients express concepts that they don't have the words for or that they are too afraid or anxious to speak about. It provides an honest representation of their thoughts and feelings that is more transparent than words alone could provide. For children who prefer to draw their responses, ask clarifying questions about the drawing and the meaning that it has for the child.

When children do not get their need for love met, they begin to seek attention in negative ways. Oftentimes, this involves attention-seeking behaviors, such as verbal or physical aggression, elopement, tantrums, or other behaviors that involve testing limits. When a child receives consequences for these negative behaviors, not only is it ineffective but it can damage the relationship between the child and adult. In contrast, proactively meeting the child's need for attention can decrease these behaviors because it communicates that we see the need and care enough to meet it, which further builds the trust-based relationship. However, if this need for love is left unaddressed, it can follow children into adulthood and result in the development of maladaptive characterological traits and even personality disorders. The **Positive Attention** worksheet can be used with children or adults to explore their use of negative attention-seeking behaviors and to consider alternative behaviors they can use to meet their needs.

In addition, the **My Needs, Your Needs** worksheet is a useful resource for clients who exhibit personality disorder symptoms as a result of childhood neglect. Oftentimes, personality disorders can develop when an individual's emotional and physical needs have been neglected in childhood, causing that individual to begin meeting their own needs—even at the expense of others. Because no one listened to or cared about their needs growing up, it can be difficult for them to listen to and care about the needs of others. As adults, they can become completely focused on meeting their own needs at all costs, regardless of the consequences this may have on others. This worksheet can help adult clients consider the impact of such overly self-seeking behavior on their relationships.

When someone has experienced emotional neglect, it can be challenging for them to acknowledge and express their emotions because they don't believe anyone will validate or understand them. In turn, they may have difficulty understanding their emotions and may struggle to find the words to express themselves. For example, when asked, "How do you feel about that?" they may respond with "I don't know." This is not an attempt to avoid the question but is indicative of their inability to access feelings that they have discounted for a long time. These clients have perfected the art of containment to such an extent that they do not allow themselves to express any emotions. Use the **Finding My Feelings** exercise to assist adult and child clients in increasing their ability to access and tolerate their emotions.

Once clients have begun to identify and accept their emotions, they can use the **Sharing My Feelings** activity to role-play sharing these emotions with a safe person who will respond with understanding and support. This allows clients to restore the use of their emotions in a healthy relationship where they are met with respect and validation. It is important to support clients as they reexperience their emotions because if they have not had access to their feelings for many years, then they may feel overwhelmed when their emotions reemerge. We want to equip clients with skills they can use to calm those feelings because if they feel flooded, they may want to return those feelings to permanent containment.

Use the **Flood Gates** handout to help adult and child clients brainstorm coping skills they can use to calm their emotions as they are released. For children who may have a harder time understanding this more abstract concept, you can have them draw a river with a dam or flood gates that can represent coping skills that slow the flow of emotions or that calm the emotions being expressed.

When a person has had their needs belittled, discredited, or ignored, they can begin to feel that they are unworthy of having their needs met. Restoring this feeling of worthiness is critical in helping clients repair attachment trauma caused by neglect. Use the **My Needs Are Important** worksheet to allow clients to explore their beliefs about their needs. When reviewing the worksheet with clients, make sure to normalize the universality of needs and to highlight the role that needs play in the development of relationships characterized by connection and attunement.

In addition, clients who experienced neglect as children may struggle with accepting constructive criticism. As children, they were so focused on taking care of themselves and on meeting their own needs that they now experience a fierce independence and often feel like no one has the right to challenge their way of doing things. These difficulties with accepting criticism can impact them at home, in relationships, and at work. Use the **Using Constructive Criticism** worksheet with adult clients to help them accept and give constructive criticism. In helping them to understand and apply this concept, it is giving them a tool for relationship success.

Clients who had to meet their own needs as children often need to have things organized and structured in a certain way to feel safe and secure. This desire for control can impact their personality, their relationships, and their daily functioning. They may need to have control at work, at home, and in social situations to feel comfortable. Use the **Healthy Control** worksheet to help clients understand the cause of this anxiety, to help them recognize when they are safe and secure, and to help them recognize when to exert control versus share it with others. We want to emphasize that control is not a negative tool but that using it at the wrong times or in inappropriate situations can damage relationships. Control has a purpose and has served clients in the past, but we also want them to recognize when they can relinquish control and allow it to rest.

Childhood neglect comes with a variety of losses, including the loss of parental trust, the loss of feeling safe and cared for, and the loss associated with having to grow up too quickly. It is important to give time and space to explore clients' feelings about these losses. Use the **Visiting My Inner Child** worksheet to have adult clients think about the child within themselves. This child most likely wanted to be cared for and to depend on adults to meet their needs but was unable to. Encourage clients to be honest with their feelings as they explore this worksheet, making sure to validate their emotions about these childhood experiences.

Next, encourage clients to think about their inner parent, the part of themselves that rose up and helped the client survive. Perhaps their inner parent took care of them when their own parent was unable to. Perhaps it served as the voice of reason that helped them make well-informed decisions. This inner parent that helped them survive is still within, and we want them to recognize it and integrate it into their persona. Use the **Visiting My Inner Parent** worksheet to help clients identify this part of themselves so they can move their story from one of grief and loss to one of strength and survival. This will increase self-esteem and promote healing as they reframe themselves as a survivor instead of a victim.

Clients who experienced parentification as children were required to take on responsibilities for which they were not developmentally ready, which can cause them to exhibit confusion about caretaking roles. They may lean more toward codependency or may try to take care of others in all their relationships because that behavior was normalized in their family of origin. Use the **Healthy Caretaking** worksheet to help adult clients find healthy boundaries and achieve balance when it comes to giving and taking in relationships. If a client identifies themselves as being responsible for meeting all of their own needs, as well as others' needs, explore this as a treatment goal to move the client toward healthy boundaries.

In order to further explore the impact of parentification on a child, clinicians can also give parents the **I Am the Parent** worksheet to help them examine their parenting style. This worksheet reinforces the important role that parents play and the impact that parentification has on a child. We want parents to think about how they can change the expectations they have for their child. If the parent is able, we want to empower them to assert their parenting skills and to serve in a capacity where they can effectively parent their child. Sometimes, though, parents may be unable to change the situation. For example, a parent may have a serious medical condition like cancer, or they may be a single parent and have limited options for finding childcare or rearranging their work schedule. In these situations, work with parents to increase their insight into the effect of parentification on their child's behaviors and feelings, which may prompt them to react with support and understanding instead of anger and frustration.

Feeling Taken Care of Again

Individuals who were neglected in childhood have had the experience of their needs not being met consistently. There are many needs that children have because they depend on adults to take care of everything, such as providing food, shelter, clothing, and love. If you experienced neglect, then one, some, or all of these needs may not have been met. Think about that experience, and consider how it may have changed your thoughts about needs moving forward. Think about your current relationships and how you negotiate your needs now.

1. In childhood, which of your needs were not met?

_____

_____

_____

2. How did this impact you or change your experience of childhood?

_____

_____

_____

3. Did you try to meet those needs yourself? In what ways?

_____

_____

_____

4. How do you negotiate for your needs to be met now? Do you express your needs to others?

_____

_____

_____

5. Is it hard or easy to trust others with your needs? What, if anything, could make it easier?

_____

_____

_____

6. How do you respond to the needs of others? Do you see and recognize their needs? Do you meet their needs when they ask you to?

_____

_____

_____

Roles and Relationships

Adults and children have different roles and responsibilities at home. Think about the adults in your family. Think about the things they do versus the things you do. How are they different? What are you responsible for? What are your parents responsible for? Put a check mark in the corresponding box to indicate whether adults or children are responsible for that particular activity.

	Adults Do This	**Children Do This**
Take care of children		
Prepare meals		
Decide bedtime		
Do the shopping		
Play		
Do chores		
Do laundry		
Pay bills		
Do homework		
Other:		

Roles and Places

Different places have different rules and expectations that you need to follow. Think about two different places that you go—like home, school, day care, or summer camp—and compare the ways you need to behave in each.

	Environment 1	Environment 2
Example: *Eating*	At home, I can eat anytime I want to.	At school, I can eat only in the cafeteria and at lunch time.
Eating		
Playing		
Listening to and following directions		
Doing chores/responsibilities		
Sharing		
Following bedtime/rest times		
Showing respect		

I Am a Survivor

If you experienced neglect as a child, you may have had to take care of yourself and/or your siblings. You may have had to meet some or all of your needs. In order to survive, you had to mature quickly so you could handle those responsibilities. Although this was not an easy experience, it allowed you to develop some strengths that molded you into the survivor you are today. Look over the following characteristics and circle the ones that best describe you.

Determined	Persistent	Courageous	Resourceful
Perseverant	Creative	Adaptable	Brave
Capable	Confident	Decisive	Dependable
Efficient	Diligent	Hardworking	Loyal
Organized	Persuasive	Protective	Responsible
Reliable	Strong	Intelligent	Tough

1. Now think about the words you circled. How have these characteristics helped you get where you are today? In what ways have these characteristics served you well?

_____

_____

_____

2. Have there been times when these characteristics have caused challenges, such as in close relationships? For example, perhaps you find yourself being overly protective of those you love, or you find yourself becoming critical of those who aren't as reliable as you are. What kinds of difficulties have you experienced?

_____

_____

_____

3. How do others react when these difficulties arise? How does that make you feel?

_____

_____

_____

4. How could you let down your guard and relax some of your character traits in certain environments? How do you think that might affect your relationships?

_____

_____

_____

Finding My Voice

Do you feel like people listen to you? Care about what is important to you? Want to help you with things that are hard? This is your chance to tell everyone what you think! If you don't want to write your answers, you can draw them instead.

1. If you had a microphone and could tell the world something, what would it be?

_____

_____

2. What is a feeling you want to share with everybody?

_____

_____

3. What is something you wish your parents knew about you?

_____

_____

4. What is a thought or an idea you want to share with everybody?

_____

_____

5. How does it feel to have everyone's attention and to have them listen to you?

_____

_____

Positive Attention

We all need attention at times because it is a way for us to feel loved. Sometimes, though, we try to meet our need for attention in negative ways. For example, we might act out in class, intentionally cause arguments, or post inappropriate content on social media. When we use behaviors that get us negative attention, it is fulfilling but has consequences that go with it. These consequences can be damaging to our relationships and to ourselves. In contrast, positive attention meets our need for attention with no consequences. Answer the following questions, and think about possible ways to get positive attention that have no consequences and that keep your relationships strong.

1. How do you try to get attention in negative ways?

   _____

   _____

2. What are some consequences that come from negative attention?

   _____

   _____

3. How do these consequences hurt you or damage your relationships?

   _____

   _____

4. What are your strengths? What are some things you are good at?

   _____

   _____

5. How could you use those strengths to get positive attention? Think of two ways you can seek positive attention for all the good things you do. Then come up with a plan to try those two things this week.

   _____

   _____

My Needs, Your Needs

When a child is raised in a neglectful environment—one in which they lack access to basic physical and emotional resources—it is normal for them to lose trust in other people's ability to meet their needs. In turn, they may become overly independent and hyper-focused on meeting their own needs as adults, even if it is at the expense of their relationships. However, everyone around us has needs too, and these needs are equally important. When we allow ourselves to focus on the needs of others—and they focus on our needs in return—all our needs are met in fulfillment. Use this worksheet to think about what happened in your childhood that may have made it difficult to meet other people's needs and how this may affect your current relationships.

1. How old were you when you first started to meet your own needs? What were some of these needs?

   _____

   _____

   _____

2. What about your childhood environment made it necessary for you to start meeting your own needs?

   _____

   _____

   _____

3. What kinds of needs do you have now? Are these needs more important than those of your loved ones? Why or why not?

   _____

   _____

   _____

4. What are some needs of your loved ones? Do you meet these needs? Why or why not?

_____

_____

_____

5. When you don't meet the needs of those closest to you, how does that impact the relationship?

_____

_____

_____

6. What would happen if you allowed yourself to meet the needs of someone close to you? How would that impact your relationship?

_____

_____

_____

7. Think of one need you could meet for someone else. What need would that be? Make a plan to meet that need and describe how doing so affected the relationship.

_____

_____

_____

Finding My Feelings

When our feelings have not been respected, appreciated, or validated, we can begin to think that our emotions are not important. We may start to feel like those emotions just get in the way and make things harder. Maybe we put them away, stuff them inside a box, push them into a closet, or try to ignore them and hope that they will go away. However, they never go away because they are inside us, a part of us. If we look for them, we will find them. And when we use them, they make our world brighter and more alive. Take the next few minutes to think about your emotions.

Now, close your eyes and think about your body. Think about the parts of you that may be hiding those feelings. Perhaps you have stored them somewhere safe, a place of honor, like your heart. These feelings are inside you, for they are inside all of us. Take a few minutes to think about where you may have placed them.

Then think about visiting that place. Don't open the door or lift the lid off the box yet. Just sit with those feelings for a moment. Think about placing your hand on the door or the lid of the box. Think about what is inside and why you have contained it. What caused you to contain those feelings so long ago? Perhaps there was a time or place where your feelings were not welcomed, understood, or accepted. Are you in the same place now, or have you moved to a different one? Do you have relationships now in which those feelings would be important and valued? Maybe it is time to bring them out and to allow them to color your world.

As you are able, think about opening that door a crack or lifting that lid just a bit. Look inside, and accept the first feeling that presents itself. Maybe allow that feeling to join you and close the door to the others, just for now. Sit with this feeling. How does it feel? Is it a happy or sad feeling? Is it big and overwhelming or smaller and manageable? When is the last time you remember experiencing it? As you simply experience this feeling, take a few moments to appreciate it and to imagine what it would bring to your world. After a few minutes, you can decide if you want to put it back into its container or take it with you. If you choose to take it with you, see what it's like to feel this emotion this week. Explore where it applies and how it enhances your life and experience of events. And if you choose to return it to containment, it will be there the next time you decide to visit it.

Now open your eyes and consider how it felt to search inside yourself and to experience this emotion. Consider returning as often as you feel comfortable, allowing other emotions to emerge each time. Eventually, one at a time, consider taking each feeling out and incorporating it into your daily life until you have restored all of your feelings.

Sharing My Feelings

Once we know what our feelings are and how we want to use them, it is healthy to be able to share them with others. This may be hard to do if you have shared your feelings and they were not respected. After you have practiced taking your feelings out of containment, use the questions below to consider whether you'd like to share those feelings with someone else.

1. Think about a past relationship in which your feelings were not validated. How was that relationship different from the relationships you have now? Can you list two or three differences?

   _____

   _____

   _____

2. Now think about a relationship in which you feel safe and cared for. Imagine sharing your feelings in that space. What would it be like? Would the other person care about your feelings? Have they expressed care or curiosity about your feelings before?

   _____

   _____

   _____

3. Practice sharing one or two feelings now with your therapist. Go ahead! Try it out! Once you have accomplished this, do you feel more prepared to try with your friend or spouse? Think of one feeling you want to share this week, identify someone you'd like to share it with, and then do that as homework.

   _____

   _____

   _____

Flood Gates

When you begin experiencing your emotions again, you may find that they begin to rush in and overwhelm you. It is like a dam that is holding back water. When a small hole opens in that dam and all the water tries to push through, there can be pressure and even an explosion as all of that water breaks free. If you have been containing your emotions for a long time and finally open a crack to let some feelings free, you may find that you experience pressure and tension as your emotions want to flood through. It is important to have some tools (or "flood gates") you can use to keep those emotions at bay or to slow their flow. When you are beginning to feel flooded by emotions you can:

1. Count backward from 10, or say the alphabet backward. This moves your brain from thinking about emotions to thinking about mathematical and analytical concepts. You are changing the side of the brain you are using, which can calm big emotions quickly.

2. Start moving. Take a walk, do five jumping jacks, or do wall push-ups. This burns the adrenaline that's released when you are starting to feel anxious or upset.

3. Do the 5-4-3-2-1 activity, which uses sensory input to ground you back to the present when you are beginning to be swept away by emotions. When you are anchored in the present, you are able to recognize that you are safe and secure in this moment, even if your feelings are telling you something else. To practice this activity, say aloud:

   a. Five things you can see

   b. Four things you can touch

   c. Three things you can hear

   d. Two things you can smell

   e. One thing you can taste

4. Color a mandala. A mandala is simply a circle with a symmetrical drawing inside of it, which you can fill in with different colors and patterns. Mandalas are very effective for soothing emotions because they require both sides of your brain to work together on the same activity. Your creative and artistic right brain (which is activated as you color) is paired with your analytical and logical left brain (which is activated as you symmetrically color in a pattern), which calms your whole brain. A couple of mandala templates are included on the next pages.

Mandala Template

Mandala Template

Worksheet (Adult or Child)

My Needs Are Important

When people have had the experience of their needs not being met, they often begin to think that their needs are not important. They may even begin to view themselves as being unworthy or unimportant. However, our needs keep us alive, so they are very important— as are you! The following are some negative beliefs people commonly develop when they have had their needs ignored. Try to counter these negative beliefs by coming up with a helpful, positive statement that more accurately reflects your worth and value. An example is provided for you first.

Example:	*My clothes were often too small for me.*
Statement:	*My parents didn't meet my needs because I was not important.*
Rewrite:	*My needs were not met because my parents' financial situation prevented them from adequately providing for me. My needs still deserved to be met.*

1. I must meet my needs on my own because others don't view my needs as important.

   _____

2. My needs are not as important as other people's needs.

   _____

3. My needs don't deserve to be met.

   _____

4. I can manage without my needs being met.

   _____

5. It's more important for me to meet someone else's needs. My needs can wait.

   _____

Using Constructive Criticism

Nobody is perfect—we all make mistakes! When this happens and someone says or does something to correct us, they can provide us with destructive criticism or with constructive criticism. *Destructive criticism* is hurtful and is intended to make us feel bad for making a mistake. In contrast, *constructive criticism* is intended to help us learn the correct way to do something by providing us with helpful feedback. It involves a correction with kindness. However, even constructive criticism can be hard to accept! Being able to accept constructive criticism and to learn from it does not mean that we are bad or that we have failed. It means that we are human and still have new things to learn.

In this exercise, you are going to explore the difference between destructive criticism and constructive criticism by coming up with some sample responses that reflect each kind of criticism. Look at the scenarios provided here, and then fill in the blanks. An example is provided to get you started.

Example: You pick up too many bags of groceries and drop one on the way into the house.

Destructive criticism: "Why do you always have to overdo it and make a mess?"

Constructive criticism: "It looks like your hands are full! Next time try taking one less bag."

What is the person trying to help you learn? To not drop a bag next time

---

1. Your boss sees you making a mistake as you stock the shelves at work and tells you:

   Destructive criticism: _____

   Constructive criticism: _____

   What is your boss trying to help you learn? _____

2. You turn in a project, which is missing a section, and your teacher says:

   Destructive criticism: _____

   Constructive criticism: _____

   What is your teacher trying to help you learn? _____

3. You are making dinner and get distracted, so you don't see the pot boil over, and your mom (or spouse) says:

   Destructive criticism: _____

   Constructive criticism: _____

   What is your mom (or spouse) trying to help you learn? _____

4. Your friend is telling you how difficult their day was, and you are distracted by the TV when they say:

   Destructive criticism: _____

   Constructive criticism: _____

   What is your friend trying to help you learn? _____

After doing this exercise, how do you now feel about constructive criticism? We all receive constructive criticism at one point or another, and accepting it will help you to grow and learn. Hopefully you have also learned how to give good constructive criticism because nobody likes to be criticized without kindness!

Healthy Control

If you have been meeting your needs and taking care of yourself for a long time, it may be hard to let someone else share the control. You may have certain ways that you like things to be done, to look, or to be organized. Perhaps having control helps you feel safe and secure in relationships. However, this can negatively affect your relationships if you are unable to share control or to find times to relax it. As with everything, having balance is healthy, and knowing when to use your control and when to relax it is important. Consider these questions as you think about your need for control.

1. Do you always need to be in control over all aspects of your daily life, or are you sometimes able to relax your control (using it as a "tool" when needed and putting it back in the toolbox when it's not)?

   _____

   _____

   _____

2. Do you need to have all of the control in your relationships? If so, how does this impact your relationships? How do others feel about you always having the control?

   _____

   _____

   _____

3. Do you trust your loved ones to hold the control and to be responsible with it? What would it look like if you were to share control?

   _____

   _____

   _____

4. How would it feel to allow someone else to share the control? To trust someone with the control?

_____

_____

_____

5. What is the worst thing that could happen if someone else was in control and did not do things your way?

_____

_____

_____

6. Could you tolerate things being different than the way you like them? Why or why not?

_____

_____

_____

7. How would it impact your relationships to share this control? How would your loved ones respond to you sharing control with them?

_____

_____

_____

Visiting My Inner Child

If you experienced neglect as a child, you had to be creative about finding ways to meet some of your needs. You had to depend on yourself more than other children your age. You may have been scared or worried at times because you were uncertain whether you would get your needs met. Perhaps you didn't get to have the same experiences as other children your age. There were things that you lost, missed out on, or weren't included in. Although you no longer look, act, or talk the same way you did as a child, that child is still a part of who you are, and that inner child helped shape the person you are today. Take a few moments to consider these things as you talk to your inner child.

Dear Inner Child,

I know it has been a long time since we talked or spent time together. But I know you are still there, inside of me, traveling with me through the years. I wanted to visit with you over the next few moments to tell you this:

I know it was hard on you when

_____.

I know you were sad about

_____.

When our parents

_____

it made you feel

_____.

Even now when I remember

_____

it makes me feel

_____.

While other children were being typical kids, you were

_____.

I just wanted you to be able to

_____.

I am sorry that you had to

_____.

I am sorry that you didn't get to

_____.

If I could go back and change anything, it would be

_____.

I know you did the best that you could because you were just a kid. And I thank you for helping me get through those hard times. I love you!

Love,

_____

Visiting My Inner Parent

In your childhood, you may have had to grow up quickly to learn about adult things so you could take care of yourself or maybe even take care of other children or adults. This experience created an inner parent within you who rose up to take care of you when no one else did. That part of you is a survivor who still lives within you! Take a few minutes to talk to that inner parent, telling them how they supported you and thanking them for helping you through a hard time.

Dear Inner Parent,

I know you are still there. You are even more a part of me now than ever before because I have grown into you. You were present at a really hard time for me and helped me through. I want to spend the next few moments with you to tell you this:

You helped me be strong when

_____.

I learned so much from you, and I see you in me when I

_____.

I could not have gotten through these things without you:

_____.

Thank you for staying with me and not leaving me alone. I feel

_____

when I think about you. I also feel

_____

looking back at what we survived. You were strong and courageous, helping me find my way to this adulthood. I want to thank you for

_____.

I will never forget how you

_____.

I know you will always be with me, and I will always take good care of you because you took such good care of me. I love you!

Love,

_____

Healthy Caretaking

If you had to take care of your parent while you were growing up, you may have come to accept or even embrace this caretaking role. Maybe your parent was ill or unable to take care of you or themselves in other ways. As an adult, you may find yourself in relationships where you are doing most of the caretaking because this feels most comfortable to you. As with anything else in life, it is important to have balance in our relationships when it comes to caretaking. It is normal and healthy for us to take care of one another, but an imbalance can occur when one person is shouldering the burden of caretaking. Think about a loved one in your life—ideally someone with whom you live or share household responsibilities—as you look at the table below. Place a check mark in the column to indicate who meets the need in your relationship.

The Needs	I Meet This Need	My Loved One Meets This Need	We Both Meet This Need
My emotional support			
My loved one's emotional support			
Dinner preparation			
Laundry			
Grocery shopping			
Lawncare			
Car maintenance			
Childcare			
Bill payments			
Household clean-up			
Household repairs			
Pet/animal care			
Other:			

Now look at where the check marks are. Are they evenly spread out, or is one person doing most of the caretaking? Are you taking care of your loved one without a balance in responsibilities? Are they taking care of you? How does this feel? What can you do to bring more balance to your relationship?

_____

_____

_____

_____

I Am the Parent

Parenting can be challenging, exhausting, and infuriating. But it can also be joyful and fulfilling. When you think about yourself as a parent and take a moment to assess your parenting skills, how are you doing? Consider the questions below, and think about what your child needs from you. Remember that children need their parents to provide for them, to protect them, and to prepare them for life. Your role as a parent is life-changing. You are important to your child!

1. What does being a parent mean to you?

_____

_____

_____

2. What are your strengths as a parent?

_____

_____

_____

3. What are some things you struggle with as a parent?

_____

_____

_____

4. How do you take care of your child? How do you meet their needs?

_____

_____

_____

5. Does your child ever take care of you or their siblings? If so, in what ways?

_____

_____

_____

6. How do you think your child feels when they have to take care of you or their siblings? Have you ever asked them? Have they told you how they feel?

_____

_____

_____

7. Your child is still growing and developing. They have a lot to learn about life and about responsibility. How do they react when they are given adult responsibilities, like taking care of themselves after school or fixing their own dinner? Do they handle those responsibilities well, or do they need redirection and prompting?

_____

_____

_____

8. When you give your child adult responsibilities, how do they behave toward you? Are they respectful? Do they follow directions?

_____

_____

_____

9. Is there anything you could do differently to relieve your child of these adult responsibilities? Is there anyone you could ask for help or something you could do differently to change your schedule or situation? If so, how do you think your child would feel?

_____

_____

_____

6
Medical Trauma

Kamy was born four weeks early. Her lungs were not fully functioning, and she spent three weeks in the neonatal intensive care unit (NICU). During this time, she experienced painful medical procedures and tests on a daily basis. While other newborns were forming attachment-based relationships with their parents, Kamy was unable to be held or comforted on a regular basis, which prevented her from forming a healthy bond with her parents until she was discharged from the hospital. As the years progressed, Kamy developed asthma and began requiring the use of a rescue inhaler. Sometimes, though, her inhaler failed to prevent or mitigate asthma attacks, requiring that she be rushed to the hospital via ambulance for breathing treatments. In third grade, a child at Kamy's school died of an asthma attack, causing Kamy to experience acute anxiety for months following the event.

At age 10, Kamy began experiencing panic attacks whenever she needed to visit the doctor, though she could not explain the source of the anxiety. She reported having a hard time breathing, experiencing racing thoughts about the doctor, and feeling hot—all symptoms of an adrenaline rush caused by anxiety. In addition, she frequently fought her mother in the morning while getting dressed due to her dislike of wearing socks and shoes. When her mother questioned her, Kamy said it was because the socks felt "weird" and her foot wasn't comfortable. Kamy's skin on this part of her body had a sensitivity that her mother could not understand.

Kamy eventually began attending therapy, and when the therapist asked if there was any history of medical trauma, Kamy's mother reported the NICU experience, but she dismissed it as unrelated to Kamy's current anxiety and sensory sensitivities. After the therapist asked additional clarifying questions about the NICU experience, Kamy's mother remembered the daily heel pricks Kamy required during the three weeks she was hospitalized. As the therapist framed the heel pricks in terms of Kamy's sensitivity to socks and shoes—talking about how the body remembers trauma—a light went off in Kamy's mother's eyes. She now had a different way of seeing Kamy's daily struggles, which changed the way she interacted with her daughter around this behavior. Instead of becoming frustrated, she approached Kamy with compassion and, together, they problem solved the sensory sensitivity.

When a child has experienced a medical emergency, a long-term diagnosis, or a medical procedure, this can create trauma that needs healing. Many children who have experienced medical trauma have a fear of doctors, hospitals, and medical procedures. They may experience anxiety symptoms that are triggered by specific sensory stimuli, such as the smell of antiseptic solution, the sound of beeping machines, the feel of latex gloves, or even the experience of pain. A child who had a serious medical procedure that required hospitalization may fear that going for a routine checkup will result in a hospital stay and painful procedures, resulting in anxiety about going to doctor's appointments. This can undermine a child's ability to feel safe with adults and to feel that adults can keep them safe because they are the ones performing the procedures that are the source of pain.

When a medical emergency happens in the life of an adult, their experience is often vastly different from that of a child because the adult brain is fully developed, allowing the capacity for higher-order thinking. Therefore, an adult who experiences a cardiac event that requires medical attention and open-heart surgery will have a different perspective of the event because they understand the necessity and purpose of the medical procedure. In contrast, children exhibit more concrete thinking and are not able to readily rationalize the source of their pain. All they know is that they are in pain and that an adult is responsible. As a result, children can develop a mistrust of adults, especially those in the medical profession, resulting in anxiety whenever a child enters a doctor's office or hospital.

In addition to acute medical emergencies, trauma can also result when a child must manage a long-term medical condition, such as asthma, epilepsy, or diabetes. It can sometimes be difficult to manage these conditions, causing children to doubt adults' ability to take care of them or to keep them safe. In turn, they may take it upon themselves to keep themselves safe instead of depending on others to do so. For example, a child who experiences uncontrolled asthma attacks or seizures may attempt to control other areas of their life in order to feel safe. They may refuse to participate in gym class or to do chores outside, and although this may look like oppositional behavior, it simply reflects the child's attempt to keep themselves safe and to avoid another medical crisis, even if it is ineffective. These controlling behaviors can impact the child's friendships and interactions with adults, as well as their relationships as they move into adulthood. Remember that when a child tries to keep themselves safe and to meet their own needs, this often looks dysfunctional and inappropriate.

Additionally, when a child has experienced a medical trauma, it is important to consider that the parent has experienced a trauma as well. Parents have felt powerless to protect their child or to save them from having to undergo painful testing and procedures, and they have experienced the anxiety of not knowing whether their child would survive a medical procedure or serious illness. In turn, parents can have symptoms of trauma that impair their functioning, and they may attempt to restore feelings of power and control by anxiously trying to protect their child from perceived threats of harm, whether real or imagined.

Medical trauma can also result when a child has a parent, sibling, or other loved one dealing with a medical diagnosis. For example, a parent struggling with cancer or another chronic condition may be unable to care for the child in the way they need. The child may even need to take care of their parent at times, creating parentification. Although it is acceptable for children to exhibit minor caretaking behaviors at times—such as when a child makes the family breakfast on Sunday morning or brings a sick parent a bowl of soup—it becomes problematic when the situation is more permanent. This can occur when a parent needs ongoing support and care, and the child is placed in the role of providing that care. It further reinforces the notion that the parent is unable to take care of the child and that the child needs to take care of themselves and their parent. This type of situation can mirror the experience of neglect for a child.

When this parentification progresses into adulthood, the individual may become codependent and look for others to take care of because that experience has become normalized. It is what they are familiar with and what feels most comfortable in relationships. In turn, they may become caretakers and sacrifice their own needs in order to meet the needs of others. To them, it feels unnatural to have another person focus on their needs and take care of them, which can impact their ability to build attunement, trust, and attachment in adult relationships. The healthy give-and-take behaviors that characterize normal relationships become a source of distress.

Finally, medical trauma can happen as young as the newborn or infant stage, which can occur when children require treatment in the NICU or PICU (pediatric intensive care unit). These babies experience painful medical procedures and monitoring when they do not yet have the verbal capacity to express their pain and needs. Often, they also do not receive the comfort needed to feel safe and secure in the midst of a trauma. We now know that it is important for babies in the NICU and PICU to be touched and held, and while hospitals try to facilitate this as much as possible, it may not be enough.

For these infants and young children, who do not yet have the capacity for language, the traumatic experience becomes encoded not as a verbal memory but as a sense memory. Their five senses collect information from the environment, like the smell of antiseptic solution or the sound of beeping health monitors, and connect that stimuli to the experience of pain. When that child then experiences those stimuli again later in childhood, it may elicit fear and anxiety. While this response may not make sense to the adults witnessing it—and the child may not recognize its significance either—it will nonetheless be associated with the feeling that adults, or their environment, are not safe.

When this occurs, as with all preverbal trauma, the most important thing to remember is that the child may not know what is upsetting them. Therefore, repeatedly asking the child to describe the trigger will be frustrating for both the adult and child. If you ask, "What just happened?" and the child cannot tell you, believe them. They do not know the answer. They simply know that they felt scared and that they needed to move. They cannot identify why. In this case, the most effective intervention is to calm the child using strategies that tap into the five senses. Have the child suck on a piece of sweet candy, listen to calming music, look at pictures of happier times, touch a grounding object (such as a blanket or toy), or smell some scented oils. Providing support and nurturing care at this time will allow the child to feel safe and to trust that adults can take care of them in this situation.

In addition, because the child does not have a verbal memory of the trauma, attempting to process the trigger can be ineffective. Instead, focus on teaching the child to listen to their body. When their brain is triggered, the alert system in their brain sends a signal to release adrenaline and cortisol. We know that adrenaline causes the heart to beat faster, the lungs and muscles to constrict, and blood pressure to rise. If we can teach children to monitor and listen to their bodies, they can begin to recognize when their body starts to exhibit these symptoms and to use that as a signal to practice coping skills. In turn, children learn an important emotion regulation skill when their bodies give them these special physical signals that they are experiencing anxiety.

As children move into adulthood, some medical diagnoses may resolve while others may continue. But even individuals whose medical issues resolve may still exhibit the need to control themselves, others, and their environment. This can cause mounting feelings of frustration and continued anxiety when individuals attempt to control things over which they have no control. In order to heal, it is necessary to help clients recognize what they can realistically control and what they cannot—and to teach them the importance of tolerating the uncertainty of that which is outside of their control. Doing so can reduce anxiety as clients learn to let go of situations over which they have no power.

Even though adults who have experienced medical trauma possess the capacity for higher-order thinking, the presence of rational and abstract thought does not always lessen the impact of the trauma. Adults can still experience medical trauma and have anxiety about medical procedures, even when they are able to rationalize the necessity for undergoing these procedures. For many adults, there is still fear about the unknown outcome or the painful recovery. Additionally, depending on their life situation, clients may not have been able to draw on resiliency factors needed to lessen the impact of the trauma, such as coping skills, self-care strategies, and supportive relationships. They may also experience medical trauma due to specific medical procedures and the urgency with which they were provided.

In fact, the specific type of medical trauma can play an important role in recovery. In their book *Managing the Psychological Impact of Medical Trauma,* Michelle Hall and Scott Hall (2017) discuss three levels of medical trauma that shape our understanding of how trauma can develop. A **level one** medical trauma is described as a planned or routine medical intervention, such as a test or procedure that's done on an outpatient or inpatient basis. It may or may not require anesthesia, but the person has advanced knowledge that the procedure will happen, has time to consider risks and make a decision about moving forward, and has met the doctor and has confidence in their abilities. Because individuals are able to prepare for the event and have some control over it, the experience is less likely to result in trauma. In working with these clients, it is important to process their understanding of the medical event both before and after it occurs. Narratives can help clients put their experience in sequential order given that they often have a fragmented understanding of the experience.

In a **level two** medical trauma, a person experiences a life-threatening or life-altering diagnosis. Perhaps they are diagnosed with diabetes and have to monitor daily insulin levels, or they receive a cancer or dementia diagnosis. This type of trauma requires clients to adjust their lifestyle, to accept new limitations, and to deal with chronic pain or uncomfortable symptoms. For those with a terminal illness, it also requires that they come to accept that their condition will result in death.

Clients with a level two medical trauma will need to process their feelings about their changing life circumstances. In working with these clients, it is important to help them recognize that while there are many things about their diagnosis they cannot control, there are other things they can control. For example, a client with diabetes has control over the frequency with which they monitor their insulin levels, which may help them feel calmer when they are worried about another hospitalization or medical crisis. Similarly, a client who has been diagnosed with cancer is in control of their ability to research treatments and to make an educated decision regarding their medical care, which may give them peace as they move forward.

A **level three** medical trauma is an unexpected and life-threatening medical event that requires a visit to the emergency room or intensive care unit, such as a heart attack, stroke, accident, or other event that causes grave injury. In these situations, the client does not have time to prepare for the event beforehand, and their outcome may be uncertain for some time. This is another situation where helping the client create a narrative can bring integration and healing. If the client was unconscious for a portion of the event, this may require talking to friends or relatives who were present to fill in puzzle pieces of the experience so the client has a clearer understanding of the event. This storytelling serves a dual purpose of processing the trauma narrative for the client while also processing the vicarious trauma of the family member who is telling the story to the client.

Finally, Hall and Hall (2017) specifically acknowledge childbirth as a medical trauma that may span across all three levels. At times, childbirth can begin as a planned medical intervention that reflects a level one trauma but can progress to a level three medical trauma if unforeseen circumstances arise. For example, the baby may go into distress and need to be delivered by cesarean section. This results in an intensive surgery that can put the mother's life at risk and that results in a longer recovery time. Even a natural delivery can result in a level three trauma if the baby becomes lodged and an episiotomy has to be performed to ensure a successful delivery.

In these situations, a mother may experience periods of panic or fear for the life of her child. In turn, she may have a difficult time connecting to and caring for her child, which can result in the child experiencing an attachment trauma within the first few weeks or months of life. When treating clients with this type of medical trauma, it is important to assess for symptoms of anxiety and depression related to the birthing experience and to assess supports that are available to the client, such as lactation consultants or visiting nurses who may be able to provide assistance to the mother. You can also identify self-care practices that the client can do, such as taking a walk outside for 20 minutes each day, sleeping when the baby sleeps during the day, and leaning on friends and family who can help out with taking care of the baby.

The following worksheets can provide a useful resource in working with individuals who have experienced medical trauma. In particular, these worksheets will help clients process their medical trauma through narrative exercises, sensory interventions, and body-based activities. Interventions are included for individuals with a closed medical trauma (in which the event has ended), as well as for those who have ongoing trauma in the form of a long-term medical diagnosis. **It is important to recognize that we cannot begin to heal from trauma until it has ended and we can reestablish feelings of safety and security.** For clients who are experiencing a chronic condition or life-altering diagnosis—in which there is ongoing medical testing, procedures, and treatments—the focus of treatment involves helping the client better tolerate uncertainty and manage anxiety.

INTERVENTIONS FOR HEALING

Regardless of a client's medical diagnosis, whether it is long-term or short-term, serious or more minor, your client has thoughts and feelings about their diagnosis. Clinicians can use the **My Medical Diagnosis** worksheet to assist adult or child clients in talking about their diagnosis and the ways it is impacting their life. This worksheet is useful for clients who have a temporary diagnosis, like Bell's palsy or gestational diabetes, or a permanent diagnosis, like chronic obstructive pulmonary disease (COPD) or epilepsy. It is also useful for end-of-life issues, like terminal cancer or liver failure.

The worksheet provides clients an opportunity to better understand their symptoms and prognosis. Many times, clients are anxious about the unknown, and educating them about their diagnosis can calm their anxiety and fears. At the very least, it can help them know what is ahead and how they need to plan or make adjustments to their life. It is also an opportunity to engage in reality testing if the client is catastrophizing about the situation. A goal of treatment is to help clients accept their diagnosis and to walk through that process with them as they continue on their journey.

For children or adults with a chronic or life-altering medical condition, clinicians can also use the **My Medical Condition** worksheet as a supplement. Thinking about the impact of a long-term diagnosis can leave clients feeling hopeless and overwhelmed. This worksheet can assist clients in exploring how their life has changed and how they are finding their "new normal."

The **My Medical History** worksheet can be used with adults or children to examine the impact of their childhood medical history. Although the client may no longer be dealing with an active diagnosis, the unresolved effects of the medical trauma may continue to affect their life. For example, they may have ongoing anxiety about medical appointments or sensory sensitivities as a result of past injuries. They may also have long-term effects related to the medical trauma, like a secondary diagnosis of asthma or learning disabilities as a result of being born prematurely.

In everything in life, there are things we can control and things we cannot control. When it comes to medical diagnoses that feel overwhelming or out of control, the temptation for many clients is to swing to the other side of the control spectrum and to try to maintain control over everything. For example, they may avoid certain activities (e.g., a client with asthma may limit physical activity in an attempt to prevent an asthma attack) and avoid medical professionals they don't trust as safe (e.g., a child may begin to scream as they enter an appointment in an effort to stop the exam). Helping clients to find balance—to recognize that there are some things they can control and others they cannot control—is key. Doing so gives them a sense of competence over that which they can control and allows them to cope with that which they cannot control. Clinicians can use the **Controlling My Health** worksheet to assist children and adults in finding this balance.

In addition, many clients with medical trauma are dealing with the uncertainty of their condition, which can be especially frustrating and anxiety-provoking. For example, a client with elusive symptoms may see several specialists and undergo extensive testing but still not have a diagnosis or treatment plan. Another client may receive a diagnosis where the prognosis is uncertain or treatment is not available. This lack of certainty and loss of control can lead clients to experience hopelessness and helplessness. In these situations, it is important to work with clients to accept and tolerate "not knowing." Use the **Tolerating the Unknown** handout to help adults and children learn ways to manage ongoing fear, frustration, and disappointment. Although they cannot change their situation, they can learn to accept ambiguity and turn their focus toward what they can control and what brings them peace and joy.

When a parent has had to contend with a medical issue—such as a terminal illness, substance abuse, mental illness, or another disabling condition—and the burden of care is placed on the child, the ensuing role-reversal can be confusing. The child may come to believe that it is normal to give up their needs in the service of others. In turn, that child can move into adulthood looking for caregiving relationships characterized by codependency. Clinicians who are working with children currently in this situation (or with adults who previously cared for their parent in childhood) can use the **Taking Care of Me, Taking Care of You** worksheet to help them explore that parent-child relationship and to examine how it differed from other relationships. The worksheet can also assess how many caregiving relationships the client has had and how deeply reinforced that dysfunctional relationship style has become.

When working with a client who has experienced a medical trauma, whether they are an adult or a child, it is important to keep in mind which of the three levels of trauma they may have experienced. For clients who are preparing to undergo a medical procedure that could reflect a level one medical trauma, use the **Planning for a Medical Procedure** worksheet to help them prepare for the event. Clients who are planning to have a colonoscopy, angioplasty, or the removal of a tumor could all fall into this category. Talk through the procedure, its risks, and their feelings about the upcoming event. Then focus on helping them identify supports and coping strategies they can use to manage anxiety symptoms and promote resiliency.

When working with a client who is experiencing a level two medical trauma, the **Regaining My Balance** worksheet can empower the client by allowing them to recognize that which they do have control over when it comes to their diagnosis. Oftentimes, when clients are diagnosed with a serious condition, such as cancer, AIDS, or diabetes, the surprise of the diagnosis can leave them feeling like they do not have control over their body or their future. This worksheet can help them find balance.

For clients who have survived a level three medical trauma, in which their feelings of safety and security were taken from them, the **Telling My Story** worksheet can allow clients to talk about the fear and uncertainty they are experiencing. This narrative intervention assists clients in taking fragments of the event and putting them in sequential order so they can develop a more cohesive picture. Oftentimes, clients experience fear when they do not have answers regarding what happened to them and how it happened, especially if they were unconscious at the time. They can have anxiety about the event happening again or feel powerless over the symptoms or conditions that have resulted. As they create their narrative with the help of family and friends, clients can develop a better understanding of what happened and try out exercises that can calm their body.

When working with clients who have gone through a traumatic birthing experience, use the **Birthing Trauma** worksheet to help them explore the traumatic experience. This intervention allows clients to tell their story, to identify where they feel they lost control, and to identify what can help them regain those feelings of control and competency. It's important to allow clients to tell their story and to validate their feelings as they express them. This safe therapeutic space may be the first time a client has had to process this trauma.

Oftentimes, individuals who have experienced a medical trauma do not feel safe when it comes to medical appointments, and they feel anxiety or apprehension when facing procedures or surgeries. This lack of felt safety is a result of an overactive fight, flight, or freeze response. When the body's internal alert system goes on overdrive, it signals the presence of threat even when there is none. For example, a child who experienced a painful medical procedure may now exhibit an overwhelming fear of doctor's offices, causing their internal alert system to activate even when there is nothing to worry about. Use the **Quiet the Alert System** handout with children and adults to explain how this alert system works, as well as **The Fight, Flight, or Freeze Response** handout to explore what they can do to find felt safety in those situations. Helping clients feel competent and in control over their fear response can empower them toward recovery.

In addition, you can help clients counter their fear response by teaching them to change the script that is running through their minds. When their brain's alert system warns them that a medical situation feels dangerous, even when it is safe, we can change the way their alert system responds by challenging fear-based thoughts with a reality-based positive affirmation. The **Changing My Thoughts about Medical Experiences** handout provides clients with a variety of positive affirmations they can use to change their thoughts about medical situations that cause them anxiety.

Often, we fear things that we do not understand. For many clients, medical situations can provoke a variety of symptoms associated with the release of adrenaline, such as fast heartbeat, sweaty palms, and a stomachache. These symptoms can feel uncomfortable and can cause clients to experience increased fear and anxiety about symptoms that were originally initiated by fear and anxiety. To help clients break this vicious cycle, it can help to provide them with an understanding of this process, including what drives it and how to stop it. Use the **Break the Anxiety Cycle** handout to provide psychoeducation on the effects of adrenaline and to present clients with coping and calming strategies they can use to break the cycle of anxiety.

For child clients, who may have a more difficult time understanding and verbalizing their symptoms, it can be helpful to use an art-based intervention, such as **My Body Is Talking**. This activity asks child clients to visually identify where their body holds tension following a medical trauma. When reviewing the exercise, it is important to notice how they conceptualize themselves. If they pay disproportionate attention to one side of their body (or draw one side of their body larger), ask clarifying questions. It may be that this part of the child's body holds significance or is the center of their discomfort following a medical trauma.

Once clients know how their body responds when it is escalating in fear or anxiety, they are better able to use tools to bring their body back down to baseline when they notice these reactions beginning. The **Calming Down My Body** handout provides examples of sensory activities clients can use to reground their body in response to anxiety or fear. Because clients who have experienced medical trauma hold memories of the trauma in different areas of their body, some clients may respond more strongly to certain sensory interventions over others. Each client is different and will have different preferences based on their body's experience of the medical trauma. Practice several interventions with clients, using activities from each sensory category, until you find some that work best for them.

When a child has experienced a medical trauma, we must recognize that parents have also experienced the same trauma from a different perspective. Oftentimes, parents feel like they have lost control over their ability to keep their child safe, which can result in vicarious trauma. Even after the child recovers, parents may engage in anxious parenting behaviors in an attempt to protect their child from further harm. This can harm the parent-child relationship by making children feel like they are being overprotected and are having unfair restrictions placed on them. To help parents find balance again, use the **Parenting and Supporting My Child** worksheet to help them process the experience of their child's medical trauma and to increase their ability to parent in a way that provides security, stability, and nurturing care.

It is also important that parents be supportive when their child is feeling anxious in response to medical trauma instead of dismissing these feelings as an overreaction. When parents validate their child's feelings and prompt them to use coping skills to regulate their emotions, this moves the child into healing and felt safety. The **Medical Trauma and Your Child** handout can help parents come to a better understanding of the need to validate their child's reaction to current or past medical traumas.

My Medical Diagnosis

When you receive a medical diagnosis, it can be overwhelming trying to understand the symptoms, treatment, and prognosis. Thinking about the diagnosis—and how it may change your life—can create feelings of anger, fear, or sadness. Take a few minutes to think about your diagnosis, what it means for your life, and how you feel about this.

1. When did you receive your diagnosis?

_____

_____

_____

2. How were you told about your diagnosis?

_____

_____

_____

3. What kind of support did you receive from medical personnel or your family? Do you feel like you need more support? Who may be able to provide the type of support you need?

_____

_____

_____

4. What do you understand your diagnosis to be?

_____

_____

_____

5. What are your symptoms? How do they impact your daily life?

_____

_____

_____

6. How do you feel about your symptoms?

_____

_____

_____

7. What treatment are you undergoing? Do you feel it is helping? Why or why not?

_____

_____

_____

8. How do you feel about your treatment? Its side effects?

_____

_____

_____

9. What is your prognosis? How do you feel about this prognosis?

_____

_____

_____

10. Are there any things you're still wondering or thinking about when it comes to your diagnosis? Describe that here.

_____

_____

_____

My Medical Condition

Being diagnosed with a life-changing medical condition can make you feel anxious or depressed. It is normal to have these feelings, but it is also important to find a "new normal" and to not allow the condition to control your life. There are still positives and things to look forward to, and finding that balance can help you cope with difficulties as they arise. Take a few minutes to think about the challenges but also the positives that your life holds.

1. What did you think and feel when you first received your diagnosis?

_____

_____

_____

2. What are your greatest fears about your diagnosis?

_____

_____

_____

3. What is the largest challenge you will face?

_____

_____

_____

4. How can you prepare for that challenge to successfully endure it? What kind of support would be helpful?

_____

_____

_____

5. How does this diagnosis impact your family or the people you care about? How do you feel about this?

_____

_____

_____

6. What are some strengths you possess that will help you to cope with this diagnosis and the challenges it brings?

_____

_____

_____

7. Who can you turn to for support?

_____

_____

_____

My Medical History

When children are required to undergo medical procedures or need to manage a chronic medical condition, it can impact their feelings about medical offices, personnel, and procedures going forward. If you experienced any medical conditions during childhood— even as an infant—use this worksheet to explore how those experiences impacted you then and may continue to impact you today.

1. What types of medical procedures or conditions did you experience as a child?

_____

_____

_____

2. Do you remember any of these experiences? If so, what are those memories like?

_____

_____

_____

3. How did your medical history impact you as a child? Is there anything it interfered with or prevented you from doing?

_____

_____

_____

4. Are there ways your medical history continues to impact you now? For example, do you have any fears, anxieties, or apprehensions about medical appointments or doctors in general? Or has it caused other long-term effects? Describe those here.

_____

_____

_____

Controlling My Health

When it comes to life, there are things you can control and things you cannot control. This is especially important to remember if you are dealing with a medical diagnosis, which can sometimes feel overwhelming and unmanageable. In this case, finding a balance between that which you can and cannot control about your diagnosis can help you find perspective. For example, you can control how you monitor your health and proactively care for your diagnosis, but you can't control the fact that you have the diagnosis to begin with. Think about your diagnosis, and answer the following questions to reflect on what you can and cannot control about it.

1. What do you worry about the most with regard to your diagnosis? What is on your mind the most?

   _____

   _____

   _____

2. Of these worries, which are within your control?

   _____

   _____

   _____

3. Of these worries, which are out of your control? What are you unable to change about your diagnosis or circumstances?

   _____

   _____

   _____

4. For the worries that are in your control, use the following chart to problem solve how you can create a plan and follow through. If your plan works, that's great! If it doesn't, then brainstorm again and find new ideas.

Define the problem: Example: *I'm afraid of injections.*	**Define the problem:**
Brainstorm ideas: Idea 1: *Call before the appointment and ask if there will be any injections.* Idea 2: *Ask a friend to go with me.* Idea 3: *Plan to treat myself to something fun after the appointment.* Idea 4: *Ask to chew gum during the injection to relieve anxiety.*	**Brainstorm ideas:**
Identify a solution: Now pick one, or three! *I will call ahead because there may not be a reason to worry. If they say I need an injection, I will ask to chew gum and then get a special coffee on the way home.*	**Identify a solution:**
Try it out! Did it help? *Getting the shot was a little uncomfortable, but it wasn't as bad as I thought it would be!*	**Try it out! Did it help?**

5. Now look at the worries that you identified as being out of your control. Look at the list below, and circle the coping skills you can use when you begin to feel overwhelmed about these things. Try practicing at least two of these skills over the next week, and see if they help you feel calmer and more peaceful.

Taking a walk	Listening to music	Watching funny videos
Talking to a friend	Cooking	Reading
Drawing	Dancing	Journaling

6. After you try a few of these coping skills, rate how effective they were on the following scale:

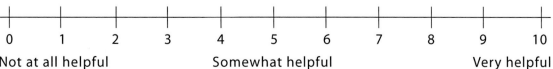

Not at all helpful   Somewhat helpful   Very helpful

Tolerating the Unknown

When it comes to medical conditions, there are times when you do not have answers. Perhaps you are waiting for a diagnosis, treatment, or the reduction of symptoms. Those answers may come this week, next month, a year from now, or longer. What will you do while you wait? How will you spend your time? Take the next few minutes to brainstorm some activities that you enjoy doing. Think of things that bring you joy or peace. These things may calm you or bring you fulfillment. They may feed your soul or feed the souls of others. A few ideas are listed here to get you started.

Cooking for your family

Gardening

Coloring pictures and taking them to a children's hospital

Watching movies by your favorite actor

Volunteering at your favorite community agency

Visiting elderly people

Reading to children at the library

After you have brainstormed a few ideas, make plans to do one of them this week. Then think about how it made you feel to accomplish this goal. There may be things about your medical situation that you cannot control, and that can be frustrating. However, there are many things in life you can control, and one of them is how you spend your time. You can choose to spend your time doing things that bring you peace and calm, that put a smile on your face or on the faces of others.

Taking Care of Me,
Taking Care of You

When a parent isn't healthy and requires caregiving, children sometimes step into that role. However, this can be confusing because parents are supposed to take care of children. Maybe you had to be responsible early on, taking care of your parent because they were having a hard time taking care of themselves. Maybe you didn't get to fully engage in your childhood. Maybe the caretaking relationship you had with your parent became comfortable, so you now look for people to take care of. Healthy relationships are based in balance where two people take care of each other equally. Answer the following questions as you think about your relationship with your parent and how it may have shaped your relationships with others.

1. Did your parent take care of you? In what ways?

   _____

   _____

   _____

2. Did you take care of your parent? In what ways?

   _____

   _____

   _____

3. What caused you to have to take care of your parent? How did this affect your childhood? How did you feel about it?

   _____

   _____

   _____

4. Are there any people you take care of? In what ways?

_____

_____

_____

5. Do the other people in these relationships take care of you? In what ways?

_____

_____

_____

6. Are your relationships balanced—meaning that both people in the relationship take care of each other equally—or does one person take care of the other most of the time? Are you happy with that arrangement? Why or why not?

_____

_____

_____

7. What would it mean to you to have someone take care of you?

_____

_____

_____

Planning for a Medical Procedure

The possibility of needing to undergo a medical procedure can create anxiety in anyone. The extent of this anxiety can depend on the severity of the procedure, its risk factors, and its possible side effects. Many times, we have anxiety about things that we do not understand or that we have unanswered questions about. If you are experiencing anxiety about an upcoming medical procedure, you can reduce the anxiety by thinking through the procedure to better understand it or by coming up with clarifying questions to ask your doctor. Use the spaces provided to help you plan for this event and reduce your anxiety about it.

1. What is the purpose of your upcoming procedure? How will the procedure be done? What questions do you have about it?

_____

_____

_____

2. What are the risks? Is there anything you can do to reduce those risks? What questions do you have about those risks?

_____

_____

_____

3. Who can you ask to find the answers you need to these questions? Perhaps the doctor's office or a friend who has gone through the same procedure?

_____

_____

_____

4. Before and after the procedure, who can you lean on for support? Who can drive you to the office, and who can bring you a meal after?

_____

_____

_____

5. If a particular area of your body will be impacted by the procedure, identify some sensory coping strategies you can use to calm your body. Below are some ideas. Circle the ones that may work for you or add your own:

- Ice any sore body parts. (Make sure you have lots of ice at home before leaving for the procedure.)

- Use calming essential oils (e.g., lavender, frankincense, ylang-ylang, rose, lemon, jasmine, chamomile, bergamot) in a diffuser or on cotton balls.

- Find a soft blanket to cocoon yourself in.

- Eat a favorite food or snack (that is compatible with your doctor's follow-up recommendations).

- Listen to relaxing music, such as classical or spa music.

- Watch a favorite light-hearted movie or show that makes you smile.

- Other: _____

6. After you try a few of these coping skills, rate how effective they were on the following scale:

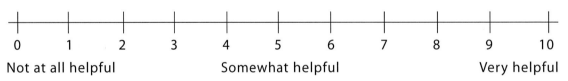

0   1   2   3   4   5   6   7   8   9   10

Not at all helpful   Somewhat helpful   Very helpful

Regaining My Balance

When you receive an unexpected medical diagnosis—one that changes your life—it can cause you to feel anxious or to feel like things are spinning out of control. It might seem like you have lost control of your life and your body. To find your balance again, it is important to identify the things you can control about your diagnosis. For example, you are in control of making decisions about treatment and deciding how you take care of your body. Take a few minutes and think about regaining your balance.

1. What things have you lost control over when it comes to your diagnosis?

_____

_____

_____

2. What aspects of your medical diagnosis can you control? For example, do you have control over your treatment? If so, in what ways?

_____

_____

_____

3. What other choices do you have? For example, are you able to manage your symptoms? If so, how are you able to do so (e.g., through diet, exercise, pain management, medication)?

_____

_____

_____

4. What other aspects of your medical condition or treatment you are able to control?

_____

_____

_____

5. Who can you talk to about your diagnosis? For example, is there someone you can connect with who has the same diagnosis? Is there a support group or national organization you can join? How might that help?

_____

_____

_____

6. If you continue to have trouble refocusing your attention away from the things you cannot control, it can help to practice calming strategies to distract your mind. Look at the list here, and circle any activities you think might be helpful or add your own.

    • Watch a favorite TV show

    • Listen to your favorite song on repeat

    • Read a chapter in a book

    • Take a walk outside

    • Draw or color a picture

    • Call a friend

    • Do a few yoga poses

    • Play with your pet

    • Eat an orange or have a glass of lemonade (which are calming flavors)

    • Other: _____

7. After you try a few of these coping skills, rate how effective they were on the following scale:

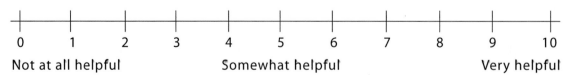

0   1   2   3   4   5   6   7   8   9   10
Not at all helpful   Somewhat helpful   Very helpful

Telling My Story

If you have experienced an unexpected and serious medical event, it is common to have symptoms of anxiety. You might have nightmares, experience panic (e.g., heart beating fast, trouble breathing), or "space out." These are all ways that your body is trying to cope with the medical emergency you survived. Use this worksheet to help your brain and mind understand what happened, and then use this understanding to allow your body to recover from the traumatic experience. Follow the prompts below to work through this process.

1. Tell your story to your therapist by describing what you remember about the medical emergency, or write it in the space here.

_____

_____

_____

_____

2. Now identify any parts of the story that are missing. Sometimes our mind forgets parts of the story in an attempt to protect us. However, it is only by putting together all the pieces of the puzzle that we can see the big picture, which brings clarity and reduces anxiety. Describe any missing pieces here.

_____

_____

_____

_____

3. Who can you ask to fill in the missing parts of the story? Your doctor? A family member or friend? With their help, fill in the blanks here.

_____

_____

_____

_____

_____

4. Once you have pieced together your story, tell it again to a trusted loved one. Choose someone you trust to support you and to respect your emotions because it may be a hard story to tell. After you're done sharing your story, describe what it was like to share the full story aloud.

_____

_____

_____

5. When you are done sharing your story, think about how your body felt during the experience. Did certain parts of your body feel physical pain as you recounted your story? Just as your mind holds on to the emotional memory of the medical trauma, your body holds on to physical memories associated with the experience. In order to find healing, it is important to give those areas special attention. Here are some ideas to help your body recover. Circle the ones that might help you or add your own:

- Massage the area with lotion, or treat yourself to a massage.

- If your doctor approves, take a walk, or do gentle exercises for that part of your body to get it moving.

- Give that part of your body a rest and prop it up with pillows.

- Complete a body scan exercise (see chapter 4) to identify where you are holding tension, and work to relax that part of your body.

- Help your lungs and heart relax by using deep breathing techniques. Imagine climbing a mountaintop. As you climb the mountain, take three deep breaths in through your nose and out through your mouth. Hold your breath for a moment at the top of the mountain as you enjoy the view, and then descend the mountain by taking three deep breaths again, in through your nose and out through your mouth.

- Other: _____

Birthing Trauma

Parents often have some idea about how they think their labor and delivery will progress, and when this process does not go as expected, it can be a surprise and even traumatic. If you, your partner, or your child experienced harm, it can be difficult to manage your feelings. You may even find yourself reexperiencing the traumatic event when you hold your child or think about the birthing process. Use this exercise to recount your birthing story and to brainstorm activities you can use to ground yourself in the present moment whenever your mind gets stuck in the trauma.

1. Use this space to tell the story of your birthing trauma, making sure to focus on your thoughts and feelings surrounding the experience.

_____

_____

_____

_____

_____

2. At what point in your story did you feel like you experienced a loss of control? What did you lose control over? What was this like for you?

_____

_____

_____

_____

_____

3. Have you regained control in those areas? For example, if you lost control of your body when you had to have an emergency cesarean section, have you have regained control over your body and your ability to make decisions about your body? If so, how did you reestablish that control? If not, what does it feel like you still don't have control over?

_____

_____

_____

4. When you think about your body and the decisions you are making for yourself and your child, what do you have control over?

_____

_____

_____

5. When you feel like you are not in control of your body, it can be helpful to practice some of the grounding techniques listed here. Circle the ones you think might work best for you, and add any others that help you feel connected to your body:

- Take four deep breaths while touching your thumb to each finger (thumb to pointer finger, thumb to middle finger, thumb to ring finger, thumb to pinky finger). Breathe in through your nose and out through your mouth.

- Take a deep breath in through your nose as you raise your hands over your head, and release the breath through your mouth as you bring your arms down to your sides.

- Do a few yoga poses and feel the stretch in your muscles.

- Use your five senses:

  ○ Touch your nose.

  ○ Put perfume or body spray on and smell your wrist.

  ○ Focus on a moving object (e.g., a buzzing bee, a passing car) and follow it.

  ○ Listen to a sound in your environment (e.g., a ticking clock, a pot that is boiling) and follow it.

  ○ Eat a peppermint candy or chew gum.

- Other: _____

Quiet the Alert System

In your brain is an alert system. It has a very important job! It lets you know when you are in danger and helps you to stay safe. When something in your environment seems threatening, your brain sends messages to the rest of your body, letting all of the parts know to be ready to protect you. Your heart may beat faster and your muscles may get tight and tense, preparing you to confront the dangerous situation that you need protection from.

Sometimes, when you have experienced something traumatic, your brain will send off alerts telling you that you are not safe, even when you are very safe. For example, maybe you had to undergo a painful medical procedure one time, and now every time you go to the doctor, you feel anxious. That's because your brain is trying to take care of you and to protect you from something painful. But it has become a little overprotective. It is trying too hard to keep you safe, and it is keeping you away from things that are unsafe *and* safe.

You can quiet your alert system and help your brain learn new ways of reacting by helping it recognize safe situations. To do so, pause whenever you are feeling anxious or afraid, and ask yourself, "What am I afraid of right now?" and then ask, "Is that thing happening now?" For example, the next time you are at the doctor's office and you notice your body giving you those danger signals (e.g., fast heartbeat, sweaty palms), ask yourself: "What am I afraid of right now? A procedure. Is a procedure happening now? No." After you have had this quick conversation with yourself, tell your alert system that it's okay. You can say, "I got this one" or "No thanks, it's okay" or "No worries, everything's fine." After a couple of times, your alert system will start to understand that you're in charge and that it doesn't have to work so hard to keep you safe. Your alert system will start to quiet, and you will be able to do safe things without feeling afraid.

The Fight, Flight, or Freeze Response

When we feel scared or anxious, the alert system in our brain prepares our body to do one of three things: fight, flight, or freeze. These responses are fueled by adrenaline. The **fight** response looks like verbal or physical fighting. Maybe you argue or become oppositional at doctor's appointments. When you feel the fight response, you can use your five senses to remind yourself that you are safe right now. If you are in a doctor's office and start to feel irritable or grumpy, here are some sensory grounding techniques you can try:

- Listen to some relaxing music

- Suck on a small butterscotch or sweet candy

The second response you may have is the **flight** response, which can look like running away or trying to avoid doing something. You may avoid medical appointments, reschedule them repeatedly, or refuse to follow medical recommendations for treatment. Adrenaline won't just go away and needs to be burned off through physical activity. If you are in a doctor's office and feel the urge to take flight, you can:

- Bounce your leg

- Tighten and then relax the muscles in your arms and legs

The last response you might experience is the **freeze** response, which involves becoming unresponsive, not answering questions, or staring into space. In medical situations, you may experience a state of paralysis and not remember what the doctor explained. The freeze response is your body's way of trying to escape something that's hard to think about. This can make it hard to interact, to answer a question or hold a conversation, or to pay attention to what someone is saying. If you are in a doctor's office and feel yourself starting to freeze, you can:

- Gently squeeze one of your fingertips

- Pull on your earlobe

Changing My Thoughts about Medical Experiences

If you have experienced a medical trauma, it is normal to be on alert or anxious about future medical situations. That's because your brain's job is to keep you safe, and even though there may be nothing scary about the current situation, your brain is still trying to protect you from something that was unsafe or caused anxiety in the past. At those times, you can use a firm and kind voice to tell your brain that everything is okay. Change the script that is running through your mind. Instead of listening to your mind say, "This is scary. This is going to be bad. I can't handle this," say a positive affirmation that reminds you of your strengths. Several are listed below. Try them out, and then create some of your own.

I've got this!

I have been through hard things before. I can handle this.

I know what is going to happen today, and it is not scary.

I'm strong.

I'm a survivor.

I trust my doctor.

I'm the boss of hard things!

Whatever happens today, I can manage it.

I am safe.

Break the Anxiety Cycle

When you feel anxious or afraid, your alert system activates, sending adrenaline through your body to prepare you to fight, flight, or freeze. The effects of adrenaline cause your heart rate to increase, your lungs to constrict, and your muscles to tighten. You may feel hot all over and have sweaty palms, a headache, or a stomachache. These physical symptoms often feel uncomfortable, which can make you feel even more anxious and cause the cycle to continue. If you have ever felt this way before, then you may already know that when your body feels this way, the symptoms can feel scary and make you feel more anxious. For example, if you have had the experience of getting medical test results that changed your life, your alert system may now trigger the release of adrenaline whenever you are waiting for test results, trapping you in this cycle of anxiety.

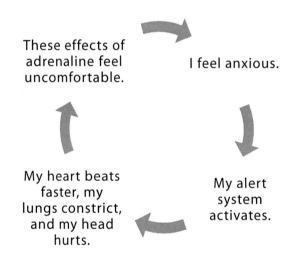

These effects of adrenaline feel uncomfortable.

I feel anxious.

My alert system activates.

My heart beats faster, my lungs constrict, and my head hurts.

To stop the cycle, it's important to understand that although the effects of adrenaline may be uncomfortable, they reflect your body's normal response to anxiety and fear. This is just how the body works. The next time you feel anxious about a medical appointment and your alert system activates, remind yourself that there is nothing wrong with your body, and then use one of these interventions to break the cycle:

- Take some deep breaths to re-regulate your breathing and heartbeat, breathing in through your nose and out through your mouth.
- Run your hands under cold water to re-regulate your body temperature,
- Tense and release some muscles in your body to help them relax.
- Move your body to burn the adrenaline (e.g., a short walk, a few jumping jacks).

You can stop the cycle! You can control your anxiety so it does not control you!

My Body Is Talking

Did you know that your body can talk to you? Are you listening? Your body can tell you a lot about YOU! Sometimes when you are anxious, scared, or afraid, your body will feel uncomfortable. Your tummy might hurt, your heart may beat faster, and you might feel hot or sweaty. On another piece of paper, draw a picture of your body, or use the template provided on the next page.

Then spend three minutes just being quiet and sitting still, paying attention to your body. How does it feel to sit in the chair? Can you feel the chair beneath you? What parts of your body are touching the chair? Is your body relaxed? Are there any parts that are tight or tense? Can you hear your heart beating? Is your mind quiet, or is it thinking about a lot of things? Try to ask your mind to be quiet so you can listen to your body.

Now, use different colored crayons to color in various parts of your body, either using the picture you drew or the template provided for you:

- Use the green crayon to color any part of your body that has had an injury or surgery.

- Use the blue crayon to color any part of your body that hurts sometimes. Maybe it hurts because you had a medical procedure in the past, and it still feels uncomfortable or painful at times.

- Use the red crayon to color any part of your body that feels uncomfortable when you are scared. Think about how your heart, breathing, head, and tummy feel when you are afraid.

- Use the yellow crayon to color the rest of your body.

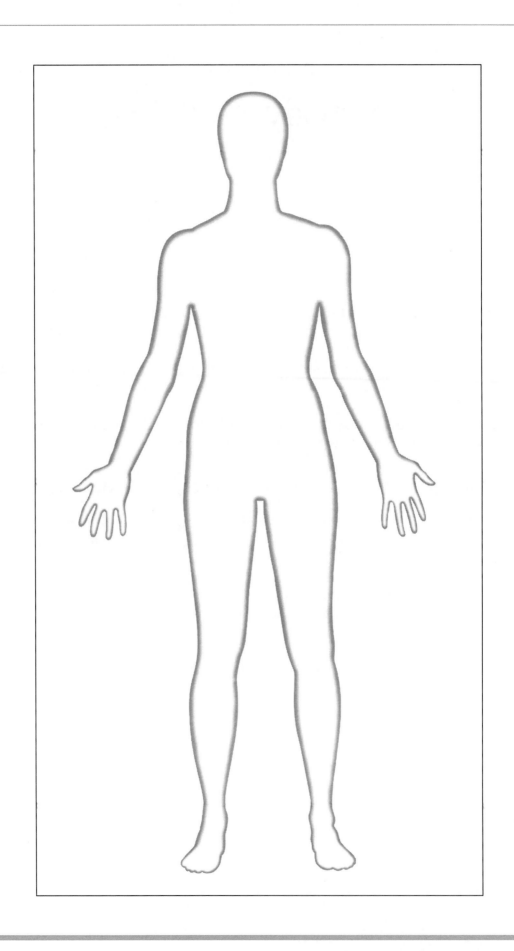

Now look at the picture as you think about these questions:

1. Do any of the colors overlap? Sometimes when we are scared, the parts of our body that hold scared feelings are the same ones that were hurt before. Did that happen in your picture? Did the green and red overlap anywhere?

_____

_____

_____

2. Notice how much of your body is colored yellow. Is it a lot of your body, or just some of your body? Maybe it feels like your whole body hurts sometimes, but in looking at your picture, you can see that some parts hurt but other parts are doing okay.

_____

_____

_____

3. What did you learn about your body? Did you learn how your body may be trying to talk to you? Did you learn how to be quiet for a few minutes and just feel your body so you can hear it talking?

_____

_____

_____

When your body starts to hurt, remember to take a few minutes to be quiet and to listen to your body. That may help that part of your body feel better or may allow you to think of an idea to help that part of your body. Now share your picture with your parents, and tell them what you learned about your body!

Calming Down My Body

When you have experienced a medical trauma, like a surgery, illness, or accident, it is important to know that your body remembers the trauma. It remembers the fear and the pain. It's for this reason that using sensory interventions—those that tap into your five senses—can calm your body when it is getting upset. These interventions allow you to take care of your body like it has taken care of you. Look at the sensory activities here, and try as many as you want until you find the ones that work best for you. You can add your own too!

1. Sense of sight

   • Watch a video of a happy memory, or imagine it in your mind.

   • Look at a picture or object that a special person gave you.

   • Focus on an object around you that you can see, like a vase or piece of fruit.

2. Sense of hearing

   • Listen to a calming sound (e.g., the rain, the beach, white noise).

   • Call a friend and listen to your friend's voice.

   • Focus on a sound you hear, such as a clock ticking or a dryer running.

3. Sense of taste

   • Eat something sweet, like butterscotch or bubble gum, to increase calmness.

   • Eat something spicy, like peppermint or cinnamon, to increase alertness.

   • Focus on the taste and texture of the next thing you eat or drink (e.g., salad, coffee, sandwich).

4. Sense of touch

- Create a sensory bin containing a variety of fabrics (e.g., velvet, burlap, silk).

- Bury small toys in a container of dried beans and search for them.

- Play with kinetic sand.

- Play with Orbeez®.

5. Sense of smell

- Smell cotton balls with various essential oils on them.

- Take in the scent of something meaningful, like your mother's perfume or your father's deodorant.

- Take a walk outside and identify two things you can smell.

After you try a few of these coping skills, rate how effective they were on the following scale:

| 0 | 1 | 2 | 3 | 4 | 5 | 6 | 7 | 8 | 9 | 10 |

Not at all helpful   Somewhat helpful   Very helpful

Parenting and Supporting My Child

If your child has experienced a medical trauma, then so have you. As your child's parent, you are responsible for supporting them and for helping them feel safe. This can be challenging to do when your child is facing a scary medical condition. You may feel anxious about your child's health and your ability to parent them at this time. However, it is important to remember that you are the largest predictor of your child's success in recovering from this trauma. The care that you provide during and following the trauma can help your child feel safe again. Answer the following questions to explore how you feel about your ability to parent your child now, and then look at the parenting recommendations that follow.

1. How has your child's medical condition changed the way you parent them?

_____

_____

_____

2. Do you feel any anxiety as a parent after watching your child progress through the medical trauma? Do you feel equipped to care for your child's needs? Why or why not?

_____

_____

_____

3. How do you manage your own anxiety? Your child will look to you to learn what to do with their own anxiety, so how you cope will affect how your child copes.

_____

_____

_____

When a child has experienced a trauma, what they need from their parents is stability, security, and nurturing care. Here are some ideas about how to implement each one of those for your child:

- **Stability**

  - Return as quickly as possible to the same schedule and routine you had before the trauma.

  - Have a regular bedtime.

  - Make sure there are healthy food and snacks available that your child can independently access when hungry.

- **Security**

  - Your child may have ongoing medical procedures. During those times, your child needs you to be present with them, in the moment, and to provide comfort and support. Being with your child in the hospital or during procedures, when it's allowed, helps them feel safe and secure.

  - Your child may express anxiety by being more clingy than usual or by reporting increased physical symptoms. Validate their feelings, and offer comfort and support.

- **Nurturing Care**

  - Encourage your child to talk about their feelings, and let them know that their feelings are acceptable. You or your child may feel angry, sad, or scared, and each of those feelings is normal in situations like this.

  - Help your child learn to calm their big feelings. If you have a hard time with this yourself, you can learn together.

  - Give lots of hugs, kisses, and healthy physical touch. For example, you can rub your child's back, place a hand on their shoulder, or play with their hair as they fall asleep. These things help your child feel comfort and increase their connection to you so they do not feel alone in their pain and fear.

Medical Trauma and Your Child

If your child has experienced a medical trauma, this can impact their ability to feel safe in medical situations moving forward. Even if your child was in the NICU as an infant and does not have a verbal memory of the experience, they still have a sense memory. Their bodies remember the way the NICU smelled, sounded, and felt. When something reminds them of that smell, sound, or sensation, they can feel triggered to a place of fear and danger. That is because the body remembers trauma. It remembers the sense of touch and the sensation of pain. For example, a little girl in the NICU who required daily heel pricks for blood samples may throw a tantrum whenever she needs to put on socks and shoes because she has a sensory memory of that pain. Her body is holding on to that trauma.

Children who hold trauma in their body act out of fear, which is why you may see fight (opposition), flight (running away), or freeze (not listening to directions) behaviors whenever they become triggered. Children generally can't verbalize the reasoning behind these behaviors, especially if the trauma occurred before they developed the verbal capacity to put the memory into words, so attempting to verbally process their behaviors will often lead to further frustration. Instead, it is important to respond with support and empathy to help your child feel safe. Find coping skills that calm and soothe them. Coping skills that engage the five senses can be most effective since your child's senses recorded the medical trauma. These sensory memories trigger your child's fear and anxiety response, so using specific sensory coping skills can help override this response.

For example, if your child is triggered by the smell of a doctor's office, have them bring a cotton ball infused with lavender essential oil that they can smell while at the office. Or if your child is triggered by the taste of a medicine, ask the pharmacist if they can add flavor to liquid medication, or offer a strong-tasting food item the child can eat after taking the medicine, such as a piece of bubble gum or a butterscotch candy. Ultimately, the goal is to create an environment where the child can find safety and heal.

7
Natural Disasters

Adam was at high school on a Thursday morning when a tornado hit unexpectedly. The sirens went off moments before the storm tore through the building, giving the teacher just enough time to get her students into the interior supply closet. When they emerged, there was destruction all around them. The building was demolished, and dozens of students and faculty had been killed or seriously injured. Although Adam's home had been spared, many of the surrounding homes in his neighborhood were gone.

In the weeks that followed, Adam experienced a variety of panic symptoms. He struggled to breathe, experienced a racing heartbeat, and was awoken by nightmares every night. When classes finally resumed at a temporary school that had been set up at the local recreation center, Adam refused to attend. His parents grew tired of prompting him to attend school and eventually placed him in a virtual classroom instead where he could log in to class from his home computer every day. Even with these accommodations, Adam continued to struggle. Whenever any alarm would sound—such as an alarm clock or a timer—Adam was instantly transported back in time and felt as if he was in the midst of the tornado again. He did not feel safe no matter how much his parents attempted to explain that he was no longer in danger.

Like Adam, many children who have experienced a natural disaster, including hurricanes, pandemics, floods, or tornadoes, can struggle to feel safe in environments that used to provide them with a sense of safety. Their school, home, or community can become a place that elicits anxiety. In addition, the uncontrollable nature of natural disasters can undermine a child's ability to trust adults to keep them safe. This is particularly the case if the adults were unable to keep the child (or themselves) safe at the time of the crisis or when navigating the aftershock. In these crisis situations, though, it is not only children who are affected. The whole family unit may lose their most intimate belongings—their pictures, their trophies, and other prized possessions that they often feel define them. They may lose their homes, their jobs, and their ability to support themselves. When people lose everything, they begin to question what their life represents.

In addition, the aftereffects of natural disasters can persist long after the event itself has passed. It may take years for people to rebuild their houses following a flood, earthquake, or tornado, and families may need to relocate to a different town altogether. The stress caused by this traumatic experience can put the body into a state of fight-or-flight, causing a flood of stress hormones to be released into the body.

Although this stress response is useful in mobilizing the body to deal with acutely stressful situations—such as surviving the initial disaster itself—prolonged elevations in cortisol and adrenaline negatively impact our body (Harris, 2018). In particular, it can result in cardiac and pulmonary disorders or hypertension. In children, this can be especially impactful because the continued release of stress hormones places a burden on the bodily organs, leading them to eventually tire from overuse. In turn, children who continue to have ongoing stress reactions for years following a trauma can reach adulthood with compromised physical health. Without the coping skills necessary to calm the stress response system, the prognosis is poor.

During these types of crisis situations, adults can help children cope by creating an atmosphere of felt safety even when there is none. Even in unsafe environments, children can feel safe if adults are in control and are emotionally consistent in their responses. When adults take care of children and meet their needs, it facilitates an environment of felt safety where the child can emotionally co-regulate with the trusted adult. However, this can be challenging when a family has experienced the collective trauma of a natural disaster. Not only is the child experiencing a trauma in this case, but so is the parent. Even parents who do not have a trauma history and who are functioning from a place of safety may experience difficulties in helping their child find healing. Parents have their own feelings about having lost their home and possessions, and they may be feeling overwhelmed themselves.

In these cases, it is acceptable for parents to express their emotions about the event—as it can normalize for the child that it is okay to feel bigger feelings—but it is important that the child does not take care of the parent emotionally. The parent and child can support each other as they share their emotions, which can strengthen their bond through their shared adversity, but parents need to lead the way. **Children cannot emotionally regulate their parents.** Parents need to emotionally regulate their children. To do so, parents may need to find supports and self-care outside of the family so they can provide felt safety to their child.

For example, a parent can ask a trusted friend or family member to watch the child for an hour or two, giving the parent the space to grieve and process their own feelings. Although this may be difficult for children who are expressing anxiety by clinging to the parent, if the friend or family member is someone the child knows and trusts, this can help the child separate even for a short time. It is necessary for parents to take this time for themselves and to have an outlet for their own feelings so they can help their child cope with theirs. Adults need to take care of themselves first before they can take care of their child.

Support and self-care are particularly important for adults who have an unresolved trauma history because the additional strain of the natural disaster may compound their feelings of being out of control. If these feelings become too overwhelming, they may experience dissociation or become frozen with fear or shock. In fact, the experience of losing everything can be destabilizing enough to result in a severe mental health crisis. Parents can lose the ability to effectively parent their child, resulting in an experience of dysregulation for parent and child alike. In these cases, it is necessary for the parent to process both traumas collectively. Trauma, regardless of the type, results in a loss of felt safety and security while also increasing feelings of sadness and fear. Therefore, we want to work with clients to restore that foundation of safety and to manage distressing feelings, as opposed to focusing on the actual facts of each trauma, so they can find stability again.

When working with families who have experienced the collective trauma of a natural disaster, it is best to involve the whole family in the healing process because they have all experienced the same event. When they heal together, this can create stronger family bonds and a healthier family. Just as children need to feel safe and secure with their parent, parents need to feel like they can keep their child safe. However, the trauma of a natural disaster can impair an adult's ability to provide that sense of felt safety as they struggle to manage their own feelings about the event. Therefore, use this as an opportunity to teach the whole family emotion regulation skills. The emotion regulation interventions presented in chapter 4 would be helpful in this situation. When family members are learning together and supporting one another, this strengthens the bonds of cohesion and allows parents to provide the safety and security their child needs to recover.

In addition, if the family has lost their home or other treasured possessions, then it can be useful to focus on what does remain: the memories they carry with them, the relationships they have with their loved ones, and the unique strengths that each person brings to the table. Identifying the strengths that each family member possesses and underscoring how these strengths can add to the family as a whole can bring hope for rebuilding and encourage individuals to move forward in re-creating their life. For example, a parent who possess strong nurturing traits can take the lead when it comes to caretaking (e.g., cooking for the family, keeping children busy with activities), while a parent who possesses excellent organizational skills can use those traits to help the family rebuild by organizing disaster supplies, applying for disaster assistance, and taking the lead in replacing lost or destroyed documents.

The following section provides several interventions to help families find healing and safety following the trauma of a natural disaster. These interventions are intended to decrease clients' feelings of lost safety and security while increasing their ability to cope with overwhelming feelings of sadness and fear. Specific family-based interventions are also included to assist the family in finding stronger bonds through collective healing.

INTERVENTIONS FOR HEALING

When a natural disaster occurs, the body often remembers sensory aspects of the event, which can cause clients to become triggered when they hear, see, taste, smell, or touch something that reminds them of the trauma. Give children and adults the **It Didn't Feel Safe** worksheet to identify sensory aspects of the natural disaster that were most frightening. Increasing awareness of these sensory experiences can help clients identify why a sight or sound might have such an impact on them.

Once clients have identified their triggers, we want to teach them coping skills they can use to navigate these triggers. Mindfulness is one such tool, which can help clients stay grounded in the present moment instead of allowing themselves to become engulfed by trauma memories. When clients practice mindfulness, they take a nonjudgmental attitude toward any thoughts, feelings, or sensations that may arise—just observing them as they come without getting stuck in them or trying to fight them. The following are several interventions that promote mindfulness:

The **Introduction to Mindfulness** activity explains what mindfulness is and provides some sensory-based mindfulness exercises that clients can practice. When introducing this activity, make sure to have a variety of sensory objects on hand that engage each of the five senses. This can include a fabric box made with felt, cotton, and burlap; a variety of sweet and spicy candies; a diffuser with several different scented oils; and a sound machine that plays various nature sounds. Try to have two or three objects for each sense, and then work through the prompts on the activity sheet.

Next, the **My Safe Place** exercise is a guided meditation that offers clients a safe place they can visit in their mind whenever they are feeling overwhelmed by emotion. It walks clients through three environments—a beach, a forest, and a garden—that they can explore using their senses. You can provide each meditation one at a time in separate sessions. If clients report anxiety in any of the prompts, use the prompts in reverse order to bring them back to the present moment.

In order to prevent clients from getting stuck in negative thoughts, you can also use the **Stay Here** exercise, which helps clients let go of any uninvited thoughts or feelings that may cause them to reexperience the traumatic event. This activity reminds clients to stay here—in the moment—whenever they find themselves getting triggered. The words "stay here" keep clients grounded to the present moment instead of allowing their mind to wander with whatever comes into awareness.

The **Mindful Movement** exercise promotes mind-body awareness as clients focus on how it feels to move their body. While clients complete this activity, check in to see what they notice in their body as they move. Do they feel comfortable or uncomfortable? Tense or relaxed? As they focus on the experience of their body moving, encourage them to free their mind of distractions and to focus their attention on how they feel physically. This can be particularly healing for clients who have experienced an injury related to the natural disaster. Since the body remembers trauma, the client's muscles, bones, and nerves can be reactive, causing them pain and discomfort. Through mindful movement, clients can access the parts of their body that are holding the trauma and begin to release the tension and trauma being held there.

Natural disasters cause extreme devastation to communities, leaving behind buildings and homes that have been damaged or destroyed altogether. When clients have experienced a fire, tornado, hurricane, earthquake, or flood that has destroyed their home, they can struggle to find feelings of safety at home again. The damage serves as a reminder of having survived that disaster and of no longer feeling secure. Even if the family is able to rebuild their home or to relocate to a completely new home, it does not mean that the family will feel safe in that home. That's because the people, places, and things involved in trauma often become associated with the experience of pain. Even a new home is representative of the place where trauma occurred, which can trigger clients to feel unsafe. Use the **A Safe Home** worksheet to help children, adults, or families think about what would help them feel safe and secure in a home again.

For clients whose home was the location of the trauma, you can also use the **Our House** activity to help them process the fear and sadness they experienced about losing their house. This art-based activity follows three prompts that ask clients to illustrate (1) their family home as it used to be, (2) their family home after it was destroyed, and (3) their new (or restored) family home. As clients complete the activity, take time to process their experience after each prompt. For example, the first prompt may elicit happy memories but may also trigger feelings of grief and loss over what is no longer. As you progress through the prompts, process how this client or family will recover. How will they rebuild? What will this look like? Are there new memories to be made? Will more fun be had again in a new house? And what will that experience be like for them?

When a family has collectively experienced the trauma of a natural disaster, you can promote recovery and increase connection and trust by involving the entire family in the healing process. To do so, use the **I Am Strong** worksheet to help each family member identify their respective strengths and then apply those strengths to the journey of recovery. After each person shares the skills and characteristics they can draw on to assist the family in rebuilding and recreating a new life, ask other family members to go around and make observations about what the person has shared. Listen to the family's discussion, and call attention to the strengths shared between family members, or point out how one person's strengths complement those of another family member.

You can also focus on strengths through the **We Are Family** activity, which is an art-based intervention that families can complete together to prompt unity and recovery. In this activity, family members are asked to create a piece of art that illustrates how they will use their respective strengths to overcome their current challenges. This intervention should reflect a collaborative drawing where each family member adds something to the picture. After the family finishes the activity, encourage them to hang the completed work of art in their home so they can look at it daily as a reminder of their courage and teamwork.

Natural disasters can take away our sense of control, even after the event has long since passed. In order for clients to heal, they must recognize what they could not control about the situation and what they can control now about their recovery. For example, they were powerless to stop the hurricane itself, but they can create an evacuation plan to use the next time a hurricane is forecast. Coming to this realization can help them gain a greater sense of control over themselves and their ability to cope. It empowers clients to recognize what they do have power over, which decreases feelings of hopelessness and helplessness that may have resulted from the natural disaster. Use the **Controlling the Uncontrollable** worksheet with children or adults to help them find a balance between coping with what they cannot control and acting on what they can control.

When a person feels helpless in a situation, it can cause them to ask, "Who is in control, and why is this happening?" For some people, this can be a moment of spiritual crisis that causes them to question their beliefs in a higher power. Even for clients who do not believe in a higher power, the magnitude of a natural disaster can prompt them to question the meaning of existence. Use the **A Spiritual Crisis** worksheet to process these concepts with clients. Seek to understand their spiritual beliefs before the crisis, how the crisis has impacted those beliefs, and whether their beliefs have changed as a result of the crisis. This is the client's journey, and our role is to simply walk beside them as we provide support, normalize their experience, and provide acceptance as they question their beliefs.

Feelings of fear and anxiety are normal after a natural disaster, and normalizing these reactions can encourage clients to talk about their feelings instead of feeling shame for their ongoing fear. Use the **Anger and Grief Together** worksheet to create a safe space where both adult and child clients can explore their emotions, specifically those related to anger and grief. Clients can keep the exercise to themselves or share their answers with the clinician. If they decide to share, ask clarifying questions and provide support and validation for the emotions they have revealed. Encourage the client to share the narrative with others who may understand.

Once you have helped clients explore their feelings surrounding the trauma, you can teach them what they can do when they feel fear and anxiety approaching. Both the **Taking Care of Me** and **Overcoming Fear and Anxiety** handouts provide several interventions for the brain and body that both adult and child clients can use to take care of their emotions. Clients can choose any of these interventions when they feel like adrenaline and cortisol are causing their brain to become clouded and their body to escalate into distress. Encourage clients to practice each intervention and to find the ones that best fit them.

Another concept that survivors of natural disasters often struggle with is survivor guilt. They don't understand why they survived and why someone else did not, and it feels overwhelming that they were helpless to have stopped the crisis that took the lives of others. This can cause distress and confusion as they try to determine why they survived and what their purpose is now. In addition, clients with survivor guilt often experience emotional highs and lows: oscillating between feeling relief that they survived and then feeling grief and sadness for families who did not. These complex emotions can cause emotional flooding or even numbness. Use the **Dealing with Survivor Guilt** worksheet for adults or children who are struggling to understand why they are still here following a natural disaster. We want to restore their ability to believe that they can make a difference and that they can help. Find ways for them to give back and to thank first responders. Help them brainstorm what they can do to help others impacted by the crisis. Be creative, and encourage them to reach out of their pain to help another.

When a family has been through a natural disaster, a parent's ability to help their child feel safe is the greatest predictor of that child overcoming that trauma. That is because an attachment-based relationship provides the foundation for healing trauma. However, in order for parents to be emotionally and physically able to help their child heal, they need to take care of themselves first. This self-care can involve talking to other families who are facing similar challenges of rebuilding, taking a walk outside to have a break from the congestion of the shelter setting, or practicing deep breathing techniques when they are becoming overwhelmed. Give parents the **Parent Self-Care** handout to point them in the direction of self-care. In taking care of themselves, they will also be taking care of their child.

Parents also need to know how to emotionally regulate themselves so they can model emotion regulation for their child. To help parents with this goal, use the worksheets in the emotion regulation section of chapter 4, as well as the **Modeling Emotion Regulation** handout provided here. Although children may not be in a safe environment following a natural disaster, parents can provide children with the sense of felt safety by making sure they themselves are emotionally regulated.

Finally, families who have survived a natural disaster can struggle to return to a stable level of functioning. However, stability and security are necessary components of trauma recovery. Use the **Tips for Living in Survival Mode** handout to help survivors of natural disasters find ways to achieve that stability on a day-to-day basis, even in unstable circumstances, so they can begin healing. Most important is working with clients to implement a predictable routine as quickly as possible, even if it is a new routine. For example, parents can reinstate some simple family rituals, such as eating dinner together and having a storytelling bedtime routine. Even if a family has lost their home and is staying in a shelter, the presence of these rituals can restore stability for the child.

It Didn't Feel Safe

When a natural disaster happens—like a flood, earthquake, tornado, or fire—it can take away our feelings of safety and security. It can cause us to have fears that we didn't have before. These fears are often stored in our five senses, which record the trauma into our brain. Think about how your senses recorded the trauma and whether those things still impact you today.

1. What do you remember hearing during the event? Do those sounds still cause a fear response for you? If so, in what ways?

   _____

   _____

   _____

2. What do you remember seeing? Do those sights still cause a fear response for you? If so, in what ways?

   _____

   _____

   _____

3. What do you remember smelling during the event? Do those smells still cause a fear response for you? If so, in what ways?

   _____

   _____

   _____

4. What do you remember feeling or touching during the event? Do those textures still cause a fear response for you? If so, in what ways?

_____

_____

_____

5. What do you remember tasting during the event? Do those tastes still cause a fear response for you? If so, in what ways?

_____

_____

_____

6. What things still feel unsafe to you?

_____

_____

_____

7. Do you have any fears related to another natural disaster? If so, what are they?

_____

_____

_____

Introduction to Mindfulness

If you have survived a natural disaster or other crisis, it is common to experience flashbacks that make it seem like you're reliving the event all over again. These symptoms can make you feel like you're in danger even when your current environment is safe. To help your brain recognize your current experience of safety, you can use mindfulness. Mindfulness involves staying in the "here and now" and focusing your attention on your experience of the present moment. You do not judge the experience, meaning that you don't criticize the way you are feeling or thinking, nor do you judge what is around you.

To introduce you to the practice of mindfulness, your therapist will provide you with some objects that tap into your five senses. Follow the prompts as you explore each object, and talk about what you are experiencing, being fully present in the moment.

- **Touch:** Hold an item with both your hands, turning it over and feeling its soft, rough, smooth, or hard texture. Describe what's in your hands, focusing on the way it feels. Move on to the next item until you have held each one and experienced it. Are there any objects you enjoyed touching more than others? Those may be particularly soothing to you and may help you feel calmer in times of stress. Wearing clothes made of those fabrics may even give you a way to touch that texture when you need to calm. If there were any textures that made you feel uncomfortable, just acknowledge that discomfort, and be aware of it when you come into contact with that texture in daily life.

- **Smell:** Close your eyes, and inhale each scent one at a time. Give yourself a few minutes to focus on each scent and to describe the experience. What does it smell like? Is the scent subtle or strong? Does the scent make you feel more relaxed, or does it energize you? If the scent triggers any positive or negative memories, nonjudgmentally allow yourself to sit with that memory for a moment—not fighting against it or getting stuck in it—and then allow it to drift away. Keep working through the different scents in the same way.

- **Hearing:** Take a few minutes to listen to each sound, closing your eyes and allowing yourself to become fully immersed in the experience. What comes to mind as you listen to each sound? Does the sound bring peace or cause tension? Allow yourself to sit with any experiences that arise. After you listen to each sound, take five deep breaths, and feel your body begin to release tension. Drop your shoulders and relax your legs. After you have worked through each sound, move on to the next category.

- **Taste:** Allow your taste buds to experience the flavors of different food items. As you place each item in your mouth, fully experience and savor the flavor, describing what is happening inside your mouth. Is it salty or sweet? Spicy or bland? Is it a bold or subtle flavor? Did it start subdued and grow in intensity? Did it fill your mouth, or are your still searching for its essence? Allow your taste buds to fully participate in the experience, exploring how each item tastes.

- **Sight:** Look at the several pictures or patterns before you. Choose one item at a time, and focus on it for several minutes. Describe what you see. Observe the colors and intersecting lines. See the different shades and the moments when the color changes in the design. If it is a picture of a place, imagine going there in your mind, and explore what it would feel like to step into that scene. Take deep breaths as you walk around the landscape in your mind. How does it feel to be in this place?

As you close this experience, how did it feel to stay in the present moment with only the things before you? Did you enjoy the exercise, or did you feel like it was more of a struggle? Did you have a hard time keeping your mind from wandering? Maybe certain sensory activities were triggering while others helped you feel relaxed and calm. Become aware and intentional about incorporating what you learned about yourself today into your daily routine. Incorporate the things that brought you peace, and be aware of the experiences that may have triggered you.

My Safe Place

This guided meditation offers you three different landscapes that you can visit in your mind to help restore feelings of safety. You can turn this into a quick three-minute practice or extend it to an hour-long practice—however long you need to reground yourself. The more you do this practice, the less time you may need to restore a sense of peace and calm in your body and mind.

Meditation 1: The Beach

Close your eyes and take a few deep breaths, breathing in for a count of four, holding for a count of four, and exhaling for a count of four. Now imagine that you are arriving at a beach. Turn off your sense of touch, smell, taste, and hearing, leaving only your sense of sight activated. Looking through your mind's eye, you can see the ocean and the cresting waves crashing against the sand. Observe where the waves meet the sand, and watch the water wash over the beach. Take in the picture that you see. Notice the colors of the blue sky and the shades within the blue of the water. Find the horizon, where the sky meets the sea, and gaze there for a minute, looking out as far as you can see.

Now turn on your sense of hearing. Listen to the sounds of the beach. What do you hear first? The sound of the waves crashing onto the shore? The calls of the seagulls as they fly overhead? Take several deep breaths as you listen to the sounds of the ocean, allowing yourself to be engulfed by the sounds. Breathe in through your nose and out through your mouth.

Now turn on your sense of smell. Taking a deep breath, smell the salt in the air. As you continue to breathe deeply, allow your body to fill with this air, letting it warm your body from your toes to your nose. Open your mouth as you turn on the sense of taste. Can you taste the salt in the air? Again, fill yourself with this cleansing breath.

As you take steps toward the water, turn on your sense of touch, and feel the sand beneath your feet. Feel the granules of sand working their way between your toes. Is the sand coarse or soft? Is it hot or cool? As you walk toward the water, begin to feel the wet and compact sand beneath you. How does it differ from the dry sand? As you approach the ocean, feel the cool water touch your toes, sending a chill through your body, even on a warm day. Feel the warm breeze on your face. Stay here as long as you'd like, as long as it is comfortable, and as long as it feels safe. When you are ready to return, you can walk back away from the beach and into your life, which is waiting for you.

Meditation 2: The Forest

Close your eyes, resting your hands in your lap and placing your feet firmly on the floor. Take three deep breaths, breathing in through your nose and out through your mouth, feeling your chest rise and fall with each breath. When you are feeling more relaxed, imagine yourself at the edge of a forest. Walk toward the trees, taking in their beauty and watching them reach high overhead. See the various shades of greens and browns that decorate the trees. Observe the green grass and underbrush at the foot of the trees.

As you enter the forest, you find a path, a trampled way through the woods traveled by those who have come before you. It will be traveled by those who follow you as well. As you walk the path, feel the grass crushing beneath your feet. Feel the leaves and branches brush your arms and legs as you walk deeper into the forest. Notice the sun does not shine as brightly, for the canopy overhead is shielding you from its warmth and rays. Feel the cool breeze that rustles the leaves. Hear the sounds of the woodland. The birds chirping, the bugs buzzing, and the small animals scampering. Hear the noise of something rustling the leaves on a bush nearby. Allow your gaze to follow the rustling leaves.

Take a deep breath as you continue walking along the path. Smell the pine and dirt and floral scents, breathing them in and filling yourself with them. You become a part of the woods as you fill yourself with its breath. Feel your shoulders relax and your eyes soften as you feel safe on the path through the woods, enveloped, protected and serene. Stay here as long as you need to, as long as you feel safe, as long as you feel protected. Then walk back out of the woods to where your present world awaits you.

Meditation 3: The Garden

Close your eyes and take several deep breaths, breathing in through your nose and out through your mouth. With each breath, imagine your world moving further behind you as you leave it for these few minutes. Clear your mind of all worries, moving them aside and making room for peaceful thoughts. Before you, you see a wall, so high and wide that you cannot see around it. Walk along the wall and imagine reaching out to touch it, feeling its firmness and strength. You come upon a wooden gate and unhook the latch, pushing it open and revealing a colorful and cared-for garden. Walking through the opening, you are surrounded by fragrance and beauty.

Slowly walk around the garden, on the path created just for you. See the vibrant red roses, the deep yellow tulips, and the bright purple lavender blossoms. Bend over to smell them, inhaling their calming scent. Look ahead and see a swing, hanging in a large oak tree. Sit down on the wooden seat and begin to rock back and forth, moving higher and higher, reaching toward the sky. Stretch your legs out in front of you and see them touch the sky. From up high, look down on the maze of paths and colors beneath you. Feel free as you watch a bird rise up to join you on your flight. Coast for several minutes before feeling the swing slow.

Allow the swing to stop and climb off, continuing down the path. Reach out and touch the delicate flowers, feeling the fragile petals and gently caressing them. See a metal bench before you and take a seat. Inhale deeply several times, filling your body with the scent of the flowers and lavender. Sit here for as long as you would like, as long as you feel safe and at peace. The entrance to the garden is just behind you, and when you are ready, you can leave through it, re-entering your life, which is waiting for you. Remember that you can always return to this place when you need to find safety, peace, or serenity.

Exercise (Adult or Child)

Stay Here

When you have been through a traumatic event, such as a natural disaster, your mind can wander off and take you back in time, making it feel like you are experiencing the event all over again. When this happens, you feel unsafe and your body experiences a fear response, even though there is no danger in your current environment. To remind your brain that you are safe right now, it can help to repeat the phrase "stay here," which refocuses your mind in the present moment instead of allowing it to travel back in time. You can say the words out loud or in your head.

To practice, lay on a mat on the floor or on a couch. Close your eyes and focus on the present moment. Listen to the sounds you hear in the room. As you inhale, focus on the smells you experience. Feel the floor or the couch beneath you. Try to remain present. Each time your mind begins to wander, repeat the phrase "stay here," either aloud or in your head. When you are feeling comfortable, seeing that your mind does respond to your prompts, allow your mind to wander intentionally. Nonjudgmentally observe any thoughts, feelings, or sensations that arise, allowing them to come and go. After a few moments, say "stay here" to bring yourself back to the present.

Once you have returned to the here and now, check back in with what you hear, feel, and smell, allowing your mind to open and experiencing the thoughts, feelings, and sensations that come to you. You can focus on thoughts for a few minutes, bring yourself back, and then focus on sensations or feelings. Repeat this cycle several times, always bringing yourself back to present-moment awareness with the prompt "stay here."

Make sure to practice this exercise in times of calm, recalling your mind back to the present moment, so you can more easily do it in times of stress. You are training your mind to follow your direction, which will allow you to control where your focus goes. Whenever you feel your mind wandering back to the trauma, you know how to bring yourself back to the present moment, where you are safe.

Mindful Movement

You can practice mindfulness as you walk or even do yoga, which improves the mind-body connection. By focusing on the way it feels to move your body and nonjudgmentally accepting the sensations that arise, you can find healing. A nonjudgmental attitude means that if you move a certain way and experience pain—perhaps it hurts, pulls, or feels uncomfortable—you treat that part of your body with self-compassion. You accept that part of yourself and even thank it for taking the pain and the hard work of healing. Think about holding this compassionate stance as you practice this walking mindfulness exercise.

Step outside and begin walking at a comfortable pace. Take several deep breaths, feeling your lungs expand and fill with air, then deflate as you exhale. Breathe in through your nose and out through your mouth. Bring into awareness how your body feels as you move it. Beginning at the bottom and working your way up, take inventory of each part. Feel the ground beneath your feet as you take each step. Notice how your feet feel as they ground you to the earth beneath you. Moving up into your calves, focus on how they feel in this moment. Feel the stretch as you take each step, just becoming aware of this sensation.

Moving up your body, feel your thighs as they tighten and relax with each step you take. Notice any tension or stress that your legs and feet may be holding. With compassion, accept the way they feel, and keep moving up into your trunk. Focus on your back and how it is holding your body up. Your core is responsible for moving your legs and making it possible for your body to move. Feel the movement in your back and chest as you walk. Notice how your stomach feels. Is it comfortable or uncomfortable? Now think about your breathing. Is it shallow, heavy, or even? Can you feel or hear your heartbeat in your ears or chest? With compassion, accept the way they feel, and keep moving up into your arms.

Now turn your attention to your hands. Are they loose and relaxed, or tightened into fists? Are your forearms quickly swinging by your sides, or moving more slowly? How does that feel? As you continue to take deep breaths while walking, shift your awareness to the muscles in your upper arms. Are they relaxed or tight? Moving up further, focus on your shoulders and neck. Are your shoulders hunched up around your ears or pushed down? Is there any pain in your upper body? Do you feel any tension or tightness? Remember to view any sensations you experience with acceptance and compassion.

Release any negative feelings you have about any parts of your body, and become more aware of how those parts allow you to function throughout the day. Continue taking deep breaths as you walk on. How do you feel? How are you viewing your body right now? How connected are you to your body in this moment? Are you more self-aware? You can practice this mindfulness exercise anytime you need to strengthen your mind-body connection.

A Safe Home

When something happens to your home (or in your home) that makes it feel unsafe, it can be a challenge to find feelings of safety in a home again. For example, if your home was destroyed by a fire or a tornado, you may still feel uneasy in your new home because of the fear that something similar will happen again. This fear is not based in imagination but is a result of a real-life experience that actually happened to you, so it's completely valid to feel this way. Use this worksheet to think about what would help your home feel safe again.

1. What about your home no longer feels safe? What is your biggest fear about it?

   _____

   _____

   _____

2. What would a safe home look like? You can describe that here or use the space on the back of this paper to make a drawing.

   _____

   _____

   _____

3. What part of this home would keep your family safe (e.g., smoke detectors to alert you to a fire or a basement to protect you from a tornado)?

   _____

   _____

   _____

4. What routines or rules could make this home feel safer (e.g., practicing a family evacuation plan or checking the smoke detectors every Saturday)?

   _____

   _____

   _____

Our House

For many people, their home is their castle, refuge, and safe place. If something happened to your home, those feelings of safety and security were taken from you. Maybe your home is no longer standing, or if it is, it doesn't look the same. It is normal to feel sadness and even anger about that. You lost something that was important. Yet you will have a home again. Maybe you will rebuild the one you lost, or maybe you will move to a different house. Follow the prompts below to express your feelings about the home you lost. For this activity, you will need poster board (or paper), pencils, markers, paint, and paint brushes.

Prompt one: Using a piece of paper or poster board and a pencil, draw a picture of the house you lost. Draw it the way you remember it. Think about the way it looked and the things you liked about it. Talk about the memories you had there. Thank this house for being there for you, for keeping you safe and protected. Thank the house for the memories it provided, and talk about your feelings for the house.

Prompt two: Now using markers, draw over the pencil drawing to show what happened to your house. How was it destroyed? What happened to it? Talk about your experiences of that day and how it impacted you to lose your home. Talk to the house about what happened that day, telling the house what you remember and expressing how sorry you are that it is gone. Take time to express and take care of your feelings. Know that it is normal for you to be feeling everything that you are right now.

Prompt three: Now use paint to cover the destroyed home and to design the new home you will move to. Will you rebuild the old house or create a new one? What will it look like? What type of memories will you make there? What meaning does it have for you that this is a fresh start? What will make this new house a home? How will it keep you safe and protected? Talk to the house, welcoming it to the family and thanking it for holding your future.

I Am Strong

You are stronger than you may realize. When you are faced with the challenge of overcoming a trauma, it can sometimes feel like you lack the skills, personality, or characteristics to successfully recover. However, you had already developed several valuable skills, personality traits, and characteristics long before you faced this crisis. You have conquered hard things before, and while this may be the largest thing you have faced, you hold the strengths within you that will allow you to be a survivor now. Look at the list of traits and characteristics below, and circle the ones that apply to you.

Hardworking	Determined	Perseverant	Resourceful	Strong
Creative	Resilient	Physically fit	Communicative	Wise
Punctual	Thorough	Appreciative	Friendly	
Responsible	Reliable	Thoughtful	Humble	
Kind	Faithful	Sensitive	Articulate	

Now look at the words you circled, and describe how each one will help you to overcome your current challenges.

Example:

Perseverant (adults): I can use this skill to help me call insurance companies, reach out to disaster-relief organizations, and contact family and friends as I search for a place to stay.

Helpful (kids): I can use this skill by listening to my parents and packing up my toys to move to a new, safe house.

_____

_____

_____

_____

_____

_____

We Are Family

If you have recently survived a natural disaster, like a fire, flood, or tornado, your family may be going through a hard time right now. It may seem like you are facing large obstacles, and it can be hard to imagine how you'll overcome them. However, you have gotten through hard things before by drawing on your strengths as a family. Focus for a few minutes on what obstacles you have previously faced together, and describe how you overcame those obstacles.

Past obstacle:

_____

_____

_____

How we overcame it:

_____

_____

_____

Now think about your current obstacles. Maybe it is rebuilding a home or your community. Perhaps it is recovering from injuries. It may also involve overcoming the fear and anxiety you experienced as a result of the natural disaster. Together as a family, follow the steps here to create a collaborative drawing of the obstacles you are facing and the strengths you will use to overcome them. To complete this activity, you will need paper, pencils, and markers.

1. Take a large piece of paper, and on the right side, draw the challenges or obstacles you are facing as a family. Start with one family member, and ask that person to draw one particular challenge or obstacle. Then pass the page to another family member and have them incorporate an additional challenge into the drawing. As each family member adds to the picture, pause to talk about how that challenge has impacted each person. Keep passing the page until no one has any more challenges to add.

2. Then on the left side of the page, draw the strengths that each person brings to this battle. Pass the page around again, allowing each family member to add their own strengths to the picture. Pause to discuss how that person's strengths can be useful in overcoming the current struggles or how they complement other family members' strengths. Continue passing the page around and adding strengths until no one can think of more strengths to add.

3. Now place the completed drawing somewhere in the house where the family will see it every day, such as the kitchen or living room. Remember that you, as a family, are fighting this challenge, not one another. You are using your collective strengths to conquer the struggle, and you are stronger together than on your own.

Controlling the Uncontrollable

When an unexpected event like a natural disaster has occurred, there are many things about the situation you could not control. For example, if you survived a tornado, you could not control that it destroyed your home or that it caused injury or death to your loved ones. This can make you feel overwhelmed, afraid, and anxious about not being in control of anything in your life. However, the reality is that you do have power over some things in life, such as your recovery, your ability to cope, your future, your work, and your emotional responses. You can learn how to control and calm your emotions when they begin to overwhelm you. Use this circle to identify what about your situation you cannot (or could not) control, as well as what you can control moving forward. By learning to cope with the things you can't control and directing your attention to that which you can control, you can start to make changes that will improve your life.

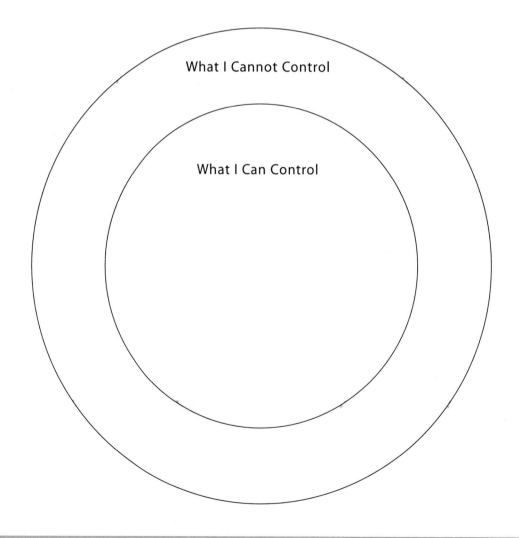

A Spiritual Crisis

When a natural disaster occurs, it can cause you to ask, "Who is in control, and why is this happening?" That is a normal question to ask when you have gone through a situation such as this. Some people take comfort and find strength in a higher power at times like this, while others become angry because they don't understand the reasons for the crisis taking place. Take a few minutes to consider the questions here, and then brainstorm who can support you in finding answers to your questions.

1. What were your spiritual or religious beliefs before this crisis? If you believed in a higher power, what aspects of life did they have power over?

   _____

   _____

   _____

2. If they are in control, how are you reconciling this crisis with that belief?

   _____

   _____

   _____

3. Have any of your beliefs changed? In what ways? How does this impact you, and what does it mean for your spiritual walk?

   _____

   _____

   _____

4. Who can you can talk to about this spiritual crisis? A pastor, priest, rabbi, or religious leader? Is there someone else you know, even if you do not regularly attend services?

   _____

   _____

   _____

Anger and Grief Together

When you have been through a crisis like a natural disaster, it is normal to have large feelings as a result. It can start to feel like your anger is overwhelming you, and you may begin to feel irritated or short tempered, like you are always on edge. You may even start to notice your relationships changing if your friends and family don't know how to handle your anger. But you have good reasons to feel angry because a lot has happened and changed in your life. Take a few minutes to record your angry feelings on the lines below. Think about all the reasons you are feeling angry right now, including all the triggers that make it hard to control your emotions.

_____

_____

_____

_____

_____

Anger is what's known as a secondary emotion, meaning that it often comes *after* another feeling—and that first feeling is almost always sadness. When you are feeling sad about a loss, you are experiencing what is known as grief. Left unchecked, that sadness and grief can grow larger each day until it becomes anger. This is especially true if you are feeling sad and don't know how to take care of yourself or don't have someone to help you take care of your feelings. Take a few more minutes to re-read what you wrote above. Look at each reason you wrote for your anger, and identify what could be causing you to feel sad about each item instead. Write those things here.

_____

_____

_____

_____

_____

Now that you know there are reasons to be sad and mad, it's important to find ways to take care of yourself when you are having these feelings. Look at the **Taking Care of Me** handout for some ideas.

Taking Care of Me

When you have experienced trauma, it is important to practice good self-care. This means taking care of you! It can involve eating healthy, getting exercise, and spending time with friends and family. However, it also means taking care of your feelings. When we have large feelings and don't take care of them, they don't go away—in fact, they usually grow bigger. That's why it is important to take care of your feelings when you first notice them. Below are a few good ways to express your emotions and to take care of them. Not everything works for everyone, which is why there are many ideas from which to choose. Practice a few of the self-care skills listed here, and keep using the ones you find helpful.

- **Write in a journal:** It can be helpful to get those thoughts and feelings outside of you and onto paper where you can see them more clearly and can then work to problem solve or calm them.

- **Draw it out:** Sometimes it's hard to talk about our feelings, but when we draw, we are able to better illustrate what we can't speak about yet.

- **Share the story:** Repeatedly telling the story of the trauma can help it lose its power. Write a narrative of the event, and share it with a trusted friend or family member.

- **Do an arts and crafts project:** Using the creative side of your brain can calm your emotions.

- **Put together a puzzle:** Using the analytical side of your brain can distract you from focusing on your emotions.

- **Get moving:** Take a walk outside or go for a swim. Combining physical activity with a sensory activity can calm your body.

- **Keep a notepad and pen close by:** Write yourself notes, and make lists to keep you organized when your thinking gets clouded by emotions.

- **Use a containment jar or box:** When you feel flooded by emotions, set aside a box or jar where you can keep these feelings. Write these overwhelming emotions or thoughts on slips of paper, and put them in the box or jar. Then once a day, for 20 minutes, allow yourself to open the lid, and take out one of the slips of paper. Use this time to fully experience the emotions you had written down. Give yourself permission to cry and express your feelings. Then put the lid back on the box or jar, and continue with your responsibilities for the day.

Overcoming Fear and Anxiety

It is normal to have fear and anxiety after you have survived a natural disaster or crisis event. That's because when you are feeling anxious, your body releases stress hormones called cortisol and adrenaline. Cortisol can make it hard to focus or concentrate, while adrenaline can make you feel like you need to move your body. It can also cause your heart to beat fast, your lungs to feel tight, and your body to feel hot. When you begin to feel anxious, here are some activities you can try to calm your body. Practice them now so you will know how to use them the next time you feel anxiety rising.

- Count backward from 100

- Spell your name: first, middle, and last

- Sing your favorite song

- Give yourself a bear hug

- Do five jumping jacks, four wall push-ups, three toe touches, two squats, and one yoga pose

- Get a cotton ball and pull it apart, focusing on how it looks and feels

- Chew gum

- Do some stretches for your body (reach your arms over your head, then down to your toes, then twist your body at the waist, moving from side to side)

Dealing with Survivor Guilt

You have survived. Some days you might feel great and full of life. Other days you may feel depressed and uncertain why you survived and others didn't. It doesn't make sense why you are here and someone else is not. It is normal to feel this way after what you have been through. One way you can work through these feelings is to find purpose by giving back to those affected by the disaster. Sometimes finding a way to give back, to help others out of the pain that you experienced, is what brings healing. For example, the National Center for Missing and Exploited Children was founded by parents whose children went missing or were abducted. Those parents felt like they had something to give to other parents. In order to find your own healing, look at the list of ideas here, and check off any ways you'd like to give back to your community.

_____ Donate clothing, food, or other household items.

_____ Support a local organization in your area.

_____ Give blood.

_____ Donate money to disaster-relief organizations, like the American Red Cross.

_____ Color pictures and take them to the hospital to decorate the rooms of other survivors.

_____ Organize a community fundraiser.

_____ Host a food drive.

_____ Find volunteer opportunities in your community.

_____ Sign up for Habitat for Humanity.

_____ Open up your home to survivors in the community who have been displaced.

_____ Other ideas: _____

Parent Self-Care

You have been through an event that has been overwhelming. Your feelings of safety and security have been shaken. And you may be feeling anxious and uncertain about what the future holds and where you go from here. At this time especially, it is important to take care of yourself.

- **Take care of yourself physically.** Make sure you are eating regularly and getting enough protein, fruits, and vegetables to keep your body healthy. Try to exercise, even if it is just walking for 30 minutes a day. When we are in a state of stress, the body releases adrenaline to help us survive. Physical activity helps burn off that excess adrenaline so our anxiety doesn't keep growing. In addition, make sure to get enough sleep. Your mind will be busy all day problem solving and will need rest at night to refresh.

- **Take care of yourself emotionally.** You have big emotions right now—fear, anger, frustration, and sadness—and for good reasons. Use your supports to take care of your emotional health. Turn to family and friends who can listen and offer love. Take the time to cry, but also find reasons to smile and laugh. Use coping skills that have worked for you in the past when you were feeling overwhelmed. Take a walk outside. Drink a cup of tea. Set aside time for prayer, meditation, or yoga. Journal or draw.

- **Take care of your family.** They need you right now. By taking care of yourself, you will be able to take care of them. Your children need you to be their safe place. They need to know that everything is going to be okay. Help them feel safe again by comforting them and helping them find hope. And if you can't find any hope for yourself, then reach out to your supports to help you find the way. You have survived hard things before. This is one more hard thing. Just remember that you are a survivor.

Modeling Emotion Regulation

When your family is living in survival mode and recovering from a crisis situation, it can be hard to parent at the same time. You may feel like you are struggling to take care of yourself and are struggling even more to take care of your children. What your child needs from you right now is safety, stability, and nurturing care. One way to provide all three of these things at once is to model emotion regulation for your child. If you are calm, then your child can be calm too. They are watching and looking to you for guidance in these uncertain times. They will mimic and repeat what they see you doing, so it is important that you show them how to cope. Here are some steps to model emotion regulation for your child at this time:

- Take care of your emotions so your child can find a safe place in you. It is important for you to show your emotions so your child knows it is okay for them to express their emotions too. It is equally important to cope and calm your emotions so your child learns to do the same in turn. It is okay to cry, but you also want to show your child how to calm down by practicing coping skills, like taking deep breaths or going on a walk. Invite your child to practice these coping skills with you so they can learn from you at the same time.

- When your child expresses an emotion, validate what they are feeling, and tell them it is okay for them to feel that way. Let them know that it is normal and that you feel the same way (if you do).

- Children need to feel close and connected to you during this crisis. Make sure you pull them in for hugs, kisses, cuddles, and snuggles (even those teenagers!) because they need to know that you are in this together. Being in close proximity can calm them without your even having to say a word. Allow them to sit with you, sleep by you, or go with you to appointments. They need comfort, and you are the best one to give that to them. This can strengthen your family bonds as your child finds comfort and closeness in you.

- Implement a routine as quickly as possible so your child can feel stable and secure. Having a predictable schedule reduces fear and anxiety because your child knows what to expect next. Although you may be staying with family or living in a shelter or motel, think about what your child's routine was before this crisis, and try to mirror it as much as possible, even though it will be different. Each day you repeat this new schedule, your child will settle into the new routine and begin to feel secure, which will also calm their emotions and remind them that you are taking care of their needs.

Tips for Living in Survival Mode

When you are living in a crisis situation, it can be hard to find any stability or security, yet that is what you need to begin healing. Here are some tips you can use to find that stability, even in unstable circumstances, so you can begin the journey to recovery:

- **Maintain routines or create new ones.** Having a regular schedule that you follow can bring stability to you and your family. You know what to expect and what comes next. This allows your brain to relax instead of continuing in a hyperalert, vigilant state.

- **Know that it is normal to have good and bad days.** You will be on a roller coaster for some time. Practice good self-care and coping skills. Find the things that bring you peace, and incorporate them into your everyday routine. Cope with the bad days, and use the good days to accomplish your goals. Give yourself and your family a large dose of grace.

- **Stay organized by making lists of things you need to get done.** Your thinking may be clouded because you are living in a crisis situation and are focused on surviving. If you make lists, then you can be productive on good days and accomplish the things that need to be done.

- **Limit your exposure to media coverage of the event.** You are living through the crisis event itself, so you do not need to be updated about it. Focus on getting through your day and completing the tasks that you need to get done. Social media can wait. Get your information from credible sources, like government agencies that are coordinating relief efforts or the American Red Cross.

- **Help someone else.** When you offer to provide support to others, it can help you feel connected to your community, and the distraction may be healthy for you. Offer to watch someone's children while they meet with relief workers. Perhaps they will watch your child in the future while you have a meeting. This develops community even in the midst of crisis and allows you to access the strengths of the larger group.

- **Follow a bedtime routine.** This will help you, and your children, sleep better. After dinner, try to slow down and relax. Complete hygiene-related tasks, read a book, tell your child a bedtime story, or have snuggle time. This communicates to your child, and to your own brain, that it is time to sleep. If you find your mind racing with thoughts, do a "brain dump" by writing down everything you are thinking about. This can clear your mind so you can sleep better, and it will give you a list of things you can work on the next day.

8

Witnessing Violence

Davon grew up in an affluent neighborhood with his parents, who were both lawyers. They were dynamic in the courtroom, arguing their cases and often winning. However, they argued at home too. They argued about how to spend their money, who should do chores, and who should put Davon to bed. Their arguments were not only verbal, but they also became physical when Davon's mom would push and shove Davon's father, eventually culminating in physical altercations when the father fought back. Davon reacted by isolating and spending time in his room whenever his parents began to argue.

Eventually, Davon's anxiety about his parents' arguments began to transfer to other adults who raised their voices. At school, his teacher would often raise her voice to get the students' attention, and when she did, Davon would get up from his desk and walk out of the classroom. He would wander the halls, trying to find a quiet place to hide like his bedroom at home. When his teacher and administrator would redirect him to return to the classroom, Davon had a hard time complying because his classroom did not feel like a safe place. He continued to have what they called "behavior problems," which required frequent school conferences with his parents. This gave his mom and dad yet another thing to argue about at home.

In the current state of our world, witnessing violence is something that has been normalized and accepted as inevitable. We are constantly exposed to behaviors that can be classified as violent, whether it's a parent threatening their child in a grocery store or a couple yelling at each other in a crowded restaurant. Poor social skills and relationship modeling abound in many communities. Movies and television place violence in front of us every day, and the internet and social media have exposed us to violence we have never seen before and could not have imagined in the past.

With advances in technology, we can watch violent events on the news as they unfold in real time. We can watch live police chases, guerilla warfare, mass shootings, and acts of terrorism. The internet in particular has made it easy to read about and witness reports of violence, but we have to remember that our minds may not be ready for this level of exposure. Because these videos are posted online, they are always accessible, and people may watch the same video repeatedly or find several other videos that recount the same event. The more that people are exposed to violence, the more desensitized they become to that same violence. The first few times they see a parent berating their child in the grocery store, they may be surprised, appalled, and horrified. But by the time they have witnessed that same event five or six times, they walk by without looking up from their grocery list. They have become desensitized. Violence becomes the norm instead of the exception. This is dangerous because the more desensitized people become to violence, the more normal it becomes, and the more people expect it.

The sections that follow will provide an overview of different types of violence to which individuals are currently exposed on a regular basis—including domestic violence, inner-city violence, mass violence, and the violence associated with certain professions—that can contribute to the experience of trauma. Whether it's a child growing up in conflicted household, a student afraid to attend school because of a recent mass shooting, or a soldier returning home from war, the end result is the same: trauma. After exploring these traumas in detail, you will find several healing interventions to help restore feelings of safety and security.

DOMESTIC VIOLENCE

A home is meant to be a safe haven, a place where people can feel safe, comfortable, and accepted. But individuals who live in a home where there is domestic violence have no refuge. The people who are supposed to protect them and keep them safe are the very people hurting them. As a result, victims of domestic violence constantly live on edge, expecting abuse to occur at any moment and never knowing what they might do or say that triggers their abuser to lash out. This impacts their ability to trust others to care about and help them.

When children witness domestic violence between their parents, not only do they come to view the abuser as an unsafe person, but they also have difficulty trusting the victimized parent. They have witnessed that this parent cannot protect themselves, much less anyone in their care, so they come to recognize this parent as unsafe as well. As children get older, they may even feel the need to protect the victimized parent and may actually intervene in an attempt to protect them from the abuser. When the parent-child role becomes conflated in this manner, it undermines the child's relationships with their parents and impacts their beliefs about relationships moving forward.

Alternatively, children may align with the parent perpetrating the abuse and may become verbally disrespectful or even physically aggressive toward the victimized parent. The child's aggressive behavior may also transfer to other environments, such as the school classroom, and continue to follow them into adulthood. It is essential to recognize that children mimic their parents' behaviors, and if aggression is modeled as an appropriate way to communicate, then they will learn to treat others similarly. In order to change the child's behavior, you must change the family dynamics. If you teach this child new social skills and emotion regulation skills in therapy—but that child goes home every night to a household characterized by continued dysfunction—it will undermine everything you are attempting to do in treatment. Therefore, it is crucial to teach the entire family new ways to interact and express themselves.

A related form of domestic violence that families may be exposed to is that which is perpetrated by a child. For example, a child may be struggling with a mental health disorder—such as bipolar disorder, autism spectrum disorder, or oppositional defiant disorder—or a substance abuse issue, causing them to verbally and physically lash out at their siblings or parents. Everyone has a right to feel safe in their own home, including parents, but in these situations, parents often feel like they do not have control of their home and cannot keep themselves or their other children safe. When another adult is violent, there is the option to leave, but when a child is violent, parents don't have the same option. In these situations, the child needs supervision and support through responsive parenting. Work with parents to put safety plans in place, and talk about what will happen if the child becomes violent. Several of the interventions provided in this chapter can assist you with this treatment goal.

MASS VIOLENCE

With the continued prevalence of gun violence in the United States, mass shootings have become increasingly commonplace in our society. While it may still cause grief and dismay, it no longer shocks people as it used to. When a dozen or more people lose their lives to a mass shooting, people shake their heads. Then they move on to their next task. Those grieving families are forgotten, and several days later, everyone is focused on something new. People have lost the ability to feel shocked by violence.

At the same time, mass violence has increased the experience of vicarious trauma as individuals watch real-time news coverage of these incidents and listen to victims' stories. People come to feel unsafe in environments similar to those where the incident occurred, which can create fear and uncertainty when individuals face the simple act of grocery shopping, going to school, or attending a concert. Vicarious trauma makes people feel scared and unsafe, causing them to alter their plans or to feel uncomfortable in places where they used to be able to relax. People are more hypervigilant and on edge. As a community, people often don't even realize that this is how they are now functioning. It is important to be mindful about the impact of vicarious trauma because, at times, it can be just as powerful as first-hand trauma.

In schools in particular, the fear of mass violence is so prevalent that it has impacted children's ability to feel safe at school. These fears about mass violence in schools are rooted in real-life experiences of having witnessed school shootings on a regular basis. That is because the rates of school shootings have steadily increased over the years, with 180 school shootings occurring in the past decade alone (Walker, 2019). Children can easily access television footage or watch videos of these incidents on their phone, which can elicit anxiety about the possibility of something similar happening to them.

Although schools have implemented efforts to keep children safe—such as active shooter drills where we yell at children to run in a zig-zag pattern or to hide in classroom closets for 30 minutes—these efforts may be unintentionally traumatizing them. While these drills may be necessary, they are scary and a sad commentary of where society is in regard to mass violence. We have to be mindful of the impact of these drills on our children and provide support at those times, as well as help children emotionally regulate after these drills. This can involve creating a "calm-down corner" in the classroom filled with books, stuffed animals, quiet toys, and craft supplies and prompting children to select an activity from this area when the active shooter drill is complete. For example, they can play with kinetic sand, squeeze stress balls, or color in mandalas. These coping activities can emotionally regulate each child and help them return to emotional baseline after a dysregulating drill.

In addition, children's brains are not equipped to process trauma the same way adult brains are, so when an incident of mass violence occurs, it is important for parents and educators to provide children with information that is age appropriate. Rather than allowing them to watch continued video footage of the incident—which can flood children with overwhelming information and create vicarious trauma—it is necessary to have a supportive conversation about the incident. Depending on the age of the child, a supportive conversation might sound like this:

> "Hey buddy. Something sad happened to some people in a school. It isn't a school near here. It is far away. But a lot of people were hurt. I wonder if there is something we can do to help? Maybe we can draw some pictures and make some cards to encourage them. After dinner, we can go to the store and get bottled water that we can drop off with our cards to the local Red Cross location."

Having this type of conversation can reduce hopelessness and anxiety because it provides children with action steps they can take to make a difference. It also moves the child a step further in helping them develop compassion and empathy for the ones who are hurting. They are reaching out with compassion while also meeting other people's needs. In turn, they feel like they are contributing to the healing that needs to begin for those impacted. As a bonus, it also helps adults feel less helpless in response to an event that is vicariously traumatizing to them as well.

INNER-CITY VIOLENCE

In inner-city environments, where crime statistics are high, violence tends to be a daily occurrence and not an occasional event. Individuals may hear gunshots night after night when laying down to sleep. Children may add several blocks to their route when walking home from school in order to avoid dangerous streets. It is not uncommon for their neighbors or family members to have been injured or killed as a result of violence.

When people are exposed to trauma and violence as part of their daily routine, it changes the way they interact with the world. For example, individuals who grow up in these communities are at greater risk to act out with violence in adulthood because this behavior was modeled to them as children. Even those who move out of the inner city continue to experience the effects of being exposed to trauma on a daily basis for years. Similarly, individuals who seek refuge from war-torn nations continue to feel the enduring effects of trauma even after finding safe asylum in a new country. They constantly fear that their life is in danger, which impacts their ability to feel safe in their own home, on their own front porch, when walking to the store, or when playing outside with their children. They feel like they need to protect themselves at all times and operate in survival mode. This constant state of stress places a toll on the body because the continual release of cortisol and adrenaline creates a baseline of hypervigilance and fear.

Children impacted by community-based violence lose their ability to feel that adults can protect them. They live in a state of fight, flight, or freeze, which can manifest in terms of oppositional behaviors, aggression, and elopement. These behaviors are particularly prevalent in inner-city schools, where students have a harder time sitting still and focusing on tasks, but it is important to see these behaviors in the child's context. If the child doesn't feel safe, then this is what we should expect. We should expect behaviors that reflect a manifestation of a child's innate defense mechanisms. Because these children lack a sense of safety, any efforts to educate the child need to take a back seat until this primary need for safety is met. Think of Maslow's hierarchy of needs. Until children feel safe, they will not be able to learn.

In these types of situations, it is critical for adults to help children find a sense of felt safety. We may not be able to change the reality of their situation—they may not live in a safe environment and may have to return to that same environment each evening—but we can help them develop felt safety by being emotionally consistent and nurturing, as well as by meeting the child's needs. Even though their environment may not be safe, we can help them *feel* safe. To do so, we can establish rituals or routines that provide security. For examples, parents can implement a daily schedule when the child comes home from school each day, which may involve eating a snack, doing homework, playing outside, and then eating dinner with the family. Similarly, teachers can create a ritual for welcoming children into the classroom that involves a special handshake or dance. They may also encourage students to take a five-minute break every hour to use coping and calming items in the classroom or at their desk.

In addition, we can help children develop healthy coping skills that promote attachment and felt safety. Instead of falling back on dysfunctional survival skills and oppositional behaviors, we can teach them functional and appropriate skills they can use when they feel afraid. For example, a child who is exposed to community violence on a daily basis may act out at school by trying to exert control over the classroom. That child may need to feel in control in order to feel safe, but we can teach them how to exert healthy control by showing them how to exercise appropriate leadership skills. For example, the teacher can invite that child to be their assistant for an hour each morning. Children need to feel close to adults to feel safe, and instead of seeking that attention negatively, we can help them learn ways to meet that need positively.

When working with youth who have gang involvement, there are some additional considerations to take into account. For many of these children, the gang meets a variety of needs that would otherwise remain unmet. For children who do not feel safe, the gang offers protection. For children who go to bed hungry or don't have clothes that fit, the gang offers access to those basic necessities. For children who have attachment traumas and don't feel like they are accepted or belong, the gang offers a sense of family. At the same time, the gang exposes children to an even higher level of daily trauma, and it removes safety and security from their community. Incarceration often follows, and it is not uncommon for most youth to try to find a way out of the gang within a year of joining (Hill, Lui, & Hawkins, 2001). However, leaving the gang culture proves difficult, and many die in the process of trying.

When working with gang-involved youth, keep in mind that many youth do not develop the motivation to leave until they have been confronted with the reality of what gang involvement is costing them (Decker & Lauritsen, 2002). Some are confronted with losses, including the death of a loved one or time lost to incarceration. Others are presented with new opportunities that may come from entering into a stable relationship, becoming a parent, getting a good job, or being accepted into college—and the fear of losing those opportunities tips them in the balance of gang desistance. Having an honest conversation about the pros and cons can help youth move forward in deciding whether or not to cut ties with the gang.

However, leaving safely is another challenge and can largely depend on a client's position within the gang. Gang members who are higher up in the organization—for example, who know details of how the organization is run—may have a more difficult time walking away because they can become a liability to the gang leadership. These clients will need increased support to walk away safely. For example, they may need to leave the area to attend college or visit out-of-state relatives.

In contrast, some clients may be on the fringe or periphery of the gang. They may serve as lookouts or runners for the gang but don't have a working knowledge of gang business. For these clients, walking away can be easier because they don't pose a threat to those in leadership. However, don't underestimate the danger involved in gang desistance based on the client's level of involvement. Once a client has decided to leave their gang, make sure to understand how the gang is structured and where your client is in that structure before creating a plan of desistance. Interventions in this chapter will help you to discern these important factors. These interventions are applicable for gang-involved youth, as well as clients who have matured into adulthood during their time in the gang.

PROFESSIONS WITH HIGH EXPOSURE TO VIOLENCE

Finally, many individuals are disproportionately exposed to violence as a result of their profession, including law enforcement officers, first responders, military personnel, and emergency room staff. They must navigate the daily occurrence of violence as they save the lives of others or put their own lives at risk in the line of duty. They go to work every day knowing that they are walking into crisis management situations where life and death will be dependent on their ability to make good decisions.

When working with individuals in these helping professions, we must recognize the toll that this takes on their bodies and minds. At a physiological level, the brain's alert system is constantly engaged, causing them to live in a state of fight, flight, or freeze at all times. While some may become desensitized to the repeated violence they witness each day, others will develop post-traumatic stress reactions that impair their ability to function. In fact, the armed forces have one of the highest incidence of PTSD, and until just recently, servicemembers and veterans were struggling to get the treatment they deserved. We must recognize the impact that violence exposure has on these clients and offer the necessary services to promote recovery.

The following section provides a variety of interventions that are useful when working with clients who have witnessed violence and are in the healing process. Many of these worksheets and exercises focus on restoring feelings of safety by helping clients identify what they can control about keeping themselves safe. In addition, certain worksheets are geared toward clients with gang involvement and are intended to help them assess their gang activity and membership and then create a plan of desistance.

INTERVENTIONS FOR HEALING

When working with families who have been exposed to domestic violence, use the **Creating a Safe Home** worksheet to open the door for discussion about what caused each family member to feel afraid and what would help them feel safe. It is important to begin this shared family session by asking that family members respect one another's feelings and preferences. As the family brainstorms how to meet each person's requests, make sure to validate each person's feelings about their experience. If a family member makes an unrealistic request—for example, asking that family members speak to no one outside the family—then process the fear behind this request and see if you can find ways to address the fear itself.

In addition, use the **New Family Rules** worksheet to help parents and children think about what new rules they would like to have as a family. When children have been taught inappropriate social skills through the modeling of violent behavior, we must re-teach these skills by creating new rules that encourage healthy interaction. The topics listed on this worksheet will help guide the family through that process. While the family is completing this activity, make sure to process why the new rule is replacing the old one. Emphasize that the goal of these new family rules is for everyone to feel safe and respected.

When working with families who have experienced violence in the home, you may also encounter situations in which the victimized parent has left the abuser and has taken the children with them, only to find that one (or all) of the children has begun to mimic the abusive partner's behaviors. This becomes a confusing situation of transference in which the parent may begin to displace the anger they feel toward their abusive partner onto the child who is now mimicking those same behaviors. This can be further complicated when the child has physical features of the abusive partner, which intensifies the trigger for the parent. In these situations, use the **My Child is Triggering Me** worksheet to assist parents in learning how to differentiate between their abuser and their child. As parents gain insight about the transference that may be happening, they can more easily self-monitor their reactions to the child.

Similarly, children who are diagnosed with certain mental disorders (e.g., bipolar disorder, autism spectrum disorder) or who have a history of trauma (e.g., as a result of being in foster care) may act out in the home because of difficulties with emotion regulation. This can impact everyone's ability to feel safe if the child is having tantrums and meltdowns that result in thrown objects or physical aggression. To help families in these circumstances, use the **My Sibling Scares Me** and **My Child Scares Me** worksheets, which are geared toward siblings and parents, respectively. The sibling version of the worksheet is intended to provide a forum in which other children in the family can express their fears and sadness in a supportive and validating environment, whereas the parent version also includes a safety planning component. Use these worksheets to help the parent brainstorm how they can help the other children, as well as themselves, feel safe.

When working with individuals who have been impacted by mass violence—including those who have lived through an actual event or who were exposed to it vicariously—it is important to recognize what the experience took from the person. Some people may feel powerless to keep themselves safe, leading them to make changes to their normal routine to reduce the chance of risk. For example, they may no longer feel comfortable going to grocery stores or may avoid large crowds. One way to promote healing is to identify what individuals can do to counteract their feelings of hopelessness and powerlessness. The **A Scary Thing Happened** worksheet asks clients to process through the event and to develop action steps to increase their sense of power and hope. Similarly, the **I Will Overcome** activity has clients identify the strengths that allowed them to survive the incident and that can help them heal moving forward.

In addition, you can restore people's belief that they can keep themselves safe by having them identify what they can control and what they can change. There are aspects of our lives over which we do have control, but trauma often makes us focus on that which we cannot control. When we can shift the client's focus to what they can do, they can regain a sense of stability. Use the **I Can Do Something** worksheet with clients to brainstorm ways they can reach out to help others who have survived the same trauma. There is healing in being able to use their pain to reach someone else. There is also healing in focusing outward to the needs of others instead of remaining focused on their own pain and sadness. All of these worksheets are appropriate to use with both adult and child clients.

The **Controlling My Safe Space** worksheet is useful when working with individuals living in unsafe environments, such as the inner city. It asks them to think about their current environment and to brainstorm how they can realistically keep themselves safe. For many individuals who reside in the inner city, high crime and violence are a reality of everyday life. These individuals may not be able to change the circumstances of their environment, but they can make certain changes to their routine and support system that increase actual and felt safety. For example, they can take a different route home from school or can check in daily with neighbors, helping each other and building community. Use the worksheet to help clients identify what they can and cannot control about their home and neighborhood safety, and then develop a plan for implementing a safe space and increasing feelings of safety.

In addition, when children grow up in inner-city neighborhoods, where they are exposed to violence on a daily basis, we can expect certain behaviors to occur in the school environment. We can expect children who do not feel safe and who are living in survival mode. We can expect children who exhibit high energy as their adrenaline remains elevated all day long. We can expect children who constantly express their fear with fight, flight, and freeze behaviors. We can expect children who do not trust adults as safe people and who do not follow directions or complete schoolwork. When adults can understand this and can see children in the context of their trauma, it becomes easier to work with children around these challenging behaviors and to educate them.

Share the **Safe Space in Schools** handout with educators working in neighborhoods characterized by a high incidence of violence to increase their ability to educate traumatized children. You can also share this handout with parents so they can advocate more effectively for their child's needs within the school building. Following this handout is a series of companion handouts that provide educators with the steps needed to (1) teach children self-regulation and social skills and (2) manage some of the more common, trauma-based behaviors that can appear in the classroom. These companion handouts, which are described in greater detail here, can be given to educators in a packet format.

The first companion handout, **Emotion Regulation in Schools**, is a resource for school professionals to teach emotion regulation skills to children. When teaching these skills, there will be some children who actively throw tantrums and melt down, which can create an unsafe feeling for everyone in the classroom. The **Tantrum Tamer** handout focuses on quickly de-escalating these behaviors by remembering that, in that moment, the child does not have control over their emotions and cannot access their thinking brain. The next handout, **Self-Regulation in Schools**, helps teachers instruct children in managing their body's energy. This will benefit children who are experiencing anxiety, related to trauma or otherwise, who have adrenaline surging in their body. Finally, the **Social Skills in Schools** handout provides educators with tools to manage inappropriate social behavior, such as bullying, within the school environment.

There are pros and cons to gang membership, as there are to any other situation or family. Therefore, when working with a gang member to weigh the costs and benefits of staying in a gang, be aware to not be disrespectful of the gang. Gang members are fiercely loyal, and there are strict codes of conduct for gang members. You can create a safe space where the client can talk about the possibility of desistance by approaching the topic with a curious attitude that conveys support and genuine helpfulness. By being nonjudgmental and exhibiting positive regard, clinicians can better help clients explore this topic. Use the **Gang Pros and Cons** worksheet to help clients talk about the possibility of desistance and make some serious decisions. Please understand that if they decide to leave the gang, that may be a life-and-death decision, and they will need an immense amount of support.

Once a gang member has decided that they want to leave their gang, you need to create a plan of desistance. Clients who are loosely affiliated with the gang may be able to walk away with minimal effort by decreasing the amount of time they spend with the gang, while those who are more involved may need to strategically put space between themselves and the gang. Use the **Assessing My Role in Gang Membership** worksheet to determine how involved clients are and how detailed their plan of desistance needs to be. Emphasize that your client needs to be honest with you about their involvement in order to help them. It will take time to build the amount of rapport that is needed for clients to trust you with this information. Be patient and continue to provide a safe, confidential space for them to talk about their activities and feelings about the gang.

After you have assessed your client's level of gang involvement, the next series of **Creating a Plan of Desistance** handouts can guide you in developing an appropriate desistance plan. Given that each situation is different, use caution when helping your client leave a gang organization. These handouts are merely intended to provide you with guidance. One of the largest factors in successful desistance is the support that is available to the client after desistance. The gang has been meeting needs for this individual for some time, and those needs will have to be filled by other supportive parties if desistance is to be successful. Brainstorm social supports that may be available in the community or through your client's family of origin. Not only do you need to familiarize yourself with potential supports in the current area, but you also need to find out this information in areas where your client may be relocating so you can make referrals for case management, mental health services, and other entitlements for which the client qualifies.

Many individuals are exposed to violence as a result of being in particular helping professions, including emergency room staff, military personnel, and first responders. These individuals have different roles and responsibilities in different areas of their life, and it can be a challenge to "switch hats." At work, they are in crisis management mode and need to function in a high-alert state, and they may struggle to separate themselves from that role upon returning home. If you are working with clients in these situations, use the **Trauma at Work** worksheet to emphasize the importance of taking a transition period each day where they can take time to mindfully switch roles. This transition period can allow them to decompress and find calm before entering into their home role. Although they need their survival skills to function at work, they can use containment to intentionally lay these skills aside in other contexts.

In addition, share the **Stress Care Tip Sheet** handout with clients in helping roles, or drop them off to your local fire department, police precinct, emergency room, or any other workplace associated with a high incidence of trauma. This handout lets helping professionals know, from one professional to another, that we recognize the work that they do and that we support them in healing from the trauma they are exposed to on a daily basis.

Creating a Safe Home

It is important for every person to have at least one place where they can feel safe, and for many people, this place is the home. However, if there has been violence in your home, it may no longer feel like a safe haven to you. Know that the violence in your home in the past does not have to predict that your home will always feel unsafe. You have some control over making your home a safer place. Your voice counts! Read over the questions below, and then share your answers with your family so, together, you can create a safe home.

1. What about your home feels unsafe or has felt unsafe in the past?

   _____

   _____

   _____

2. Who is in charge of making the rules in the home? Do you trust that person to keep you safe now? Why or why not?

   _____

   _____

   _____

3. What would have to change for your home to feel safe? Do you think those changes will really happen? Why or why not?

   _____

   _____

   _____

4. What new rules could you have at your house to make it feel safe?

   _____

   _____

   _____

5. How do you think the rest of your family will feel about your ideas?

   _____

   _____

   _____

New Family Rules

Sometimes we have family rules that are not written down. These are things we have learned by watching others or by repeating ways of interacting. These rules may not be healthy or kind, so it's important to think about how we treat one another as a family. Take some time as a family to brainstorm what you'd like the new rules to be in each of these areas. Then work on practicing the new rules until they become the old family rules!

1. **Communicating:** How will we talk to one another? What tone of voice will we use? What kind of words will we say to one another?

_____

_____

2. **Physical Contact:** How will we touch one another? Can we roughhouse, or is it hard to tell the difference between that and fighting? What are some acceptable forms of touch, and which forms of touch are not okay?

_____

_____

3. **Expressing Emotions:** When we are angry or sad, how can we express those emotions without hurting someone else with our words or with our hands? What will be acceptable ways to express our feelings at our house?

_____

_____

4. **Following Directions:** What expectations will we set when it comes to following directions? What types of directions will parents versus children need to follow? If we want to do something different than what is asked of us, how can we make that request? What consequences will there be if someone doesn't follow directions?

_____

_____

My Child is Triggering Me

If you are a parent and have lived in a domestic violence situation, then your child may have learned inappropriate social skills and may now mimic the behavior of the abuser. When your child now behaves in these ways, it can remind you of the person who hurt you and can make you feel triggered. For example, if your partner called you derogatory names right before becoming physically abusive, then you may become triggered when your child does the same. That's because your child's behaviors transport your mind back to a time when you weren't safe, which causes your body to have a stress or trauma response.

However, your child is not the same person as your abuser. It is important to be aware of this so you can make choices in the moment that keep you calm and consistent—because that's what your child needs from you in order to find their own calm. Look at the chart below, and compare your child's behaviors to that of your abuser. Then brainstorm ways you can react in this situation so you can separate your feelings for your abuser from your feelings for your child.

Behavior	My Partner	My Child	What's the Difference?
Example: *Yelling*	She yelled when she was accusing me of cheating.	He yells when he wants a snack or is told NO.	My abuser yelled because she didn't trust me, whereas my child yells because he doesn't know how else to express his frustration.

Behavior	My Partner	My Child	What's the Difference?

When you notice your child behaving in a way that triggers you, try one of these interventions to remain calm:

- Say to yourself: *It's not the same.*

- Take five deep breaths.

- Say to yourself: *I'm okay.*

- Walk away for five minutes, step outside, and breathe deeply in through your nose and out through your mouth.

- Spray perfume or cologne on your wrist and smell it.

- Count backward from 10.

My Sibling Scares Me

Sometimes we live in a home where our brother or sister is having a hard time. Often that means we are having a hard time too. Whether our sibling is struggling with tantrums, meltdowns, or aggression, it can cause us to feel unsafe at home. Home is supposed to be a safe place, so if you're having a hard time, it's important to talk to your parents about your feelings because they can help. Fill in the blanks below, and share your responses with your parents in a family session so your therapist can help your family problem solve your fears.

Dear _____,

I want to share something with you that is very important to me. I think that, as part of this

family, my feelings should be heard. I feel _____ about our family because

_____.

I get scared when _____

_____

because _____.

I feel mad when

_____

because _____.

I wish our family

_____.

I want things to get better because _____.

Thank you for listening to me and thinking about my feelings.

Love,

_____

My Child Scares Me

Some children require more from us emotionally and mentally as parents. If you have a child who is struggling at home—who escalates and becomes violent when they feel upset—your home may feel unsafe to both you and your other children. It is important to know that some children need more attention and time to de-escalate. To return your home to a place of safety, you need to know what to do at those times and to also know what your limits are as a parent. Answer the questions here to explore what you can do to create safety again, and then formulate your own safety plan to keep you and your children safe.

Step 1:

1. At what times does your child scare you? Are they aggressive? Do they threaten to hurt themselves or others, and do they act on these threats?

_____

_____

_____

2. What have you tried to do that has not worked in helping your child?

_____

_____

_____

3. What have you tried to do that has worked in helping your child?

_____

_____

_____

4. Who have you asked for help? What was that experience like for you? Was it helpful or unhelpful?

_____

_____

_____

Step 2:

Fill out the template below to create your safety plan.

> When my child becomes unsafe (toward themselves or others), I will call the following numbers (e.g., hotlines, therapist, police):
>
> _____
>
> _____
>
> _____
>
> And I will take the following actions (e.g., leave the house with the other children, verbally disengage from the argument):
>
> _____
>
> _____
>
> _____

Step 3:

Have a conversation with your child where you clearly state these plans:

> "If you _____,
>
> then I will _____."
>
> This way, your child will know what to expect. You must be consistent and follow through every time in order for your child to understand that you are serious and that this aggressive behavior needs to stop.

A Scary Thing Happened

If an incident of mass violence has happened to you or someone you love, it can be a scary thing. It can make you feel hopeless and powerless. One way to find healing is to take back your sense of power and hope by recognizing what you already have control and power over. You are stronger than you know because you are already a survivor. You used courage and perseverance to get through that hard time. Use this intervention to think about how the event impacted you and what steps you can take to regain hope and power.

First, use the spaces here to describe what happened. Share the incident as fully as you can.

_____

_____

_____

_____

_____

Now it's time to regain your power and control. You may not have had control over what happened, but you have complete control over your recovery. Using the sentence starters here, think about how you can use your strengths to find hope and overcome your fears:

- I am a survivor because I am still here. I can use this strength to

_____.

- I have courage because I persist every day, even when it is hard. I can use this courage to

_____.

- I have power because there are things that I do control, like

_____.

- I can use my inner strength to recover and overcome my fear by

_____.

Exercise (Adult or Child)

I Will Overcome

You are stronger than you know! You have a survivor spirit rooted in strength and courage. Take a few minutes to think about your survivor spirit. What does it include? What are the different parts of it that helped you survive this hard time? Draw a picture in the box below to represent your survivor spirit. It can be abstract or more concrete, but let your creativity flow.

I Can Do Something

When you have experienced a traumatic event, it can take away your feelings of control and make you feel powerless. However, there are things that you do control—there always are. One thing you can control is being able to reach out to other survivors. You have something to give. Look at the list below, and put a check mark by all the activities you can help out with. You can even brainstorm some of your own ideas. Then make a plan to do them.

_____ Take bottled water to your local Red Cross office.

_____ Color pictures, and take them to the hospital for those wounded and their families.

_____ Give blood.

_____ Offer to babysit for a friend who was affected.

_____ Offer a listening ear.

_____ Sit in silence with someone, just being present.

_____ Gather needed supplies from your neighbors and donate them.

_____ Write "thinking of you" cards, and drop them off at the local Red Cross office.

_____ Offer to mow someone's lawn if they have been at the hospital.

_____ Take a meal to a friend who was affected.

Now you think of a few ideas:

_____

_____

_____

_____

_____

Controlling My Safe Space

There are several things you cannot control about your neighborhood and its safety. For example, you cannot control the crime rates, the behaviors of others, or the availability of public transportation. However, there are other things you can control and change. You can control your safe space by growing a feeling of community in your neighborhood, by staying on streets that feel safe to you, and by deciding whom you will spend time with (or whom you allow your child to spend time with). Take some time to think about the differences between what you can and cannot control, and create a realistic plan for how you can create a safe space in your home or neighborhood.

1. What about your home or neighborhood does not feel safe? What do you worry about when it comes to your safety?

   _____

   _____

   _____

2. Of these worries, which are out of your control?

   _____

   _____

   _____

3. Of these worries, which are within your control?

   _____

   _____

   _____

4. What can help you to deal with the worries that are out of your control? What coping skills can you use when you begin to feel overwhelmed about these things?

_____

_____

_____

5. What actions steps can you take to address the things that are in your control? For example, what can you do to make the inside of your home a refuge, a safe place where you can relax?

_____

_____

_____

6. What can you do to feel safe when you need to go out into the neighborhood?

_____

_____

_____

7. Are there other people in the same situation? How can you support one another?

_____

_____

_____

8. Think about a safe place you can go to for a while if your home becomes more unsafe. Where would that be? A relative or friend's home? Describe the circumstances when going to their home would be a good idea.

_____

_____

_____

Safe Space in Schools

When children have experienced trauma—and this number is alarmingly on the rise—it can impact them in a number of ways. You can expect:

- Children who are living in survival mode because they do not feel safe.

- Children who are trying to keep themselves safe and meet their own needs in dysfunctional and inappropriate ways (e.g., through manipulation and attention-seeking behaviors).

- Children with high energy levels and poor impulse control due to the adrenaline that is constantly surging throughout their bodies.

- Children who express their fear with constant fight (oppositional behavior), flight (running away), and freeze (not following directions) responses.

Attempting to educate these children is challenging because these trauma responses often get in the way. To address the impact of trauma, you must build trust-based, attachment-focused relationships with these children first. You need to teach them appropriate self-regulation and social skills before attempting academic instruction. Therefore, consider pausing academics for the first two weeks of school to create a foundation for the rest of the academic year. Although other incidents will happen throughout the school year, and you will have new students join the class, you will have provided most of your students with the tools needed to face these oftentimes ongoing challenges:

- Teach emotion regulation skills to all children.

- Teach healthy social skills to all children.

- Allow children to help decorate the classroom and put up bulletin boards. This increases student ownership over their classroom and decreases classroom destruction.

- Establish "safe spaces" in the classroom and throughout the school where children can use coping skills independently. Allow the students to help set up these areas, and have them try out various coping skills at these stations throughout the day.

Once you return to academics, children will catch up quickly because they now see the adults they are working with as safe people, and their classroom feels like a safe space. The handouts on the next several pages will provide you with the tools needed to accomplish these goals.

Emotion Regulation in Schools

When children learn how to regulate their emotions, they can more easily calm themselves when they are upset. Children need to be able to do this in all of their environments: at home, in the community, and at school. By teaching emotion regulation skills at school, you can reduce tantrums and meltdowns, which will equate to more learning and less stress for educators and other students. To teach children emotion regulation skills and provide the foundation for a peaceful classroom, follow these three steps:

Step 1: Teach children about what emotions they have. Many children believe they only have a few emotions, but we want them to know that they have a variety of emotions. One book that can teach children about their emotions is *The Way I Feel* by Janan Cain (2000), which helps them begin to differentiate and label their emotions correctly. For example, anger is an emotion that is often accompanied by sadness, so when a student describes feeling mad, you want to ask what they could also be sad about. Similarly, children will sometimes say they feel mad when that anger is hiding disappointment or frustration. When we increase their vocabulary and give them words to use, this helps their brains synthesize and categorize information differently.

Step 2: Teach children how to express their emotions appropriately. It is okay to feel angry, but it is not okay to express that anger by hitting someone else. All feelings are okay, but how we express those feelings can result in consequences. We want to teach children to express their feelings in healthy ways. For example, frustration is a common emotion that students experience because of the challenges that come with learning new things, so you want to think about appropriate ways that your students can express that frustration. In addition to increasing their feelings vocabulary, you can teach them to bounce their leg when they are frustrated to release pent-up energy, or you can encourage them to pull apart a cotton ball at their desk. (Both of these strategies are silent and do not distract others.) Once you have taught them appropriate ways to express emotions, remind them to use these techniques when you see them becoming dysregulated.

Step 3: Teach children how to cope and calm emotions. We need to calm negative, as well as positive, emotions because even a child who is excited can distract a classroom and face consequences. When emotions feel big, we can decrease their size by calming them. To do so, create a calming corner or table at the back of your classroom that offers a variety of coping tools, such as coloring books, kinetic sand, a sound machine with headphones, or a bucket of fidgets. You can put a three- or five-minute time limit on the calming corner, and you can also use a ticket system to ensure children are not there all day. For example, at the beginning of every week, give each student five tickets to use any way they want. They can use all five tickets on one day or one per day for five days. Students with tickets left over at the end of the week can trade them in for something in your school's token economy or reward system. If children have experienced trauma or have sensory input needs, and may need to calm more frequently, you may issue them extra tickets each week if they are effectively using the area to calm down.

Tantrum Tamer

Children who have experienced trauma have difficulty managing large feelings and may throw tantrums or have meltdowns when their feelings escalate. It is important to remember that, in that moment, the child is moving into a fear response characterized by fight, flight, or freeze behaviors. Their emotional brain is in control of their responses—not their logical, thinking brain. With this in mind, you can calm a child in the midst of a tantrum by following these three C's:

1. **Calm:** During a tantrum, do not give instructions and expect children to follow them. Their emotional brain is in control, and you must calm that part of the brain first. Offer coping skills, especially those of a sensory nature, since the child may have experienced something with their senses that triggered them to feel unsafe. Invite the child to play with kinetic sand or Play-Doh®. Have the child walk the halls with you to burn off adrenaline. Your only purpose in this moment is to calm the child, not to process or correct their reaction.

2. **Connect:** Once the child has calmed down, remind them that you are a safe adult. If possible, try to initiate eye contact. If the child tolerates it, reach out by placing your hand on their shoulder or by giving them a fist bump. Acknowledge that they have calmed down and that you are proud of them for getting control of their emotions. Remind them that you are a team and that you are here to help problem solve the behavior together.

3. **Correct:** Now that the child is calm and you have reestablished a connection with them, move to correction. Problem solve what happened. Help them connect their thoughts, feelings, and behaviors. Ask the child to model what appropriate behavior would look like or to restore what they destroyed. Give them options for apologizing to those impacted by their behaviors (e.g., a verbal, written, or drawn apology), and remind them that they are not alone. You are there to help them learn new ways to manage their emotions.

Self-Regulation in Schools

All children have energy. Some have low levels, and some have high—especially those with anxiety or ADHD. When children's bodies are flooded with adrenaline, the fastest way to help them self-regulate is to incorporate some movement. Here are ideas to help children learn to manage their energy:

1. **Teach children that they have speeds.** We all have three speeds in which we release our energy: fast, medium, and slow. For example, we express energy quickly when we go for a run. We express it somewhere in the middle when we walk through the grocery store to find several targeted items on our list. We express it slowly by walking in a pool. You can teach children about these different speeds by offering a few activities across three days. On the first day, take them out to the parking lot and have them walk around it three times: fast, medium, and slow. Have fun with the exercise, laughing and playing as you walk with them in exaggerated, slow steps. On the second day, take them back out and have them skip around the parking lot three times: fast, medium, and slow. On the third day, have them hop around the parking lot three times: fast, medium, and slow. This repetition helps their brains learn a new concept. After practicing these activities, talk to your students about when it is appropriate to use each speed. For example, they can use the fast speed when playing tag on the playground, they can use the medium speed walking in the school hallway, and they can use the slow speed when moving around desks in the classroom.

2. **Teach them how to express energy anywhere, anytime.** Children may have excess energy that they need to expend many times throughout the day, and if they do not know how to express that energy in a healthy and appropriate manner, they can have a hard time doing so without earning consequences. One effective way to burn off extra energy is to have students bounce their leg when sitting at their desks. Another option is to have students silently manipulate a small fidget toy at their desk or squeeze a stress ball with their hands. These techniques do not distract others or make noise, and it's something they can do anytime.

3. **Make space for them to expend energy in the classroom.** Using construction paper, set up a circuit station in the back of your classroom that provides instructions for different activities corresponding to each piece of colored paper: Do five squats (red), do four jumping jacks (orange), do three wall push-ups (yellow), do two high jumps (green), do one waist-twist (blue). This strategy allows students to burn off energy without consequences. They can get up from their desk, go to the back of the classroom, and do the circuit to expend energy. The added benefit is that exercise increases neuroplasticity, or softens the brain, which makes it ready to receive new information that is being taught.

Social Skills in Schools

If a child was taught inappropriate social skills, they may think it is okay to be disrespectful, to push others, to take things, or to call others names. These behaviors may result in the child being labeled a "bully." Since social skills are learned behaviors, the best way to change those behaviors is to re-teach them. Within the school setting, you can effectively teach these skills by having a 30-minute "lunch bunch" session for several weeks. Using the format provided below, you can address a different social skill each week:

1. **First 10 minutes:** Meet, greet, eat, and check in.

2. **Second 10 minutes:** Talk about the topic for the day. For example, if the topic is respect, you can:

   - Define respect: How do students define in their words? What body language and facial expressions denote respect?

   - Have everyone share an example of disrespectful behavior.

   - Share how it feels to be disrespected.

   - Share an example of respectful behavior, making sure to write down each example on a slip of paper.

   - Share how it feels to be respected.

3. **Third 10 minutes:** Act out the respectful examples included on the strips of paper, making sure to have fun, laugh, and learn together.

Other social skills topics you can include in subsequent lunch bunches include: listening, following directions, sharing, compromising, using kind words, and keeping your hands to yourself.

Gang Pros and Cons

Everything has pros and cons, including gang membership. For example, there are things that are positive, good, and fulfilling about the gang family, such as having a place where you belong and get your needs met. At the same time, there might be things that are challenging, hard, or negative about it too, such as seeing friends get hurt or killed and spending time (or dealing with the threat of spending time) in jail. Take a few minutes to think about the pros and cons of your gang membership, and then consider how they add up.

Pros	Cons

Assessing My Role in Gang Membership

Once you have decided that leaving the gang is your goal, the steps you take in that direction will depend on your level of involvement with the organization. Think about your role in the gang as you ask yourself the following questions.

Section 1

1. Do you know about crimes the gang has committed? _____

   (If the answer is *yes*, move to section 2.)

2. Do you know the names of the leaders of the gang, or have you met them? _____

   (If the answer is *yes*, move to section 2.)

3. Does your gang have a policy or history of hurting those who leave the gang or hurting their families? _____

   (If the answer is *yes*, move to section 2.)

If you answered *no* to the above questions, then you are most likely loosely affiliated with the gang. The steps in the **Creating a Plan of Desistance: Level 1** handout may be helpful for you.

Section 2

1. Have you committed crimes for the gang? _____ Were those crimes felonies? _____

   (If you answered *yes* to the second question, move to section 3.)

2. Did you commit crimes that involved crossing state lines? _____

   (If the answer is *yes*, move to section 3.)

3. Are you responsible for collecting gang dues and other business related to the running of the gang? _____

   (If the answer is *yes*, move to section 3.)

If you answered *no* to these questions, then you are most likely closely involved with the gang. The steps in **Creating a Plan of Desistance: Level 2** handout may be helpful for you.

Section 3

1. Do you hold a position of leadership in the gang (i.e., do people report to you)? _____

2. Do you work directly with the gang leaders? _____

3. Are you aware of the inner workings of the gang and their business? _____

If you answered *yes* to any of these questions, then you most likely play an important role in the gang. The steps in the **Creating a Plan of Desistance: Level 3** handout may be helpful to you.

Creating a Plan of Desistance: Level 1

Once you know where you stand within the gang organization, you can make a plan for desistance. It is important to know that once you leave the gang, you will need support to help you follow through with your plan. This is not a one-time activity but one that you will need to intentionally follow for months or years. Understanding that level of commitment, plan your desistance by considering these steps:

Step 1: Remove Barriers: Think about things that may prohibit you from leaving the gang and problem solve them. Is your romantic partner or best friend still involved, or are they giving up gang membership with you? Do you have other family members who are in the gang, like a sibling or uncle? Think about how you'll explain to them that you are leaving. Instead of talking about it directly, it is best to mention that you are just busy doing other things. Role-play having these conversations so you are ready.

Step 2: Be Busy: Think about what activities you can do that take you away from the gang. Do you need to look for a job so you can say that your employer is keeping you busy? Think about what kinds of jobs will provide for your needs and will help you to be independent from the gang. You can also consider attending college classes or getting your GED so you can tell the gang that you are busy with classes and homework.

Step 3: Find Social Supports: Think about ways that the gang supports you now. How can you replace those supports? For example, if the gang provided you with money, can a new job meet that need instead? Did the gang provide a family for you? If so, what people could you identify as family? Who can fill those roles?

Step 4: Change Your Identity: Think about how you identify with the gang. Do you have tattoos that need to be removed or covered? Do you wear colors that you need to change? How does your thinking identify you with the gang? What are the priorities of the gang? (Are they your priorities?) What are the beliefs of the gang? (Are they your beliefs?) Who are you apart from the gang?

Step 5: Set Future Goals: Think about your life five or ten years from now. Where will you be working, and what will you be doing? Where will you be living? Who will be living there with you? Imagine your life as you want it to be. Now work with a trusted counselor to problem solve the steps you need to take to get there. Do you need an education or an employment apprenticeship? What are the next steps to create this dream life?

Creating a Plan of Desistance: Level 2

Once you know where you stand within the gang organization, you can make a plan for desistance. It is important to know that once you leave the gang, you will need support to help you follow through with your plan. This is not a one-time activity but one that you will need to intentionally follow for months or years. Understanding that level of commitment, plan your desistance by considering these steps:

Step 1: Remove Barriers: Think about risks that you or your family members will face as you leave the gang. Then brainstorm how to increase safety and security for yourself and your loved ones. Share your plans with your loved ones if you feel like you can trust them to be supportive. Can you carry pepper spray or mace? Can you take a different way home from school or work? Can you check in with family members more often?

Step 2: Be Busy: Think about activities you can do that will consume a lot of your time and that will place you in a different area of the city. Research and apply to colleges or apprenticeship programs. Look into financial aid packages that will help you pay for this education. Enroll in GED classes at a college and talk about how busy you are taking classes and studying. Role-play how you will tell your fellow gang members about these activities.

Step 3: Find Social Supports: Are there any programs that can support you in your desistance? For example, Boys & Girls Clubs of America or other community-based organizations may be able to encourage you and hold you accountable to the changes you want to make. You can also join a sports team to have another place where you belong. If you are on parole or probation, talk to your probation officer and let them know your plans. You could also reach out to a religious leader, pastor, or priest for support.

Step 4: Change Your Identity: Think about outward and inward signs of gang membership that identify your involvement. How do you view yourself? Who are you apart from the gang? What were your likes and dislikes before the gang? Can you pursue any of those interests now? Is there a particular way that you walk, talk, dress, or present yourself that may need to change?

Step 5: Set Future Goals: Gang membership involves a present-focused mentality: Survive today. Push yourself to think in a future-focused way. In ten years, what do you want your life to look like? Who will you be as a person? Start working on those physical and character goals now. Ask a trusted helping professional to help you brainstorm what the next steps are to achieve that life. The world is open to you, and the possibilities are endless.

Creating a Plan of Desistance: Level 3

Once you know where you stand within the gang organization, you can make a plan for desistance. It is important to know that once you leave the gang, you will need support to help you follow through with your plan. This is not a one-time activity but one that you will need to intentionally follow for months or years. Understanding that level of commitment, plan your desistance by considering these steps:

Step 1: Remove Barriers: You will most likely need to leave the area without warning anyone. Think about people who are important to you and how you may want to say goodbye in a meaningful way. Perhaps you can take your mother out to dinner or spend a special day with your younger siblings. It is important to not share your plans with anyone you do not trust. Only reveal your plan to one or two trusted people who can help you formulate and follow through on your plan. Make these preparations with safety in mind, and be mindful not to make any changes to your normal gang activity routines. Any changes could alert the other gang leaders that something is different for you.

Step 2: Carefully Plan: Create a plan that will allow you to leave the area. Remember that the fewer people who know, the safer you will be. Your loved ones will be safer too because they can honestly answer that they do not know where you are. Gather money to buy a bus or train ticket. Think about an area or a city where you have relatives or non-gang affiliated friends. Take a backpack with a few essentials in it but nothing that would draw attention. If your gang has identified that something is different with you, they may be watching you, so keep this in mind.

Step 3: Find Social Supports: Think about the supports that you will need in your new home. If you are traveling to an area where you do not have family or friends, look into shelters or emergency housing so you know where to go when you get into the town. Ask your clinician to help you find a case manager, therapist, and other supports who can help you settle into your new home. Your clinician can make referrals before you leave town so they are in place when you arrive. Remember to take important documents with you, like your photo identification, birth certificate, and social security card, so you can apply for services and employment.

Step 4: Change Your Identity: Think about how you can remove any gang affiliations when you arrive in your new home. If you have tattoos, consider having them covered or removed. If you have been wearing certain colors associated with the gang, then consider changing your look. You want to be a different person when you start over, especially if you are leaving a gang that has national reach. Consider how you think about yourself. Is your identity that of a gang member? What are other things about you that you are proud of or that set you apart? Do you have other talents and gifts? Write a sentence about your new identity, and keep it in your pocket, pulling it out often to remind yourself of who you are now.

Step 5: Set Future Goals: When you start over, you will have a clean slate. You will be able to be anyone you want to be. Think about who that is. What is important to you? What do you want to spend your time doing? Do you want to go back to school? Hold a certain job? Think about the steps you will need to take to get there, and then take that first step. You can be anyone you want to be. You can do anything you set your mind to—because look at what you just had to do in desisting from your gang!

Trauma at Work

When you entered into your helping profession, you chose a job that prioritizes the safety of others over your own. What that means is that, at times, your work environment is not a safe place for you. You work hard to remove threats from the lives of others, but that work is challenging, and it takes a toll on your mind and body. It is important to remember that you have two different roles: one at work and one at home. The role you play at work is that of a helper who saves lives, whereas the role you play at home is one of a parent, spouse, sibling, child, or friend. These two roles have very different responsibilities. Take a few minutes to think about who you are in each of these roles, and describe them below.

Who I Am at Work	Who I Am at Home

Now think about the contrasts and contradictions. How do you manage and compartmentalize these two roles? If you think about family life on the job, that can be dangerous for you. And if you think about the job at home, that can cause you to not be fully present with your family. Here are a few ideas for compartmentalizing. Try them out and then brainstorm some of your own:

1. **Have a transition period on your way home:** Stop for coffee. Play your favorite song on repeat and sing along. Call your favorite person and decompress about the day.

2. **Have a transition period at home:** Let your family know that you need 30 minutes when you come home before you interact with them. Take this time to change roles. Take a hot shower. Lay down for 20 minutes. Read a chapter in your favorite book. Watch one funny episode of your favorite show.

3. **Create a containment box:** At home, keep a containment box nearby that you can use for work. When a work-related thought pops into your head, write it down and put it into the box. That way you don't forget the thought, you just put it away until it is time to think about work. At your job, keep a containment box for home. When a home-related thought pops into your head, write it down and put it in the box. This will allow you to focus on your job responsibilities and to think about your family on your way home.

Stress Care Tip Sheet

The work you do is important, but it is just as important to take care of yourself. When you have been exposed to trauma or have been in stressful situations, practicing self-care can boost your resiliency. Practice the following tips for good mental health.

Tip #1: Exercise

When you are in a crisis situation, the alert system in your brain releases large amounts of adrenaline into your body to help you respond to and survive the situation at hand. Adrenaline makes your heart race, your blood pressure rise, your lungs constrict, and your muscles tense. That adrenaline won't go away until it's used, so burn it off through physical activity.

Tip #2: Eat Healthily and Get Good Sleep

When you are exposed to stressful situations, your alert system also releases large amounts of cortisol into your body. Eating green vegetables, fruits, and protein—and getting eight hours of sleep each night—can help your brain recover from that cortisol overload.

Tip #3: Connect in Relationships

Relationships bring healing when we have experienced something traumatic or stressful. A healthy relationship is a safe place where you can share your emotions and receive validation and comfort in return. A healthy relationship makes you feel secure and improves your mental health.

Tip #4: Practice Coping and Calming Skills

Find things that help you find your own peace and serenity, then do them every day. When your body and mind are exposed to large amounts of stress, you have to compensate by also incorporating large amounts of peace and joy in your life. Incorporate activities into your day, at two-hour intervals, that bring a smile to your face. Stop and get a favorite coffee. Look at a picture of a loved one. Take a walk at lunchtime. Make the time to take good care of you.

Conclusion

Trauma is a part of our society. It is interwoven into the very fabric of communities. It has touched most of us in one way or another. Although the world may never realistically be completely healed and free of trauma, we can take steps to decrease its impact. We can teach clients coping skills they can use throughout the day to stay at emotional baseline. We can work with them to incorporate physical activity into their routine to burn off the adrenaline released in a high-anxiety state. We can help them develop healthy relationships that are characterized by attachment and attunement. We can teach them to problem solve the things that are in their control and to cope with the things that are not.

We also have to pay particular attention to our children, who are experiencing trauma at higher rates now than ever before. Children have a right to feel safe and cared for. As a community, as a society, and as a world, we need to protect our children from harm. As adults, we need to think about the impact that our decisions and choices have on children. If children experience harm, we must create safe places where they can heal. We have to teach them emotion regulation skills by being emotionally consistent ourselves. We must lead the way for them because they won't know how unless we show them.

As a mental health professional, it is essential that you also practice self-care so you can continue providing the emotional care your clients need. Imagine that you are a bank. You are constantly making large withdrawals from yourself to invest in others. This means that you must have a large balance from which to work. If you have been making continuous withdrawals without making any deposits, then your balance will soon become depleted, and you may not be equipped to work with a challenging client who walks through the door. In order to make continuous withdrawals, you must also make continuous deposits to maintain a large balance and avoid burnout.

How do you make deposits? By practicing excellent self-care. This means taking care of yourself before taking care of others. You need to possess the insight into what relaxes and calms you. Take a few minutes to think about what brings you peace. You may already know and have implemented self-care into your everyday routine. Find what you love and make time to do it every day. Part of self-care also involves taking time to engage in relationships that feed your soul. Relationships provide support, nourishment, and validation when we need it the most. You spend so much time investing in others, but who invests in you? Identify those relationships that bring you laughter and joy—that you find comfort and support in—and then spend time with those people. You cannot help your clients to connect and find fulfillment in relationships if you do not have those relationships yourself.

If you have any trauma in your own background, then self-care also involves taking the time to heal your own trauma first. You cannot show someone how to walk down a road you have not been down yourself. You won't know the twists and turns, the rocky climbs, or the steady pace of the marathon. You have to learn how to pace yourself in the process—stopping along the way for necessary rest and nourishment breaks—so you can arrive at the end. Although you may still experience vicarious trauma as you walk the path with clients who are healing their own trauma, it will not impact you as deeply when you take care of yourself first. Doing so provides you with the reserves needed to serve as a safe container for your clients' emotions and to lead them to healing. It makes you a better clinician and a healthier individual. So take good care of yourself!

References

American Psychiatric Association. (2013). *Diagnostic and statistical manual of mental disorders* (5th ed.). Arlington, VA: Author.

Black, M. M., Walker, S. P., Fernald, L. C. H., Andersen, C. T., DiGirolamo, A. M., Lu, C., … Lancet Early Childhood Development Series Steering Committee. (2017). Early childhood development coming of age: Science through the life course. *Lancet, 389*(10064), 77–90.

Bremner, J. D. (2006). Traumatic stress: Effects on the brain. *Dialogues in Clinical Neuroscience, 8*(4), 445–461.

Cain, J. (2000). *The way I feel.* Seattle: Parenting Press.

Decker, S. H., & Lauritsen, J. L. (2002). Leaving the gang. In C. R. Huff (Ed.), *Gangs in America III* (pp. 51–70). Thousand Oaks, CA: Sage Publications.

Felitti, V. J., Anda, R. F., Nordenberg, D., Williamson, D. F., Spitz, A. M., Edwards, V., Koss, M. P., & Marks, J. S. (1998). Relationship of childhood abuse and household dysfunction to many of the leading causes of death in adults: The Adverse Childhood Experiences (ACE) Study. *American Journal of Preventive Medicine, 14*(4), 245–258.

Hall, M. F., & Hall, S. E. (2017). *Managing the psychological impact of medical trauma: A guide for mental health and health care professionals.* New York: Springer.

Harris, N. B. (2018). *The deepest well: Healing the long-term effects of childhood adversity.* New York: Houghton Mifflin Harcourt.

Harvard Health Publishing. (2011, March). *Understanding the stress response: Chronic activation of this survival mechanism impairs health.* Retrieved from https://www.health.harvard.edu/staying-healthy/understanding-the-stress-response

Herman, J. L. (1992). *Trauma and recovery: The aftermath of violence—from domestic abuse to political terror.* New York: Basic Books.

Hill, K. G., Lui, C., & Hawkins, J. D. (2001). *Early precursors of gang membership: A study of Seattle youth.* Juvenile Justice Bulletin. Washington, DC: U.S. Department of Justice, Office of Juvenile Justice and Delinquency Prevention.

López-Zerón, G., & Blow, A. (2017). The role of relationships and families in healing from trauma. *Journal of Family Therapy, 39*(4), 580–597.

Neria, Y., Nandi, A., & Galea, S. (2008). Post-traumatic stress disorder following disasters: A systematic review. *Psychological Medicine, 38*(4), 467–480.

Nugent, N. R., Sumner, J. A., & Amstadter, A. B. (2014). Resilience after trauma: From surviving to thriving. *European Journal of Psychotraumatology, 5,* 1–4.

Rettner, R. (2010, August 5). Brain's link between sounds, smells and memory revealed. *Live Science.* Retrieved from https://www.livescience.com/8426-brain-link-sounds-smells-memory-revealed.html

Siegel, D. J., & Hartzell, M. (2003). *Parenting from the inside out: How a deeper self-understanding can help you raise children who thrive.* New York: Penguin Books.

Strenziok, M., Krueger, F., Gopikrishna, D., Lenroot, R. K., van der Meer, E., & Grafman, J. (2011). Fronto-parietal regulation of media violence exposure in adolescents: A multi-method study. *Social Cognitive and Affective Neuroscience, 6*(5), 537–547.

van der Kolk, B. (2014). *The body keeps the score.* New York: Penguin Books.

Walker, C. (2019). 10 years. 180 school shootings. 356 victims. *CNN.* Retrieved from https://www.cnn.com/interactive/2019/07/us/ten-years-of-school-shootings-trnd/

Weathers, F. W., Blake, D. D., Schnurr, P. P., Kaloupek, D. G., Marx, B. P., & Keane, T. M. (2013). *The Clinician-Administered PTSD Scale for DSM-5 (CAPS-5).* [Assessment]. Retrieved from https://www.ptsd.va.gov/professional/assessment/adult-int/caps.asp

Weir, K. (2014). The lasting impact of neglect. *Monitor on Psychology, 45*(6), 36. Retrieved from https://www.apa.org/monitor/2014/06/neglect

Wolfe, T. (1976, August 23). The "me" decade and the third great awakening. *New York Magazine.* Retrieved from https://nymag.com/news/features/45938/